Anthropology and Archaeology

A changing relationship

Christopher Gosden

London and New York

First published 1999
by Routledge
11 New Fetter Lane, London EC4P 4EE

Simultaneously published in the USA and Canada
by Routledge
29 West 35th Street, New York, NY 10001

Routledge is an imprint of Taylor & Francis

© 1999 Chris Gosden

Typeset in Goudy by
J&L Composition Ltd, Filey, North Yorkshire
Printed and bound in Great Britain by
TJ International Ltd, Padstow, Cornwall

British Library Cataloguing in Publication Data
A catalogue record for this book is available from the British Library

Library of Congress Cataloging in Publication Data
Gosden, Chris, 1955–
    Anthropology and archaeology: a changing relationship/Chris
Gosden.
      p. cm.
    Includes bibliographical references and index.
    1. Anthropology—Methodology. 2. Archaeology—
Methodology. 3. Ethnoarchaeology. I. Title.
GN33.G68 1999
301'.01—dc21   98–50480
            CIP

ISBN 0–415–16249–1 (hbk)
ISBN 0–415–16250–5 (pbk)

To Emily and Jack

Contents

Illustrations

Figures

Tables

Preface

One possible way to write this book was as a volume entitled 'Anthropology for Archaeologists'. A book with this title already exists (Orme 1981), as do others with similar aims (Hodder 1982). As well as not wanting to cover old ground, I soon became convinced that to explain anthropology to archaeologists was not possible. Books have been written on statistics for archaeologists, for instance, as these two disciplines have had largely separate histories and only the slightest of mutual influence. This is patently not the case with archaeology and anthropology, which have been and remain linked intimately, albeit in different ways in various parts of the globe. The only way forward seemed to be to look at the interrelationship of the two subjects and how each had provided contexts for the other.

Interlinkage has been closest in North America, although it can be argued that now the two elements of the joint discipline are somewhat estranged. In Britain and elsewhere in Europe there has been a fluctuating relationship between the two, so that at the end of the last century, when an evolutionary scheme held sway, they were almost indistinguishable, but early in this century they parted company. It is a major part of my argument that social anthropology was set up in Britain, by people like Malinowski, using strategies of institutionalisation which deliberately emphasised and exacerbated the difference between the two. Thus, even at periods when the two subjects parted company, one was still defined in terms of the other, even though this was a definition through difference. Today there is *rapprochement* in Britain, but distance in North America, Australia and New Zealand, where relations have been more cordial in the past.

For these reasons, which will be elaborated in the body of the book, it is impossible to write a book on anthropology for archaeologists as this would imply the relationship of two separate entities. Instead I have dwelt on the mutual history of the two, although the main emphasis is to provide an account of anthropological concepts and trends which may be of use to archaeologists. This emphasis is legitimate, I think, as archaeology has been an importer of anthropological ideas and suffered a balance of trade problem due to the lack of export of archaeological results and theories. Things are changing, however, and in many areas anthropologists are becoming more aware that it is impossible to approach the present without a knowledge of the past and that much of this past is prehistoric and thus only accessible through archaeology. The general emphasis on anthropology has meant that I have given a more consistent and coherent account of that discipline than I have of archaeology, where my account of history, theory and method has been most full for periods when archaeology has been most dependent on its sister subject. My stress on the relatedness of archaeology and anthropology has made for a book with considerable historical emphasis. Part I contains the historical material. The last three chapters concern the present scene and this is contained in Part II.

My interest in writing this book has arisen from my personal history and the result has, of course, been shaped by what I do or don't know. I am currently teaching in the joint archaeology and anthropology degree at Oxford, which is set up to explore the relationship between the two disciplines rather than give an exclusive grounding in either one. Therefore the issues I will be exploring in the book are those foremost in my mind whilst teaching. In my work to date I have attempted to combine archaeological and anthropological approaches. My doctoral work was on pottery trade in central Europe during the Iron Age, where I used anthropological information on exchange to interpret archaeological evidence. I have worked for the last ten years in Papua New Guinea, where I excavated a series of sites but also collected genealogies, oral histories and information on changing forms of exchange and ritual. Through this work I have become particularly interested in the history of colonialism and colonial contact in the Pacific and elsewhere. This experience in the field has made me aware both of the links between the two disciplines, but also their differences, which centre around long- and short-term timescales. Anthropology, for example, can look at structures of meaning as they exist in the present; archaeology can provide a long-term perspective on the development of systems of meaning and the general conditions through which human meanings can be generated. Consequently, it is both similarities and differences between the two disciplines that I would like to explore in this book.

I would not have written this book had I not been teaching in the joint archaeology and anthropology degree at Oxford and I am very thankful to all my colleagues. A number of people have particularly influenced my views and these include Marcus Banks, Jeremy Coote, Elizabeth Edwards, Howard Morphy and Andrew Sherratt. Peter Rivière read all of the historical section and made important suggestions on overall directions and corrected some errors of fact. He also suggested the example with which I start chapter 1. Mike O'Hanlon, David Wengerow and Peter White read differing amounts of the manuscript and made important comments. Lynn Meskell has been very helpful in discussions on gender and globalism, as was Stephanie Moser on professionalisation. Patrick Blackman has read the whole thing and made many changes in expression and content. I wrote the first half of the book whilst a Visiting Fellow in the Research School of Pacific and Asian Studies, Australian National University between January and September 1997. I am very grateful to John Chappell, then head of department of Archaeology and Natural History, for his support and to Wal Ambrose, Atholl Anderson, Jim Fox, Don Gardner, Jack Golson, Matthew Spriggs and Glenn Summerhayes for discussions which have contributed directly or indirectly to this book. I thank the University of Oxford for giving me sabbatical leave during 1997. Sandy Fowlie was helpful throughout. Special thanks go to Julia Cousins for the load she bore at the Pitt Rivers, which made the writing of the second half of the book possible. Most especial thanks go to Jane Kaye, Emily and Jack.

Acknowledgements

I am grateful to the Pitt Rivers Museum for permission to reproduce the cover photograph and Figure 2.1 (B2219Q). I am grateful to University of Nebraska Press for permission to reproduce Figure 3.1 (J. Green, ed., 1979, *Zuñi: Selected Writings of Frank Hamilton Cushing*: Map 1). I am grateful to the American Museum of Natural History for permission to reproduced Figure 3.2 (F. Boas, 1907, 'Second report on the Esquimo of Baffin Land and Hudson's Bay', *Bulletin of the American Museum of Natural History* 15: 371–570, Figure 202). I am grateful to Constable and Co. Ltd. for permission to reproduce Figure 4.1 (W. H. R. Rivers, 1914, *Kinship and Social Organisation*: Diagram 3). I am grateful to Routledge and Kegan Paul for permission to reproduce Figures 4.3 (Malinowski 1929: Figure 1). I am grateful to Routledge for permission to reproduce Figures 6.2 and 6.3 (from Gilchrist 1994: Figures 41 and 64). I am grateful to Cambridge University Press for permission to reproduce Figures 3.4 (Childe 1930: endmap), 4.4 (Leach and Leach 1983: Map 1), 5.1 (P. V. Kirch, 1989, *The Evolution of Polynesian Chiefdoms*: Figure 75) and 5.7 (D. Feil, 1987, *The Evolution of Highland Papua New Guinean Societies*: Figure 2). I am grateful to the Royal Anthropological Institute for permission to reproduce Figure 4.2 (RAI2075). I am grateful to Holt, Rinehart and Winston for permission to reproduce Figure 5.2 (Service 1971: Map 2). I am grateful to W. H. Freeman and Co. for permission to reproduce Figure 5.3 (from Willey and Sabloff 1980: Figure 120). I am grateful to Aldine Press for permission to reproduce Table 5.1 (Lee 1968a: Table 6). I am grateful to *American Antiquity* for permission to reproduce Figure 5.4 and Table 5.2 (Binford 1980: Figure 4, Table 2). I am grateful to University of New Mexico Press for permission to reproduce Figures 5.5 and 5.6 (Renfrew 1975: Figures 10, 12). I am grateful to Duckworth for permission to reproduce Figures 5.8 and 5.9 (Friedman and Rowlands 1978: Figures 1 and 5). I am grateful to Harwood Academic Publishers for permission to reproduce Figure 6.1 (MacKenzie 1991: Map 3). I am grateful to University of Washington Press for permission to reproduce Figure 6.4 (Duff 1975: Figure 29). I am grateful to Chicago University Press for permission to reproduce Figures 3.3 (H. E. Driver, 1969, *Indians of North America*: Map 2), 7.4, 7.5, 7.6 and 7.7 (Morphy 1991: Figures 3.1, 10.2, 10.10, 10.11). I am grateful to the Guildford Press for permission to reproduce Figures 7.1, 7.2 and 7.3 (Moore 1996a: Figures 1, 17, 24).

1 Anthropological archaeology and archaeological anthropology

'Stone Age tribe flees bushfires in Brazil' was a headline carried by a number of British newspapers in March 1998. During this month bushfires raged through the savannah and rainforest of Roriama Province of northwest Brazil, due to a drought said to be caused by El Niño. What does the newspapers' use of the term 'Stone Age' mean? Stone Age evokes echoes of the land that time forgot; portions of the globe and groups of people by-passed by the major currents of history; the survival of the past in the present. In a different age, the journalists might have used the word 'primitive' more freely, as this is partly what they meant: Stone Age tribes represent a prior stage of human history, superseded elsewhere, but still preserved by the isolating wilderness of the Amazonian rainforest.

The reports, in fact, referred to a number of rainforest groups, the best known to the western world being the Yanomami, documented through the writing and films of Napoleon Chagnon (1997). This area of Brazil has a long and complex history, both of colonialism and pre-colonial times (Rivière 1995). It is ironic that one of the most famous scenes from Chagnon's films, shows an axe fight, in which metal axes are used. Metal tools were introduced centuries ago and complex interactions have taken place between all sorts of different groups leading to the exchange of material culture and ways of life. The Yanomami and their neighbours are not Stone Age in a literal sense: they do not use stone tools. But neither are they Stone Age in a metaphorical sense, being as fully a part of the modern world as the inhabitants of New York or Tokyo. They have been propelled into the modern world through creating a history as complex, dynamic and varied as anywhere else. Theirs is not an isolated culture, but one with multiple links to rainforest and savannah groups.

However, the inaccuracy of the statement is not its interesting aspect, but rather that it was made at all. How is the phrase 'Stone Age tribe' immediately understood by people reading the news at their breakfast tables in Britain? All these readers would know that they do not live in the Stone Age. The same newspapers tell them that they live in the age of the Internet and the jumbo jet. They are not modern, but post-modern. On the other hand, they know Stonehenge originated in the Stone Age, a phase of life long past in Britain and many other places. Stone Age tribes in Brazil are made doubly distant, inhabiting a remote part of South America and a period of prehistory simultaneously.

The term 'Stone Age' succeeds in evoking such images because of several centuries of writing about the distant past and the distant present. Much of this writing is now carried out by archaeologists and anthropologists, although this academic work builds on a longer tradition of accounts by explorers and antiquarians (Pratt 1992). The immediacy of the phrase is partly a success story for archaeology and anthropology: our concepts are in general use. It is obviously also part of our failure, if such a progressivist view of world history still has common currency. But concepts such as the Stone Age are elements of the joint histories of archaeology and anthropology. An important route to understanding the distant past and the distant present by those of European descent has been to make constant metaphorical links from one to the other. Prehistory was constructed through extended analogies with people living in the present. For instance, tribal people who made and used stone tools in the Americas were models for understanding the phases of European prehistory before the use of metal. As we have seen, intellectual recycling can now take the analogy back to its American point of origin, but with overtones of European prehistory attached.

There has been a complicated trade of concepts and discoveries between archaeology and anthropology over the last five centuries, such that the history of one would have been totally different without the other. Archaeology and anthropology can be seen as a double helix with their histories linked, but distinct. In this book I hope to explore the reasons for this joint heritage and separate identities, and the implications this heritage has for pursuing both subjects in the present.

Anthropological archaeology

'Archaeology is anthropology or it is nothing', is a statement with which many archaeologists would strongly agree. As a statement of disciplinary identity, it is odd, contradictory and not at all straightforward. It seems somewhat unusual to define one discipline in terms of another. As far as I know, no one has ever said anthropology is archaeology or it is nothing. Not to define archaeology in its own terms appears intellectually lazy, bad academic politics and lacking in disciplinary self-confidence. However, people who take this view are not giving up their disciplinary identity. Instead we are indicating that archaeology is part of a broad field of study, composed of archaeology, social/cultural anthropology, physical anthropology and linguistics. This larger field is often known as anthropology, which is taken to be the study of all aspects of human life, past and present. Within anthropology, conceived broadly, social/cultural anthropology studies the people of the present, originally concentrating on so-called small-scale societies but increasingly focusing on the structures of life in the west as well. Social/cultural anthropology uses the method of participant observation, which involves immersing oneself in the life of the group being studied, learning their language (if necessary) and producing some sort of synthetic account of the experience. This is something very different to the excavation and analysis of archaeological evidence, or the study of language as such, or the bodily aspects of human existence and evolution. This book is about the relationship between archaeology and social/cultural anthropology, within the broader field of anthropology.

When I started this book, I thought it was a hopeless task, but now I know I was being optimistic. Part of my optimism was wanting to include an account of physical anthropology, although I was realistic enough to know that I could only mention linguistics in passing. My sin of omission in leaving out physical anthropology came about when I realised the magnitude of the task and it would take another book to explore the three-way relations between archaeology, social and cultural anthropology and physical anthropology. I have taken the dishonourable route of leaving out any systematic discussion of physical anthropology at all.

It also needs mentioning that social/cultural anthropology is very varied, as already implied by my joint designation. For reasons I hope will become clear as the book proceeds, there have been shifting definitions of anthropology over time. Some people have stressed the social structure provided by kinship as being the key element of life to be studied: these were self-proclaimed social anthropologists. For others, the crucial factor is culture, which ranges between the material objects that people make and use, to their sets of beliefs and views of the world. Today it is probably true to say that culture is in the ascendant, although there is much overlap and many sensibly decline to waste too much effort defining any dividing line too closely, as it is impossible to decide where society stops and culture starts or to give relative weight to each. Nevertheless both terms are in common use to designate slightly different forms of anthropology and this needs acknowledging. Other terms of importance are 'ethnography' and 'ethnology', which tend to refer to the observable aspects of a society encountered by the anthropologist in the field, the basic data observed (to use a scientific metaphor). Ethnographic data are synthesised back home and combined with theory to produce a rounded anthropology. Ethnography was often seen as the equivalent of excavation and therefore somewhat looked down on as basic toil, whereas the really worthwhile activity was the synthetic and comparative work of anthropology carried out on the data. Today, with a greater emphasis on material culture and practical action in general, ethnography is less of a second-class activity and there is some overlap between cultural anthropology and ethnography.

In a some ways it makes no sense to attempt to look at the relationship between archaeology and anthropology, as neither are single entities. There is much internal variety, with archaeologists defining themselves as scientific, ecological, historical as well as anthropological. Also, there are differences in the meaning of anthropological archaeology in different times and varying places. In order to give a sketch of this variety I shall look at the divergent meanings given to the term 'anthropological archaeology' on the two sides of the Atlantic and how usages in north America and Britain have changed over time. This will be a limited history covering the last forty years, the period in which current positions and debates have been defined; the longer-term history of the last 150 years is considered later in chapters 2 to 5.

Anthropological archaeology in North America

It was Willey and Phillips (1958: 2) who wrote that 'American archaeology is anthropology or it is nothing.' It is worth noting that they limited the statement to America and it would not have been true in any sense to say the same of British archaeology at the time. This statement had been true since the time of Boas at the end of previous century, who emphasised the combination of social anthropology and archaeology needed to uncover the culture history of local areas (see chap. 5). However, Willey and Phillips wrote when a contrasting to view to that of Boas was emerging within a new evolutionary synthesis. 'Anthropology is fundamentally a generalizing and comparative discipline' (Willey and Sabloff 1980: 1), whose ultimate aim was to understand and explain the processes underlying culture change. It is no coincidence that the article seen as the starting point for the New Archaeology was entitled 'Archaeology as anthropology' (Binford 1962).

This article, written in Binford's impenetrable style, said that archaeology could and should participate in the study of the evolution of human culture. Given that anthropologists have only a small range of variability to study in the shape of extant cultural systems, archaeology would, in fact, have the major part to play and was the only discipline that could look at really long-term change and come out with broadly based generalisations about human behaviour. His view of archaeology was as an holistic discipline, which could look at the whole of human culture. Such a view was in contradiction to the oft-expressed criticism that 'you cannot dig up a kinship system'. While Binford agreed that this was true and thus archaeologists were never going to be the same as anthropologists, he did feel they could identify all aspects of past change as well as the fact that changes happened for different reasons and at varying rates in specific elements of the cultural system. Artefacts and features have a systematic relationship to the total extinct cultural system and this relationship can, potentially, be understood. Following Leslie White he divided these elements of the cultural system into three types: the technomic, sociotechnic and idiotechnic. The first of these was technology, the extensions of the human body by which people extracted energy from the environment and processed it. The sociotechnic was to do with people's social identity within the group and the manner in which groups were given cohesion in such a manner as to use their technology efficiently. Ideotechnic artefacts created a symbolic milieu in which people were acculturated. It is necessary for archaeologists to establish relations between these different sets of artefacts, which should be expressed in statistical terms. The relationships could be expressed ultimately against the background of exceptionless generalisations or laws.

Binford felt that the ultimate aim of archaeology is to generate and apply laws of human behaviour through combining the evolutionary theory of White with the systematic study of archaeological materials. Thus although the theory came from anthropology the major contribution in data would come from the archaeologist, the only discipline with the evidence from which to generalise about long-term change and long-distance relationships. These optimistic hopes left unprobed the tricky question of the relationship between past and present forms of life and of understanding the past through analogy with the present. Binford (1972: 18) acknowledged that most ideas about the organisation of culture in the past have come from the study of human variability in the present. This obviously was not good enough if that past was truly different from the present, as interpretation based on observation in the present could only render the past in the shape of the contemporary world. The way out of this which was consistent with the philosophy of science employed at the time was to use analogies from the present as hypotheses to be tested against remains from the past (Binford 1967: 1), presumably with the possibility that quite a number of such hypotheses would be proved wrong. The more limited and specific the analogies were, the less chance they had of being pertinent. To build strong and rounded analogies 'Archaeologists must be trained comparative ethnographers' (Binford 1972: 18). This was a sentiment echoed by Richard Lee, a social anthropologist, one of a number brought in to comment on the work of the archaeologists: 'if every African prehistorian spent a field season working with the Kalahari Bushmen (or the Australian Aborigines), this experience would immeasurably enrich his understanding of all levels of African prehistory' (Lee 1968b: 345).

Binford took his own advice to heart and carried out intensive studies with the Nunamiut, an Alaskan Inuit group (Binford 1978, 1980) and less intensive studies elsewhere. He hoped to use specific observations on butchery of carcasses or behaviour around a hearth to interpret Palaeolithic remains, making the assumption that in all cases people would behave in a functionally efficient manner and not be influenced, for instance, by culturally specific attitudes to dirt in depositing their rubbish round a hearth. By positing an emphasis on efficient function Binford hoped to come up with a series of cross-cultural generalisations which could allow an understanding of the specifics of the past. But in making these observations, he became rather more bound up in testing and verification of his hypotheses than he did in building theory (Shennan 1989). On a larger scale, Binford developed the global hunter-gatherer model, which looked at how such things as technology, storage and sedentism amongst hunter-gatherers today varied with latitude, finding that those at highest latitudes in cold environments had to be most efficient in their technology and storage (Binford 1980, Lee 1968b). He used such observations to understand Palaeolithic evidence and this is a line of work that has been extended by others (Kelly 1995).

Anthropological archaeology of this type is still current in North America. Writing the first editorial to the journal *Anthropological Archaeology* in 1982

Whallon emphasised the generalising theoretical purpose of anthropological archaeology. He defined 'Anthropological archaeology as the study of organizational and evolutionary process in human cultural systems' (Whallon 1982: 2) and hoped that 'we ultimately may see the development of a systematic and rigorous understanding, on both short-term and long-term timescales, of human cultural organization and evolution' (Whallon 1982: 1). Many of the articles that have appeared in the journal subsequently have followed these lines, essentially those laid down by Binford twenty-five years ago. It seems fair to say that the majority of prehistoric archaeologists in North America would still see themselves as anthropological archaeologists within a functionalist and generally evolutionary framework (although the same would not be true for historical archaeologists). However, social/cultural anthropology has moved a long way from Leslie White, as we shall see in the course of the book. This means that there is little in common between prehistoric archaeology and anthropology so that there is a wider gap between the two disciplines now than at any time over the last 150 years.

Anthropological archaeology in Britain

Rather the opposite is the case in Britain. Since the demise of the evolutionary synthesis in the late nineteenth century (chaps 2 and 3) there has been little contact between prehistoric archaeology and anthropology. In the recent period David Clarke in *Analytical Archaeology* asserted that 'archaeology, is archaeology, is archaeology' (Clarke 1968: 13). Shennan (1989: 833) sees this work as an attempt to combine the end of the Childean culture tradition and a new cultural archaeology, which was looking at the birth, growth and death of archaeological entities, such as artefact assemblages. Such an archaeology comes out of work on seriation, battleship curves and the like and was contained within the framework of the Three Age system, rather than the evolutionary framework of White, which could immediately link it into the anthropological concerns of the time.

An anthropological archaeology was something of a novelty in Britain and, unsurprisingly, owed a lot to influences from across the Atlantic. These came either in the form of the New Archaeology itself or through the influence of evolutionary anthropologists, such as Sahlins (1958, 1963) and Service (1962, 1971). The social archaeology of Renfrew (1973a, 1973b, 1975, 1984) was an attempt to chart the movement from band, to tribe, to chiefdom to state in the archaeological evidence using the evidence of trade, or the distribution of monuments. Even though anthropological models were used, for looking at social hierarchy or forms of trade and exchange, there was never a sense that archaeology and anthropology were part of the same general study of humanity. Renfrew made efforts to distinguish social archaeology and social anthropology: anthropologists are reliant upon learning language and from there go on to kinship and the general structure of society. For social anthropologists many things were obvious, such as the size of the social unit, its political organisation, roles and statuses, which were at the top of the social archaeologist's list of things to find out (Renfrew 1984: 9–10). Archaeologists also stressed material culture, which social anthropologists had become less interested in since the decline of ethnography (Renfrew 1984: 10). This was an accurate depiction of British social anthropology at the time, which was going through a structuralist and symbolic phase.

It is interesting to contrast the reactions of anthropologists on either side of the Atlantic to new moves within archaeology. The anthropological commentators on the Binfords' *New Perspective in Archaeology* (who included Lee, Devore, Fried and Harris) were generally very positive towards the aims of the New Archaeology, which accorded with their own evolutionary anthropology. Leach, who was one of the main importers of French structuralism into British anthropology, made notorious comments on a collection of New Archaeology papers put together by Renfrew (Leach 1973), which set back relations between the disciplines considerably. Leach stressed the fragmentary nature of the archaeological evidence on the one hand, and the infinite variety of human cultures on the other. He concluded that ethnographic analogies and parallels were very hard to use with any confidence in archaeology. When Renfrew talked about Neolithic chiefdoms in southern Britain on the basis of the distribution of monuments 'social anthropologists in this audience were quite unimpressed . . . ethnographic parallels suggest at least half a dozen alternative possibilities and none of them need be right' (Leach 1973: 767). He concluded that: 'It seems to be that the wise archaeologist should steer away from trying to do the kind of social anthropology which the professional social anthropologist knows to be quite impossible' (Leach 1973: 768). So much for anthropological archaeology!

In Britain in the 1960s and 1970s the position of anthropological archaeology was complicated. There were many who wanted nothing to do with anthropology, either for Clarke's well-argued reasons or because many practitioners of archaeology had always felt more allegiance to history and had local, rather than generalising concerns. Anthropological archaeologists had common aims with anthropologists in North America, but found few at home sympathetic to an evolutionary view of human culture. Also, the stress on theory within anthropological archaeology cut it off from some areas of the discipline, so that Classical archaeologists, for instance, were sceptical of the jargon and abstractness of those who espoused a generalising, anthropologically oriented approach (Morris 1994, Renfrew 1980). This situation has changed considerably over the last twenty years, when moves in both archaeology and anthropology have brought convergence. Post-processual archaeology has embraced a social theory essentially the same as that of any anthropologists. Anthropology (or parts of it) has moved away from the abstract structuralist analyses carried out by Leach and others towards material culture, the body, art, technology and landscape. Pretty well all anthropologists acknowledge the decline in the belief in the 'ethnographic present' and the need to integrate history into their analyses. In many parts of the world

8 *Anthropology and archaeology*

without long written records, rounded and long-term histories can only be created through the use of archaeology. The result of these moves within archaeology and anthropology is an unprecedented unity in some parts of the two disciplines, in terms of teaching and research, as alluded to in the Preface.

For instance, Chris Tilley's (1996) *An Ethnography of the Neolithic*, which interestingly makes many of the same points Leach did (cross-cultural generalisations are impossible, life is about signification), is a sophisticated account of the uses that archaeologists can make of anthropology. He addresses the paradox that if life was undoubtedly different in the past from anything that exists at present, how far can we use anthropological ideas drawn from the present to enter the strangeness and difference of the Neolithic? Tilley uses notions like personification and exchange, mainly drawn from Melanesian ethnography, as means to think his way into the world of Neolithic Sweden and Denmark and to use these as props which he can discard once he has gained entry into the past. Of course, he is not entirely successful in this and his Neolithic has a distinctly Melanesian feel to it, but the strength of his account (like the strength of archaeology as a whole) is to concentrate on the long-term uses of artefacts and monuments to construct and transform social relations.

In Britain there is currently a closeness between archaeology and anthropology which has not been seen since the late nineteenth century when the two disciplines were one, within an overall evolutionary framework (chaps 2 and 3). This is reflected in Ingold's final editorial in *Man* where he sees social/cultural anthropology, biological anthropology and archaeology as 'forming a necessary unity' (Ingold 1992: 694). 'Thus anthropology *needs* archaeology if it is to substantiate its claim to be a genuinely historical science' (Ingold 1992: 694). The contrast with Leach's comments twenty years earlier could not be greater. In North America, by and large, the opposite has happened, especially as far as prehistoric archaeology is concerned. Much prehistoric archaeology is of a rather dogged processual type, still pursuing many of the themes laid down in the early 1960s. Anthropology has moved a great distance from the evolutionary framework, with the rise in the importance of the study of cultural forms and a reflexive approach to the subject (chaps 3 and 4). There is very little common language to create communication between the two subjects, although things are very different in the area of historical and colonial archaeology where themes of politics, power and material culture allow considerable overlap between archaeology and anthropology. In South Africa, Australia and New Zealand, where archaeology grew up in the post-war period within a processualist milieu, there is a suspicion that models drawn from anthropology will overwhelm the scantness of the archaeological evidence, making it impossible to think about the different nature of the past (White with O'Connell 1982: 215). The state of relations between archaeology and anthropology is currently very interesting world-wide and well worth exploring and it is now necessary to state what my approach to these issues will be.

My approach to the special relationship

To start from a negative point of view: I find specific analogies between present and past dubious, whether this is at the level of the individual artefact, economic formations or the shape of society as a whole. The old synthesis of evolution, whether that of the nineteenth century or the mid-twentieth is inherently progressivist and laden with ethnographic assumptions. I feel that ethnoarchaeology is immoral, in that we have no justification for using the present of one society simply to interpret the past of another, especially as the present is often seen as a latter-day survival of stage passed elsewhere in the world, for instance where hunter-gatherer groups from Africa or Australia are used to throw light on the European Palaeolithic. Societies ought to be studied as interesting in their own right or not at all.

Having got these negative points out of the way, I see many justifications for looking at the relationship between archaeology and anthropology. The first is that they have linked histories and the development of one has always influenced changes in the other. Second, archaeology and anthropology have overlapping subject matter, so that ideas and evidence from one can feed into the other.

In order to appreciate the linked histories of the two subjects, try the following thought experiment. Imagine what archaeology would look like if there had never been any writing on gift exchange, kinship, symbolism, gender or a host of other subjects, from an anthropological point of view. It is impossible to see what our interpretations of the Neolithic of Europe or the Middle Woodland period in North America would look like in the absence of any anthropological writing. Anthropological thought is infused into all strands of archaeology, way beyond those who would style themselves as anthropological archaeologists. Archaeology would not be impossible in the absence of anthropology, but it would be so radically reconfigured that it is impossible to know what it would look like. Slightly more surprisingly, the converse would also be true. Without archaeology we would still be working with a short chronology, a version of the biblical timescale for Europeans and the time depth of oral or written history for other parts of the world. There would no notion of human evolution and no knowledge of the Mayas, Mesopotamians or prehistoric Marquesans. Long timescales and complex prehistories are an implicit part of any anthropology, even if they get no explicit mention by those supposedly only interested in the here and now. It is fascinating to see how many references there are to the prehistoric past in the ethnographies of Papua New Guinea, for instance, even though the majority of the anthropologists working there have no real knowledge of the prehistory of the country.

Looking at the mutual influence of the two disciplines, it is tempting to say that it is frameworks of thought developed in anthropology which are important to archaeology, whereas it is the results of archaeology which have made the most impact on anthropology. However, once the joint history of the two disciplines is considered in more detail we can see that this is not true, as there has been a subtle process of mutual definition over the last century or more, with sometimes positive and at other times negatives influences. These complex mutual histories are explored in the first section of the book, comprising chapters 2 to 5.

The second justification for looking at the relationship between archaeology and anthropology is that they are part of the same endeavour. This is not to say that archaeology and anthropology are part of a grand generalising discipline of anthropology which can make statements about all of human life, past and present, as was said by the new archaeologists. Instead I feel that the two disciplines are mutually entangled in a complex manner and the full complexity will only come out in the body of the book itself, specifically in Part II, looking at the present relationship. A few of the broader themes can be introduced here. First of all there is the political context of the two subjects. The most important element of this context is that both subjects are the products of colonialism. Over the last 500 years a mass of observations of other parts of the world have been made by soldiers, missionaries, colonial officers and traders, which were complemented by more systematic observations by professionals over the last 100 years. The context in which these observations were made were colonial encounters and the people observed were seen to be natives, with all the intellectual baggage inherent in this term. This may seem straightforwardly so for anthropology, but is this true of archaeology? Part of my argument is that knowledge of parts of the world hitherto unknown, especially the Americas which were not discussed in classical sources or the Bible, opened up the possibility of prehistory which was quite different to anything known from the Romans onwards. The best way to think of this difference was by extended analogy with the newly discovered natives, and prehistory had inherent within it the prejudices of colonial observations. Added to this was the social scene of intellectuals from at least the sixteenth century onwards, in which the same people would discuss the discoveries of the Americas and observations at Stonehenge without making great discrimination between them.

However, recently much has changed and these changes have run through both disciplines equally. Up until the last thirty years, both archaeology and anthropology were unselfconsciously the study of the rest by the west. Anthropologists saw themselves as going off to small, distant and isolated communities in order to document primitive societies, which were of interest primarily because they were different from our own. Now it is seen that we live in a global culture, in which all groups are linked into transnational structures. Anthropology has come home and can study shopping centres in north London or television soap operas in north America, just as well as kinship or ritual in Africa or South America. The difference of the Other can derive from an exoticising frame of mind and a stress on the quaint peculiarities of other cultures. These and other changes have led to a reassessment of what anthropology is about and one of the most profound elements of change is a shift in the type of knowledge produced, from a systematic, scientific set of generalisations about other cultures to a profound reflection that our own ways of life and habits of thought are unusual in a world context. Not only may liberal, humanist thought not be all that helpful for understanding other cultures, it might be unhealthy in our attempts to live in our own. Archaeology also partakes of this cultural unease and the long duration of 4,000,000 years of human evolution does more than anything else to throw present ways of life into perspective. By concentrating on other forms of life and thought, both archaeology and anthropology can help to unpick our own.

These changes have come about within the context of a new rise to confidence and political activity by indigenous peoples. In many parts of the world it is unthinkable (not to mention illegal) to excavate sites without getting permission from local communities first. Part of the process of getting permission is an assurance that the work will be carried out in manner sensitive to local concerns which may well involve land claims, based on a continuing attachment to land. Archaeology can be seen, legitimately or not depending on your point of view, to provide evidence for a group's occupation of the landscape over the long term. It is not just anthropologists who now have to take notice of the concerns of the present and, as these concerns will be expressed in local cultural idioms, archaeologists have to be sensitive to cultural constructions of the world and the past, areas traditionally the domain of the anthropologist. Added to which not all study is by academic outsiders, with local people recording their own oral histories or sacred sites, so that there is increasing debate between western-trained academics and those with different cultural routes to the past or views of the present.

Examples of the entanglement of archaeology and anthropology to the point where they are inextricably bound together could be multiplied and will be as the book progresses. However, one last area is of vital importance and that is the need to locate the present situation within a sequence of longer-term change. Anthropologists are increasingly aware that the traditional eighteen months of fieldwork provides a snapshot of society, which it is difficult to understand in isolation. The need for historical context is especially acute in areas of the world with short written histories. For instance, in Papua New Guinea oral histories or early explorers accounts only cover the last 500 years at most out of at least 40,000 years of human occupation. The changes brought about by colonialism are impossible to understand without this longer time perspective, which only archaeology can supply. Thus there is a growing need for an archaeological anthropology and with it a framework within which dialogue between the two disciplines is possible.

One of the main aims of the book is to outline the possibilities for such a dialogue, but, in keeping with my overall historical approach, we have to set the present in a longer time perspective and this includes times when the two disciplines have ignored each other or talked different languages as well as periods of détente. It is to this longer-term history that I now turn.

Part I

Histories

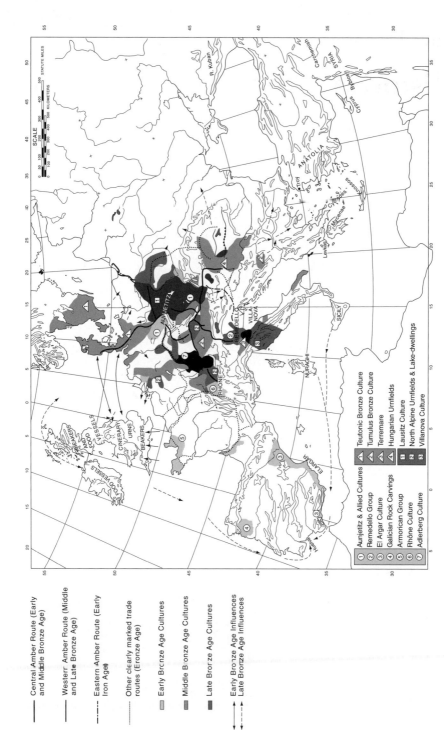

Figure 2.1 Childe's view of prehistoric cultures in Europe

2 Colonial origins

Orders of difference

This chapter explores what might be called the prehistory of the disciplines of archaeology and anthropology, that is the period before they became institutionalised subjects of teaching and research with their own methodologies, expectation of results, forms of training and academic departments. In time this consideration takes us from the beginning of the modern colonial period in the fifteenth century to the end of the nineteenth century. Much of this period saw Europeans coming to terms with forms of life quite different from their own and these encounters caused much reflection on the nature of human life in general and European lives in particular.

How do you convince someone that you have witnessed impossible events and that there are creatures and happenings abroad in the world of which no one at home has dreamed? This is an essential problem for anthropology and to a lesser extent for archaeology.

> The first thing one noticed was how long its nose was! It was like a wart-less conch-shell, stuck onto [his face] by suction. How big its eyes were! They were like pairs of telescopes, but the irises were yellow. Its head was small; it had long claws on its hands and feet. It was over seven feet tall and was black in colour. . . . Above its forehead it'd shaved a spot on its pate about the size of an overturned sake cup. Its speech was incomprehensible to the ear; its voice resembled the screech of an owl. Everyone ran to see it, mobbing the roads with abandon. They thought this phantasm more terrible than the most ferocious monster.
>
> (Unknown Japanese chronicler of seventeenth century, quoted in Toby 1994: 326–7)

This monster turned out not to be a much-feared Buddhist demon, but the first Jesuit priest to land in Japan in 1543. Although not all that destructive and dangerous in its personal characteristics, the creature did represent hugely dangerous forces which were to bring death and dispossession to many throughout the world, balanced by huge gain to others. These forces we know cumulatively by the relatively innocuous term 'colonialism'.

Both archaeology and anthropology are the outcomes of colonialism, the academic reflex of physical attempts to understand and control. The early history of both disciplines is intimately bound up with colonial expansion and a mass of encounters between widely different cultures. The encounters were at first sporadic, leading to mutual amazement, anecdote and rumour as to what had taken place, as the above Japanese incident shows, but quickly became more patterned. As the modern global structure of poverty and massive wealth developed, so did more structured accounts of what was happening on both sides, with those of the victors being more dominant.

In telling this story I use the term 'Europe' deliberately. Although not as unitary a concept as my usage here implies, Europe is a central concept around which orders of difference were created in the early years of the colonial encounter and then exported to other colonial countries in the form of notions of the west and western civilisation, where these latter terms have historical and cultural, rather than geographical, meanings. In order to understand others, we must have some notion of ourselves and both self and other are looked at in a complex process of mutual definition. Both archaeology and anthropology have been instrumental in defining Europe and the west in terms of their contemporary position and historical antecedents. In turn, these terms have been central to the self-definition of the two disciplines: we have complex, interacting histories which we need to touch on here, but cannot possibly exhaust.

What I shall tackle first in this chapter is the breakdown of the medieval worldview of Europeans through the process of colonialism over the last 500 years and how the shock of encountering totally different ways of life was gradually codified into a body of thought and a particular set of discussions about the past and the present. The major theme of this discussion and one of the main themes of the chapter as a whole is that cultural difference is not an absolute and obvious quality but one which is produced through the specifics of an historical set of encounters and deriving out of the joint logics of cultural forms: thus the subtitle 'orders of difference'.

Schwarz (1994: 1) makes the important point that for one culture to attempt to understand another culture which is new to it, there must be an implicit ethnography made up of a selective understanding of the self and the other. Novel experience is approached through existing categories of thought and these categories will inevitably have to be rethought in the face of unimagined possibilities. The contact between two cultures will derive from the cultural logics of both the participants and will be a process rather than an event, perceived differently by people on each of the two sides depending on the class, gender, age and so on of the individuals involved.

Let me start by taking a few historical liberties. For the purposes of this discussion I shall take 1492, the year Columbus 'sailed the ocean blue', as the start of the colonial period and the end of the medieval age. This is a generalisation that will be qualified later on, but provides a useful starting point, as does the notion that the broad-scale mapping of the world by Europeans was completed by Cook in the 1760s and 1770s. These two generalisations also carry within them an indication of how the centre of gravity of European colonialism shifted from Spain and Portugal in the early period to Britain, Holland and France later on.

Many writers make the point that in the medieval period both the geography of the world and its anthropology were derived from the Greeks and Romans (Pagden 1982, Phillips 1994). Geographical knowledge comprised the eastern Mediterranean, much of Asia, parts of Africa and the north Atlantic. It must be pointed out that no individual or group would have had a total map of all these areas and, for instance, the north Atlantic was really only known by the voyaging Irish and Vikings. Also, compared to the Mongols, European knowledge of Eurasia was very poor. As a western peninsula of Eurasia Europeans knew areas adjacent to them, but had no knowledge of Southeast Asia and very little of China and India. China was almost unknown to Greece and Rome and, although the Romans had a good knowledge of India, in the post-Roman period contacts broke down and this knowledge decayed. The voyages of Marco Polo (1271–94/5) were a real shock, especially in his accounts of China, which was a society recognisable to Europeans through the existence of cities, money, trade and law, but also infinitely strange. And even though added colour may have been provided by a professional writer in 1300 when his account was composed, it was the basic strangeness of the subject matter that was compelling, plus the shock of discovering that a large and populous area of the globe had been hitherto unknown. The east started to take shape in the European imagination as a region of fact and myth, to do with both holiness and immense riches. The two were combined in the mythical person of Prester John, a supposed Christian king of the east with immense wealth and power, who would come to the rescue of Christendom against the infidel once he realised its plight (Phillips 1994: 26). Also, the medieval world derived the main features of its geography from Classical sources, such as the notion of a spherical earth (whose circumference was very imperfectly known) and the existence of hot, temperate and cold zones. All the known world was in the northern hemisphere. However, there was a notion of great southern continent to counterbalance the lands of the north. The only major idea that was totally lacking was a concept of America (Phillips 1994: 31).

Pagden (1982) makes the point that in discovering the New World Europeans had to classify before they could see and they could only do this through existing categories of thought. In the medieval and early modern periods these categories derived from the Greeks. For the Greeks, and especially for Aristotle the most influential philosopher for medieval times, humanity was a unity but some people, the barbarians, lacked fully operational reason and were like children. The reasons for this lay not in the nature of the people themselves, but derived from the social forms in which they lived. These people were 'natural' in that they were governed by passions and not thought, and this was in turn because they were unconstrained by civil society which ruled through reason. Christianity added an extra term to the equation through making barbarian and pagan synonymous terms. Pagans lived in a state of turmoil and sin, they were slaves to their passions and needed to be saved. Salvation could only come about through external forces such as European intervention, and this model was very much developed during the Crusades. The medieval world has been characterised as 'a persecuting society' (Moore 1987), intolerant of perceived deviance inside or out. The Crusades encouraged notions of European expansion and the importance of spreading Christianity so that all should be given the chance of salvation. The Crusading ideal provided a poor model for meeting with other cultures.

Not only was there a need to spread Christianity, there was also the major problem for the Spanish and the Portuguese in the Americas of what right they had to rule in areas with which the crown had no historical connections. The answer was provided by a combination of Aristotle and the Bible. European powers had not so much a right to rule, but a duty, in order to impose the ordered rational existence of civil society and to provide the possibility of salvation to those otherwise denied it. Right from the start we have the notion of the White Man's burden, one of the ultimate ironies of colonial rule.

From the voyages of Columbus onwards the medieval worldview suffered enormous challenges leading gradually from 'generalised accounts of human behaviour in terms of individual psychological dispositions to an ethical sociology grounded in empirical observation . . . [and distinguished] by anthropological and historical relativism' (Pagden 1982: 1). This is the story we need to trace: how it has come to be taken for granted that all social forms live by their own logics and have ways of life which are internally consistent and which cannot be judged by a single Greco-Christian standard.

The world encountered by Columbus was both more and less strange than expected. 'I have not found the human monsters which many people expected' (Columbus quoted in Phillips 1994: 25). The travel literature from the ancient world onward was filled with odd semi-human creatures with heads on their chests, a single foot or who lived on a diet of human flesh. It is possible to see these as projections of European fears about the world and when none of these things turned out to be true it caused a great deal of thought about the unity of humanity, both physically and psychologically. And it was not only Europeans who encountered these dilemmas.

In order to find a thread through these complex histories I will use, as a device, a consideration of two collections of artefacts central to the development of anthropology and archaeology in Britain and representative of moves elsewhere to understand the new world.

A tale of two collections: part 1

People attempt to make sense of the world through cosmologies: abstract schemes which specify the ideal order of the universe, the position of things and people within the universe and the correct set of moral relationships and actions which should pertain between people and things. Cosmologies are not just abstract intellectual entities, but have practical consequences through informing peoples' actions and helping them to make sense of changing circumstances. One means of making sense of the world is through ordering collections of objects seen to be representative of various aspects and sets of relationships within the world. And a constant thread through colonial relationships is the attempt to make sense of those relationships through collections of objects.

Strictly speaking, collections pre-date colonialism. The late medieval world saw a number of European collections in royal treasuries and churches. Jean de Berry (1340–1416) in France had a collection of artistic treasures, which also included objects from the natural world and human products not considered to be 'high' art. Collections such as this fitted into a broader tradition of keeping saints' relics and pieces of the True Cross, one role of which was to make the marvellous manifest within the world. However, it was during the fifteenth and sixteenth centuries that European collections really became popular. The fall of Constantinople to the Turks in 1453 caused large numbers of artefacts and manuscripts of eastern or ancient origin to flood into the west, brought by those fleeing the fallen city. Once peaceful relations were set up with the Turks, Constantinople created a conduit between east and west, bringing many exotic and expensive items, which helped increase Europe's curiosity and greed concerning the Indies. Columbus's attempt to reach the Indies in his four voyages between 1492 and 1504 started a steady flow of goods from the Americas into Europe. Vasco da Gama's voyage around the Cape of Good Hope led to the setting up of the Portuguese East Indian colonies in 1500 and when Magellan and his crew crossed the Pacific between 1519 and 1522 this meant that all the major European sea-faring trade routes around the world were in operation and the amounts of non-European goods coming into Europe started to rise.

These were often seen as marvels and fitted within the medieval tradition of making the marvellous tangible, with the major difference that the marvellous was now the product of human beings rather than divine power. The Medicis, for instance, tried to capture the essence of the New World through their collections and Cosimo (1519–74) had objects from South America, Africa, India, China and Japan (MacGregor 1983b). These early collections are now extremely important in establishing the patterns of colonial interactions and trade in a concrete manner. Almost all the earliest material from the Far East and the Pacific came from sixteenth-century Portuguese ships and the commercial nature of the artefact trade is shown by the existence of shops such as the 'Magasin des Indes' in Lisbon and 'Noah's Ark' in Paris. Dutch trade with the east really started in the seventeenth century and made Amsterdam an important centre of collections and sale of artefacts. By the end of the six-teenth century MacGregor (1983b: 73) estimates that there were over 250 collections of natural history in Italy alone, and by this time the Jesuits were using their expanding global network to make large collections. Most of these collections were not for public view, but were seen and discussed by the aris-tocratic and bourgeois intelligentsia. However, in 1671 Basel set up the earliest municipal museum in Europe, which made some public access to the collec-tions possible. Prior to this, at the University of Leiden, collections had started in 1593 for the purposes of scholarship and these combined skeletons, specimens of natural history, ethnographic artefacts and Egyptian and Roman antiquities. Also, Worm (1588–1654) set up collections at the University of Copenhagen to give teaching about the nature of human variability an empir-ical and non-speculative basis.

There seems to have been something of a split between Mediterranean and central Europe, where collections were mainly in aristocratic hands, and west-ern and northern Europe where many of the collections were made by mem-bers of the middle classes and the growing public institutions. The collection I am going to focus on is that made by the Tradescants, father and son, between the late Elizabethan period and the seventeenth century. The Tradescant collection, or 'cabinet of curiosities' as it would have been known to its collectors, has been described as 'a characteristic product of its age, sim-ilar to many cabinets of rarities to be found over a large part of the European continent' (MacGregor 1983b: 90). It is typical not just for the objects that it contains but also for the patterns of travel and connection through which the Tradescants put the collection together.

John Tradescant the elder (c.1577–1638) assembled most of the collection in the late seventeenth century and bequeathed it to his son John the younger (1608–62) who made some additions. The Tradescants were gardeners, holding an important place in the history of gardening through the plants they intro-duced to Britain from Europe, Africa and the Americas. Just after the death of Elizabeth I, John the elder worked for a series of wealthy employers, laying out gardens on their estates and stocking them with novel and exotic plants. Between 1609 and 1615 John worked for Robert and William Cecil (the Earls of Salisbury) at Hatfield House in Hertfordshire, creating a new garden and making trips to Flanders and France to seek new plants. He became friends with Jean Robin, founder of the Jardin des Plantes in Paris, and came back with lime trees, vines, red and white currants, roses and bulbs, all of which were rare and some of which had never been seen in Britain before and had been gathered initially through colonial contacts. In 1615, in the employ of Lord Wotton of Canterbury, he made a trip to Russia and brought back many plants, but also objects of interest for his own collection. In 1620 he went to Algiers and may have voyaged as far as Constantinople, although this is uncer-tain. He lived at Lambeth for the last ten years of his life and in 1630 was made Keeper of His Majesty's Gardens, Vines and Silkworms. By the time he died Tradescant's house at Lambeth was known as the Ark, due to its famous collections. It was obvious that by the end of his life he was extremely well connected in British society and used this system of patronage and connection to further his collections, receiving objects from the king, the Salisburys, Buckingham and so on, as well as through his own journeys. One example of an important connection is Sir Dudley Digges, with whom Tradescant went to Russia and for whom he planted a garden in 1616.

Digges was a man who made his money through colonial ventures. He sponsored five expeditions to find the northwest passage between 1610 and 1616 and was a Director of numerous companies, including the East India Company, the North-west Passage Companies and the Virginia Company, and was connected to the New England Venturers, the Muscovy Company, the Bermuda Company, the Baffin Venturers and the Hudson Venturers. Through all these connections artefacts, as well as money flowed, some of which made their way to Tradescant. Digges is exemplary of Tradescant's connections and beyond that of the network of people through which objects and information circulated between the metropolitan centres of Europe, which created and maintained interest in other parts of the globe and a body of knowledge about the world. It is worth noting that similar networks remained important until the nineteenth century and beyond, and became the mainstay of a nascent anthropology.

Tradescant the younger must have inherited some of his father's connections and made trips to Virginia in 1637, 1642 and 1654; it is likely that the family owned plantations there. In the late 1640s John the younger established a friendship with Elias Ashmole, a leading intellectual, who was interested in the collections and their future use. By this period the collection contained items from all the known continents with many objects from America and Asia and a smaller number from Africa, with the Pacific being least well represented. Within these areas more detailed patterns of connections are shown, so that the African material comes mainly from the area between Senegal and the mouth of the Congo, with very little coming from East Africa, which was much less visited by Europeans. The first published catalogue of the collection dates to 1656 carried out by Tradescant in collaboration with Ashmole and Dr Thomas Warton. Public display of the collection for educative purposes became more important as time went by, to the extent that Tradescant had to answer a charge from the Royal Office of the Revels in 1661 for 'making shew of severall strange creatures' (MacGregor 1983a: 14).

Tradescant died in 1662 and left his collection to Ashmole's care, although the circumstances of this bequest caused some anguish to his surviving wife, who contested this element of the will. However, the collection did pass into the hands of the wily Ashmole, who by then had become a founding Fellow of the Royal Society in 1660. Ashmole wanted the collection to form the basis for the study of philosophical history and, as a graduate of Brasenose College, gave the collections to the University of Oxford. Twelve cartloads of material were sent to Oxford and became the basis for the first public museum in

Britain when the Ashmolean opened in 1683. Robert Plot (1640–96) was the first Keeper of the museum and his salary derived solely from the income from entrance fees. He was replaced by Edward Lhwyd in 1691 and both Plot and Lhwyd have figured in the histories of archaeology, as we shall see below. Ashmole himself died in 1692 and encouraged donations to enlarge the holdings of his museum until the end.

The Tradescants' collection and its role as a foundation for the Ashmolean Museum (where much is still on display) represents multiple histories and anthropologies. First of all there is the very stuff of anthropology, the meetings between Europeans and Native peoples through which items were originally obtained through barter, gift or theft. As mentioned above, the study of collections such as these can give realistic insights into the pattern of such encounters and their results. Second, there is the realm of gift exchange of exotica of many types through systems of hierarchy and patronage of early modern Europe. The 1656 catalogue of the Tradescant collection contains considerable detail on the movement of objects from the king at the top of the system of patronage down to the middle-class Tradescants through many intermediate rungs. Here material culture acts like a barium meal showing us the mouth, oesophagus and digestive tract of the body politic of early modern Europe and much work could be done using anthropological methods to document this anatomy. Lastly, through Ashmole the collection passes into another history, that of institutionalisation. The Ashmolean was the first museum in Britain to serve the public (of a 'better' sort) and scholars, portraying the world to them in a systematic and systematised manner. As we shall see in more detail below, institutions act to codify knowledge and to put across particular stories, which, by accident or design blot out the telling of other stories. The Ashmolean Museum was an early point in a long history of the creation of academic institutions which has given us the world people live, learn and work in today. I shall now move on two centuries to a later point in this history, skimming over much that has happened in between.

Pitt Rivers, like the Tradescants before him, made an extensive ethnographic collection and gave it to Oxford University, exactly 200 years after Ashmole's gift, in 1883. Between Pitt Rivers and the Tradescants is a gulf of time which saw the movement from colony to empire, all the thought of the Enlightenment, the recognition of European prehistory and much more. As a thread to follow through these complicated passages of history I shall examine the concept of Europe, which grew up in this time, partly through distinction from the rest of the world.

The problem of Europe

Ian Morris has recently made the point that the development of the archaeology of classical Greece is involved with a 200-year project of understanding 'Europeanness' (Morris 1994). The same argument could be extended to both prehistoric archaeology in Europe and anthropology done from Europe over the last 500 years. The late medieval European world thought of itself as Christendom and it is only with the decline of the Church in the early modern period that the more secular notion of Europe came to the fore. Europe was from the first an unlikely and incoherent entity: 'The problem of the "other" has always been the problem of Europe or rather the fear that its heterogeneous origins would forever condemn it to a political disunity of impotence' (Rowlands 1987: 559). Attempts to define Europe took two routes. The first was negative: to define Europe in terms of what it was not, through the Other. The second was to look for origins in either the prehistoric period or the Classical world of Greece and Rome, or both. As we have seen from previous discussion, the definition of the Other is always connected to definition of self and increasingly other parts of the world came to represent parts of Europe's past. There is no more representative statement than Locke's, 'In the beginning all the world was America', with the implication that Europe had passed through a series of stages since it had stopped being America. Over the centuries the past stages and ages that Europe had passed through became more apparent to Europeans, adding to their sense of self-definition.

It is only in the last 500 years that Europe has realised that it has a real prehistory – a long period of time prior to the written records of the Greeks and the Romans during which people lived lives totally unlike anything known from more recent periods. One of the arguments I shall make here is that the discovery of prehistory as representing truly different forms of life was only possible through the discovery of the Americas and beyond, areas which were unknown to the Ancients, not mentioned in the Bible and only barely imagined before their discovery. The existence of really different forms of life in the present opened up the possibility of still more different ways of life in the past. So the discovery of prehistory was not due to the existence of specific analogies between stone tool using groups of the present and the past, although these were important, but rather the New Worlds of the present enabled people to imagine the Old Worlds of the past. It is obvious that anthropology has been brought about by colonial encounters, but this is equally true of prehistoric archaeology in which our imagination gropes in the wake of cross-cultural encounters.

The first interest in prehistory coincided with the start of the colonial period, except that this was no real coincidence, but more of a causal connection. Leland (1503–52) became the King's Antiquary in 1533, some forty-one years after Columbus's first voyage and the Society of Antiquaries was formed in 1572 showing that there was considerable public interest in the unexplored past. In the following century more systematic investigations were carried out, such as those by Aubrey (1626–97) who mapped and investigated both Stonehenge and Avebury, both of which he considered to be druidical temples, thus showing some awareness of a pre-Roman past.

At first the discovery of people who had no metal tools, but only stone, in areas of the world like America and the Pacific led to what is known as 'degenerationism'. This is the idea that those groups which wandered far from the centre of the world, Europe and the Near East, must have degenerated from their former state of civilisation to a lower state. However, as time went by more people were inclined to Locke's opinion that there had been a prior age of stone throughout the world and those still using stone were survivals rather than the product of degeneration. This view included the possibility that the earlier Stone Age had also been found in Britain and that the stone tools found by antiquaries were human products from a bygone age. Robert Plot (1640–96) in the Ashmolean Museum, looking at the Tradescants' collections complemented by subsequent acquisitions, compared British stone tools with hafted axes from recent North America and said that the more recent examples provided the means of studying the prehistoric British artefacts (Trigger 1989: 53). As the seventeenth century went on, there was a growing feeling that the modern age had surpassed the Classical world in technical capability and knowledge and if history could be seen to have progressed on from the ancient world then it was possible that there was history prior to historically recorded times.

In the eighteenth century such views were commonplace and William Stukeley (1687–1765) classified different types of monuments and settlements in work supported by the Royal Society. He came to realise that there was a series of prehistoric periods in which particular monument types had been created by different peoples inhabiting southern Britain (Trigger 1989: 62). This started to address the main difficulty: the lack of a relative chronology, although this problem was only really solved in the nineteenth century. Thomsen (1788–1865) was given the job in 1816 of classifying the Danish collections and he worked out a sequence based on closed grave groups and stylistic series of artefacts, which became known as the Three Age system, where prehistory was divided into Stone, Bronze and Iron. This system, still with us today, was the first one to provide Europeans with the possibility of a long prehistoric period filled with change and inventiveness, so that a sense that there was a long pre-Classical history was fleshed out by some notion of what that history included.

However, prior to the impact of Darwinism and the construction of really long prehistoric chronologies, which we will look at later, prehistory would have added an extra dimension to the European worldview without being central. It was the Classical world which people saw as directly ancestral to themselves, created and reinforced by a Classical education and complemented by the Grand Tour and the artefacts brought back to the British Museum, the Louvre or the Altes Museum in Berlin. Until the late eighteenth century the classical world really meant Rome to most, but from the end of the century there was a rediscovery of Greece, which quickly became central to notions of Europeanness.

A crucial figure in the rediscovery of the Greeks was Winckelmann, who went to Rome as Librarian and President of Antiquities at the Vatican in the 1760s. He constructed the first chronological scheme for Greek statuary, although he never went to Greece. Of more general importance was his influence on a range of German thinkers such as Herder, Goethe, Fichte and Schiller whose writings introduced Germans and Europe as a whole to the idea that Greeks were central to European civilisation. These ideas became institutionalised in the later eighteenth century with the development of the concept of *Altertumswissenschaft*, in which a critical but positive response to the work of classical Greek artists and writers became central to the education and aesthetic responses of many Europeans. The German university system, through centres like Göttingen, had a positive influence on both French and British universities and increasingly both Greek and Latin were needed to gain university entrance.

As a university degree became a vital step towards a successful career, Greek and Latin became central to the aspirations of many, creating a powerful, even irresistible, combination of aesthetics and ambition. It is instructive to compare the fate of ancient Egypt as an element of European origin to that of Greece. Egypt was also discovered by Europeans from the late eighteenth century onwards, with massive impetus given in 1798 by Napoleon's Egyptian campaigns, in which he had a small army of 167 scholars. Egypt quickly came to be seen as the original fount of civilisation (later to be joined by Mesopotamia), but as possessing a sterile wisdom, which needed the vitality of the Greeks to transform it (Morris 1994: 20). The ultimate proof of European superiority lay in the fact that European powers ruled Egypt in the modern age, rather than vice versa. The relationship of Egypt and Greece has been explored in large and provocative books by Bernal (1987, 1991) and the relegation of Egypt to the Orient and therefore to a position of no real historical importance, is taken by Said (1978) as historical support for his argument that Europeans have used the Orient as a second-rate and clichéd Other, through which to bolster their own sense of superiority.

Europe gradually created itself through constructing a new history. A sense of dynamism and confidence was central to this history, as was the idea that the modern wellspring of productive energy was a combination of barbarian vitality, evidenced through prehistoric artefacts, and Classical aesthetics, poise and rationality. Europe always has been a contested entity in thought and through war, but Europe as an idea has been vital in giving some sense of self which could act as a mirror to the Other and as a complex series of justifications for rule over the Other. This sense of European progress and superiority peaked in the nineteenth century when much of the intellectual effort can be seen as a careful and infinite elaboration of the superiority of Europe. This history, distasteful to us now, is also crucial to our identity today and it is to this history we now turn.

A tale of two collections: part 2

Pitt Rivers (1827–1900) was an exemplary Victorian. Part of the scientific elite, he belonged to the mainstream of intellectual Victorian society through birth, marriage, interests, prejudices and preconceptions. This may have had made him a less than attractive character, but it does mean that he exemplifies many vital currents in Victorian society. The intellectual milieu in which Pitt Rivers grew up is a complex one. Utilitarianism, which sought the greatest good for the greatest number of people, and was the basis for a radical politics and philosophy, went into decline as the nineteenth century progressed, overwhelmed partly by the imperial notions that not all were born equal; some were born to govern and others to be governed. This was a notion of progress which could be applied both to the present and the past.

The Great Exhibition of 1851 at Crystal Palace, which brought material from all over the Empire, was seen by many as a snapshot of the state of the human race. Prince Albert said that if the role of humanity was to conquer nature to their use then the purpose of the Exhibition was to give a 'true test and a living picture of the point at which the whole of mankind had arrived in this great task, and a new starting point from which all nations will be able to direct their further exertions' (quoted in Stocking 1987: 3). The obvious conclusion that many drew was that not all have progressed at the same rate, and this either reflected on people's innate ability, so that some were more able than others, or on the potency of the social arrangements in which they found themselves. Thus the civilisations of the east, although capable of producing works of great art and taste were essentially static compared to the dynamism of Europe, weighed down by bureaucratic or theocratic structures.

Enlightenment thought had focused on the essential unity of all people and 'civilisation' was a singular term in the eighteenth century, but became plural in the nineteenth (Stocking 1987: 18). Not that this was a totally negative move: the eighteenth century worked with a set of progressivist assumptions too and in insisting on a single scheme of progress for all of humanity denied the possibility of real differences between people, social formations and cultures. Relativism, that is the notion that different groups really are different in their logics of social life and the fundamental assumptions they make about the world, is a product of the nineteenth century. However, this idea came together with the view that difference can be given a valuation and the pinnacle of human progress was seen to be represented by the industrial machinery in the west wing of the Great Exhibition, and the powers of the rational mind which had created such overwhelming productive power.

Pitt Rivers absorbed these progressivist notions at a young age and particularly the link between technology and progress. It is said that the Great Exhibition caused him to start collecting ethnographic and archaeological material (Chapman 1985: 16), so that from the first one of his guiding principles may have been that simple societies produce simple technologies. Pitt Rivers and others like him may have been pre-adapted to respond well to Darwin's ideas of evolution when *The Origin of Species* first appeared in 1859. Darwin's ideas were not totally revolutionary but they did crystallise many currents of middle nineteenth century thought and give them a theoretical basis. Darwin's basic idea was descent with modification, such that every offspring differed slightly in its characteristics from its parents and these modifications either made it less or more suited to survive in ever changing environments. Those individuals whose chances of survival were greatest, had the best probability of passing on their characteristics (Darwin had no notion of genes, as such) to their young and these characteristics became more common in the population as a whole. Change was through small, incremental steps and was brought about by the essentially random interactions of ever changing environments and ever changing sets of species. Change was random and had no special direction, except for the fact that the history of life as a whole seemed to be towards greater complexity of organisms and thus their interactions.

These ideas were immediately taken up and applied (not without some modification) to the sociocultural sphere. Stocking has characterised classical social evolutionism as follows:

> that sociocultural phenomena, like the rest of the natural world, are governed by laws that science can discover; that these laws operate uniformly in the distant past as well as in the present; that the present grows out of the past by continuous processes without any sharp breaks; that this growth is naturally from simplicity to complexity; that all men share a single psychic nature; that the motive of sociocultural development is to be found in the interaction of this common human nature and the conditions of the external environment; that the cumulative results of this interaction in different environments are manifest in the differential development of various human groups; that these results can be measured, using the extent of human control over external nature as the primary criterion; that other sociocultural phenomena tend to develop in correlation with scientific progress; that in these terms human groups can be objectively ordered in a hierarchical fashion; that certain contemporary societies therefore approximate the various earlier stages of human development; that in the absence of adequate historical data these stages may be reconstructed by a comparison of contemporary groups; and that the results of this 'comparative method' can be confirmed by 'survivals' in more advanced societies of the forms characteristic of lower stages.
>
> (Stocking 1987: 170)

Stating these ideas baldly and briefly has the danger of making them appear more unitary than they were. Many have pointed out that evolution was not so much a coherent paradigm, but a dominant metaphor through which the middle classes made sense of the world and it is no accident that there is a considerable resonance between social Darwinism and the economics of imperial capitalism in which unrestricted competition and the survival of the economic fittest were basic concepts.

As we shall see, these ideas sum up succinctly Pitt Rivers' views of the world and his use of material culture to exemplify these views. Pitt Rivers lived not just in a world of ideas, but in a social setting which accepted these ideas and proselytised for them. The middle and late nineteenth-century intelligentsia formed a close-knit group, with its own feuds and factions, but also its own clubs and kinship networks. The social Darwinists were related not just intellectually, but through marriage. All the major figures knew each other, regularly dined together and went to the same scientific meetings. The role of Pitt Rivers' connections and institutional affiliations is typical and gives us real insight into the social milieu in which ideas were proposed and propounded. Pitt Rivers married into the Stanley family in 1853, who were at the heart of political and intellectual life in England at that time. Through them he was proposed for the Royal Geographical Society in 1859, through which he met many returning travellers who were important for his collecting activities. He was also a member of the Society of Antiquaries, the Anthropological Society and the Geological Society, and he played an active role in the British Association for the Advancement of Science from the 1860s onward. He became a member of the Royal Society in 1876 proposed by seventeen members, including Darwin. Pitt Rivers not only had strong intellectual reasons to adopt Darwin's ideas, but also compelling social ones.

Pitt Rivers is famous for having first used the term 'typology' and ordering his material into types rather than by geographical area. After 1859 he saw parallels between his own work and that of the naturalist and he attempted to develop series which showed the evolution of types of artefacts, usually items of technology, from simple to complex (Figure 2.1). The initial spur to this was a visit to Dublin in the 1860s where he met William Wilde (Oscar's father) who had re-organised the collections of the Royal Irish Society to exemplify changes in both material forms and the sorts of societies producing those forms. This typological and evolutionary ordering marked Pitt Rivers' collection out from those of the British Museum, which started in 1753 with sixty-two cases of ethnographic material from Sir Hans Sloane, with the addition of material from the eighteenth-century voyages to the Pacific by Cook and others, which was ordered by regions of the world and not put into some more global evolutionary sequence.

Such an evolutionary sequence achieved greater importance in the eyes of Pitt Rivers through the archaeological discoveries at Brixham Cave, near Torquay in Devon in 1858. Here for the first time were found stone tools of undoubted human origin with the bones of extinct animals. The excavations were carried out by William Pengelly, sponsored by the Geological Society, of which Pitt Rivers was a member, and the site was visited by many of the leading figures of the day, including Charles Lyell, the founding figure in British geology. There had been a long debate about the antiquity of human origins and a series of possibly ancient sites had been raised and dismissed. But in that empiricist age, seeing was believing and visits to Brixham Cave convinced many for the first time that human origins went back a long way. The findings at Brixham dealt the final blow to the biblical chronology, in which the world was said to be 6,000 years old, and added an extra resonance to Darwin's ideas and their implications for human history when they were published the fol-

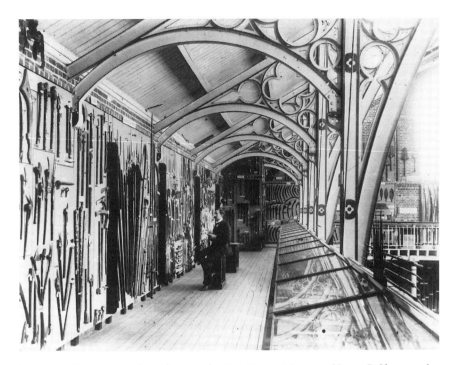

Figure 2.2 Typologies of artefacts at the Pitt Rivers Museum: Henry Balfour in the upper gallery (Pitt Rivers Museum)

lowing year (Trigger 1989: 93–4). No one knew how old the remains at Brixham were, but the fact that people had coexisted with extinct animals, combined with Darwin's gradualist approach to species evolution, change and extinction led people to think in terms of hundreds of thousands of years, and perhaps even longer, to cover human evolution.

The biblical chronology was not the only one to be discredited through these findings. Since the late eighteenth century much work had been carried out on historical linguistics, since the realisation that many of the languages of Eurasia might be related within a single family, known as the Indo-European family. The recognition by the British judge William Jones, whilst stationed in India, that Greek, Latin and Sanskrit were related, was paralleled by the discovery that the gods talked of in those three tongues were combined in the same pantheons, leading to the possibility of a linked history of both language and culture. If these languages might derive from a common language, which no longer exists, so might also the cultures. The study of comparative philology, through the systematic comparison of words and grammar between related languages, led to the construction of family trees in which different languages diverged from the ancestral forms giving rise to diversity from initial unity. The development of comparative philology, or linguistics, seemed to provide the basis for a real ethnology, that is the controlled historical study of different races and cultures starting from the basis of linguistic similarity and difference. Thus the development of linguistics was intimately tied to initial moves into anthropology and archaeology. Furthermore, in the pre-Brixham Cave days, when it was possible to sustain a short chronology, the obvious historical depths that linguistics could probe made it possible that much, if not all, of human history was covered by linguistic data. After Brixham the scope of linguistics was limited in terms of the proportion of human history it covered and other means of creating long historical sequences had to be sought.

The solution that occurred to Pitt Rivers and others was that material culture might encompass much of human history. Many of the objects in his collection were relatively recent, although archaeological material existed side by side with ethnographic. However, if you accepted, as Pitt Rivers did, that all the stages of human history were represented on the earth today, then artefacts from the lowliest groups on the evolutionary ladder, such as the Tasmanian aborigines, gave a direct insight into the Palaeolithic period of Europe, glimpsed through the finds at Brixham Cave and elsewhere. Pitt Rivers had two sorts of historical aims in mind for his collection. The first was to demonstrate the general history of humanity through a series of generalised stages, using the evolutionary metaphor of simple to complex. The second was more regionally specific and looked for origins of particular peoples from centres of origin and subsequent diffusion through similarities in the forms of the material things (Chapman 1985: 40). In this manner material culture could cover all the ground that philology previously had and more, giving us an insight into the earliest stages of human existence and the subsequent development of cultures and races. In this task, archaeological and anthropological material was treated equally; both were indicators of the grounds for present-day diversity and diversification.

Pitt Rivers was not only interested in understanding the nature of human evolution on the basis of material culture: he also wanted to educate others into the rightness of his views. His collections were seen as instruments of education, especially of the working classes, who should be shown not only the details of the scheme Pitt Rivers had worked out, but should also absorb the message that all change was gradual and incremental and, by implication, any attempt at revolutionary change was bound to fail. This conservative message was put across to the public when his collection was displayed in the working-class area of Bethnal Green in 1874 and subsequently when it was moved to the Museum of Natural History in South Kensington in 1878. There followed long wrangles about the eventual fate of the collection, in which the disputatious nature of Pitt Rivers' character came out. Eventually, the collection was given to the University of Oxford in 1883, which put up money for the collection to be housed behind the University Museum. Also in 1883, Tylor was made Keeper of the University Museum and was given the added title of Reader in Anthropology the following year.

Tylor's was the first teaching post in ethnology in Britain and the collections were used as the basis for some of his lectures. Tylor's views would seem to be totally compatible with Pitt Rivers'. In 1871 he had written *Primitive Culture*, one the most influential versions of an evolutionary view of world history. However, by the late 1880s Pitt Rivers had fallen out with Oxford University and all the members of the museum that bore his name, mainly over lack of control over his collection, but he also complained that Tylor's lectures were too focused on myth and religion and did not deal enough with material culture.

This was the slender basis on which British ethnography, which included elements of both anthropology and archaeology, was institutionalised. The work of Pitt Rivers provided the basis for a growing public knowledge of other parts of the world. The beginning of teaching anthropology in British universities is connected with his Museum, even though Tylor's lectures had a small audience and a qualification in anthropology was not possible until the next century.

A comparison of Pitt Rivers' and the Tradescants' collections is instructive in showing how much the physical and intellectual world had changed. However, one element provides a thread of continuity and this was the network of colonial connections which provided objects and information to intellectuals in the metropolitan centres. The colonial world had expanded hugely by Pitt Rivers' day to include colonies in Australia, the Pacific, India and the interior of Africa which were unimagined by the Tradescants. These colonies were fused into an overarching colonial structure, unlike the scattered plantation and mining-based colonies of the seventeenth century. But the set of connections was still between anthropological amateurs, albeit knowledgeable and enthusiastic ones, at home and abroad, and it was this network which provided the basis for anthropology over the first centuries of the colonial world.

The big difference between the Tradescants and Pitt Rivers is that the former created a cabinet of curiosities, an unusual and interesting set of artefacts, but ones which did not fit within a developed intellectual scheme. For Pitt Rivers his artefacts were exemplary of an evolutionary human history and they were used to help him, and other members of the scientific elite, to understand and to educate the general public into the lessons of that history. Darwin's ideas were crucial in structuring a general feeling of the progressive nature of humanity into a coherent programme of research and investigation, which stretched all the way from the natural world to the variety of human types and groups. Objectionable and Eurocentric though we may find this scheme today it did give form to a mass of observations, which in the Tradescants' days were still disordered, as Europeans tried to make sense of changing orders of difference, which made them reassess their own and others' place in the world.

However, although the Victorians had more stability in terms of an intellectual framework there was still a shapeless quality to anthropology and archaeology in the late nineteenth century, due to the fact that most of the major players were amateurs and had many other interests and occupations. Tylor was unusual in dedicating most of his life to ethnography, as was Pitt Rivers' concentration on ethnography and archaeology in the latter part of his life. They are transitional figures between a period of excitement and intellectual ferment in the middle of the century and the more regularised intellectual climate that came to exist at the beginning of the present century. The notion of fieldwork in both archaeology and anthropology was crucial to the development of both subjects and it is to fieldwork that we shall turn in the next chapter. This will take us through the hundred years from Pitt Rivers and Tylor to the present.

3 Instituting archaeology and anthropology

The role of fieldwork

In the late nineteenth century anthropology and archaeology were both part of a general evolutionary scheme, but in this century they have diverged. The reasons for this divergence tell us a considerable amount about the nature of the methods, theories and social milieu of each discipline, providing insights that could not be had if each were looked at in isolation.

The foundation of a new discipline requires two sets of developments. The first concerns the so-called source-side of the discipline: the bodies of evidence to be investigated. Such investigations require a set of distinctive questions to be formulated to tackle the new research area, which may in itself require theoretical advances to be made. Also, methodologies have to be available which are relevant and sensitive to the data being investigated so that meaningful results can be obtained. The second crucial aspect of a new discipline is to put a social structure in place which consists of institutions, specialist journals and conferences, students who can learn from the pioneers within the discipline and the possibility of a satisfying career structure (Moser 1995: 41). I shall argue that the development of fieldwork methodologies was the crucial development on the source-side which gave each discipline its own unique set of evidence, with separate potentials and problems. Not only did each subject define its own empirical domain through fieldwork methods, fieldwork was used as a crucial element of political strategy within universities to argue that separate departments ought to be set up to train people in the emerging subjects. The use of fieldwork as an argument for disciplinary identity was more obvious within anthropology and it is true to say that anthropology distanced itself from archaeology rather than the other way round.

In order to provide a broader context for looking at the creation of archaeology and anthropology as subjects within universities, we can look at how the birth of disciplines has been studied more broadly. One of the myths about academia is that it is a disinterested pursuit of truth in which it is the validity and efficacy of the ideas that is important and not the personalities, positions of power or career structures of the people putting forward the ideas. Older, purely intellectual histories of disciplines were replaced by those which considered the social context of academic life, through the networks set up amongst groups, rivalries between various factions and institutions and the overall culture of disciplinary life. A stress on social factors in the production of knowledge helped make an excellent polemical point, but the whole notion that ideas are important to the growth of disciplines tended to be discarded with the concept of the disinterested, otherworldly academic. Of recent years a more balanced approach is taken to the history of disciplines, in which it is the combination of methods, theories and social forces which create and maintain subject areas. In this chapter I want to look at the double helix of ideas and institutional structures in both archaeology and anthropology. Considerations of theories and approaches cannot be exhausted in this chapter and will be continued in the next. I will give somewhat more stress to anthropology than archaeology, given the overall aim of the book.

Disciplines, professions, cultures

In looking at the growth of different disciplines we need to consider a number of overlapping subject areas. First, we need to re-emphasise the point that disciplinary histories are neither purely intellectual or solely social, but both. The emphasis on the social side of intellectual life has produced a series of fascinating studies of how academic communities work (Barnes 1986, Knorr-Cetina and Mulkay 1983, Latour 1987, Pinch 1986). These replaced the early notion that science was distinct from the rest of human activity, with the idea that scientific activity was enmeshed in daily concerns and routines just as in any other area of life. In looking at social embeddedness many have found an anthropological notion of culture useful:

> life in science, like the rest of human life, means belonging to a culture. And like the rest of human existence science presents us with an endless variety of cultures, each one occupying its own region of the scientific world, each speaking its own mother tongue and finding communication with other cultures difficult, each tradition-bound with its special craft skills, which are acquired almost inarticulately, by example, in master-pupil relationships.
>
> (Nickles 1989: 227)

Such a notion of culture is especially useful as it looks not just at social connections between people and groups, but also the physical and mental skills and activities of which people are capable. The idea can be extended still further to include the notion of cosmology: views of the way in which the world works, the correct sets of relationships between things and people within the world and a sense of the moral rightness of these relationships. If each culture has its own cosmology it could be said that each had their own notion of truth. This idea is encapsulated in the term 'social epistemology', which explores the idea that truth derives from a cosmology and a shared common sense. For instance, feminist critiques of scientific endeavours attempt to expose male biases, such as an emphasis on rational thought and deductive logic, the tendency to analyse by breaking a problem down into parts, rather than more holistic forms of analysis, and an insistence on control over natural or social phenomena. Certainly, scientific approaches which did not hold these ideas, implicitly or explicitly, would look very different from most science practised to date and would create completely different expectations as to what constituted a valuable result from a piece of work. Foucault and those following him have emphasised the dual meaning of the word 'discipline', as both a structured area of enquiry, but also as habits of thought which are taught in strict manner and are hard to break out of.

Archaeology and anthropology can be seen as two sets of cultures, which are not unitary but like a confederation of tribes, which can agree temporarily at least on what constitutes right forms of action and procedure and have enough language in common to communicate. As with any set of cultural forms relationships within and between the two disciplines are not static and change as method and theory alters and one generation is succeeded by another.

Like any culture, disciplines need to be related to the landscape and the ecology within which they live. The natural habitat of the academic discipline is the university and the history of universities is part of a larger history of professionalisation. Professionalisation is the term used to look at the rise of the professions, which are so dominant in the much of the modern world. Professions range from career civil servants, to doctors and lawyers and also academics. The rise of professions occurred during the last two centuries and is tied in turn to the increase in the numbers and power of the middle classes. There is a vast literature on professionalisation (see McMahon 1984). A major feature of all professions is that they have regulated entry, so as to maintain standards and protect the status that accrues from membership. Formal means of regulating entry are through examinations and being voted into societies. Informal means, which are at least as important, are through codes of dress and address, accepted forms of behaviour and a willingness to sacrifice engagement in other areas of life in order to put in the time and effort required to be seen as full participant in the group. These informal means set up barriers of exclusion along the lines of class and gender, with the result that from their inception to the present most professions have been dominated by middle class men.

Institutions can be seen as a major means of regulating access to the professions and throughout this century the function of universities in giving out degrees and other forms of qualification has been crucial in regulating entry into academia (Table 3.1). The professions of archaeology and anthropology did not exist in the amateur world of the nineteenth century. The societies and clubs, such as those to which Pitt Rivers belonged, had restricted entry but conferred no qualifications or license to practice. This gave way to a landscape dominated by the universities as means of training and entry into archaeology and anthropology, which grew up alongside the old network of learned societies and clubs. There are anthropologies to be explored in this world either at

Table 3.1 Some of the major historical events in the institutionalisation of archaeology and anthropology

	Anthropology	Prehistoric Archaeology	Classical Archaeology
1850	Great Exhibition, London 1851	Disney Professor, Cambridge 1851	
		Chair of Archaeology, Copenhagen 1855 (Worsaae)	
1860			Cairo Museum, 1863
			Palestine Expedition Fund 1865
	Peabody Museum, Harvard 1866	Musée d'Antiquités, St Germain-en-Laye 1867	
1870	Anthropological Institute, London 1872		
	First edition Notes and Queries 1874, plus regional Committees to gather information Ecole d'Anthropologie, Paris – six chairs founded by Broca 1876		
	Bureau of American Ethnology 1879		Archaeological Institute of America 1879

1880

Pitt Rivers first Inspector of Ancient Monuments 1880
Naturhistorisches Museum, Vienna 1882

American School of Classical Studies, Athens 1881
Museum of Classical Archaeology, Cambridge 1883
Egypt Exploration Fund 1883

British School in Athens 1887
University of Pennsylvania Museum 1887
Chair of Classical Art and Archaeology, Oxford 1887

Anthropology given full section status, BAAS 1884
Pitt Rivers Museum, Oxford and Tylor first lecturer in ethnology 1884
Museum für Völkerkunde, Berlin 1886

1890

Edwards Chair of Egyptology, London 1892 (Flinders Petrie)

Haddon appointed lecturer in anthropology 1895

1900

Institute of Archaeology, Liverpool 1904

Diploma of Anthropology, Oxford 1906

Diploma of Anthropology, Cambridge 1908

School of American Studies 1908

Table 3.1 (contd)

1910	Chair of Ethnology, LSE 1910 (Seligmann)	Museum of Archaeology and Ethnology, Cambridge 1910	
1920	Chair of Anthropology, Cape Town 1921 (Radcliffe-Brown)		Oriental Institute, Chicago 1919
	Tripos in Anthropology, Cambridge 1926 Chair of Anthropology, Sydney 1926 (Radcliffe-Brown) Chair in Anthropology, LSE 1927 (Malinowski)	Abercromby chair, Edinburgh 1926 (Childe) Disney Professorship Cambridge salaried 1926 (Minns)	
1930	Chair of Social Anthropology, Oxford 1937 (Radcliffe-Brown)	Institute of Archaeology, London 1937 (Wheeler)	Society for American Archaeology 1935

1940

Chair of Archaeology of the Roman
Empire, Oxford 1946 (Richmond)

Chair of European Archaeology, Oxford
1946 (Hawkes)
First full-time Director, Institute of
Archaeology, London 1946 (Childe)

Chair of Anthropology, Manchester 1949
(Gluckman)

1950

the macro-level of modes of kinship, relatedness and enmity between institutions and people, or at the micro-level where ethnography can be carried out on the lifestyles and mores of academics at work (Latour and Woolgar 1986).

Between the 1890s and the First World War both disciplines developed their own field methodologies, which showed each could gather large bodies of data on present-day societies on the one hand, or from archaeological sites on the other. This amassing of systematic bodies of evidence caused the two disciplines to diverge (especially in Europe). Second, the decline of the evolutionary metaphor, linked in turn to the dying out of the Victorian Darwinists, meant that there was no unitary theoretical structure within which to combine archaeology and anthropology: they tended to develop their own bodies of theory at precisely the point they were becoming institutionalised within universities. Again this split was more marked in Europe than North America, as we shall see.

Instituting anthropology

For many years there was myth about the origins of anthropology which was both pervasive and persuasive and it centred round the person of Malinowski. Malinowski had, according to this origin story, which was partly of his own telling, invented the methodologies and procedures of fieldwork which allowed anthropologists access to large, detailed and (importantly) verifiable bodies of information about non-European peoples. Accounts of kinship, ritual, trade and sexual activities could form the basis for a comparative science of anthropology which allowed those of European descent to reflect on their own ways of life and on the variety of the human world around them. Such accounts were to be distinguished from the second-hand data gathered by armchair ethnographers, like Tylor and Pitt Rivers, in both its detail and reliability. Such a fund of information clearly necessitated the setting up of a separate area of study, social anthropology, which alone had the fieldwork methods and theoretical apparatus to generate and analyse detailed evidence of ways of life unlike our own.

Let us look a little more closely at the myth of Malinowski, which is not totally devoid of truth, before we consider why it is now less convincing than it used to be. Malinowski (1884–1942) was born to a Polish intellectual family and studied physics and philosophy before arriving at the London School of Economics in 1910 to study under Westermarck and Seligman. He published a monograph on the Australian Aboriginal family and when the British Association for the Advancement of Science met in Sydney in 1914, Seligman arranged a travelling fellowship for Malinowski to attend as secretary to the recorder of the anthropological section. From there Malinowski travelled to Papua New Guinea to seek out an area in which to do intensive fieldwork and went first to Mailu an island on the south Papuan coast, where the London Missionary Society had had a station since 1894 headed by Saville.

Malinowski carried with him into the field the fourth edition of *Notes and*

Queries on Anthropology, for the use of Travellers and Residents in Uncivilized Lands. These had first been put together by the British Association for the Advancement of Science, mainly at Tylor's instigation in 1874. As their title implies they were guides to colonial officers, missionaries and travellers as to how to structure their enquiries into local cultures and contained both general sections on methods and approach, but also questionnaires on language, customs and physical anthropology (including the sorts of measurements of people's bodies thought to be most informative). Malinowski had the 1912 edition, substantially rewritten by Rivers (whom we shall encounter below), who as a result of his own field experiences in the Torres Strait Islands, between Australia and Papua New Guinea, stressed the need for intensive study over weeks and months rather than days, the desirability of learning the language, and the importance of collecting genealogical information. *Notes and Queries* derived from a tradition of armchair ethnography in which people in the metropolitan centres of the empire collated and synthesised from enthusiastic amateurs out in the field. As we saw in the last chapter, such a tradition had a history going back at least to the early voyages of exploration, but it also continued through the professionalisation of the discipline, with a final (seventh) edition planned, but not completed, in the early 1970s (Stocking 1996: 440). This is a reminder that even once established on a professional basis, academic anthropology was only part of the discipline as a whole.

On Mailu, Malinowski had a difficult relationship with the missionary Saville and distanced himself partly because of this. This led him to discover that the benefits of investigations done 'while living quite alone amongst the natives' was 'incomparably more intensive than work done from white men's settlements or even in any white man's company' (Malinowski 1915, quoted in Stocking 1996: 252–3). He went on to emphasise that discussions accompanying actual events, like gardening, trading or ritual, were much more valuable than accounts at a distance from the actions described – for instance, a discussion with local people about how to rid his house of the ghosts they felt were haunting it revealed a lot of information on magic and belief previously hidden from him. His stay in Mailu was at the root of his fieldwork methods, known subsequently as participant observation, in which the ethnographer involves themselves in local life, becoming as much a part of it as cultural distance will allow.

Malinowski's most famous fieldwork was carried out on the island of Kiriwina, in the Trobriand Islands off the eastern tip of Papua. He stayed here for two periods in 1915 and 1916–17. During the first visit he started off in the government compound, which after ten years of direct rule had a jail, a hospital, twelve white residents, a large pearl industry and 120,000 coconut trees planted by the Trobrianders under orders from R. L. Bellamy, the resident magistrate. When Malinowski arrived missionaries had been in the general Massim area for twenty years and the last local warfare had occurred fifteen years previously. The area had changed considerably, something not emphasised by Malinowski, who concentrated instead on the 'traditional'

elements of the life he was observing. After five months Malinowski was suffi-
ciently adept in Kiriwinan as to only need the occasional phrase of pidgin and
at this point he moved from the government station to Omarakana, where he
pitched his tent in the middle of the village. Through his situation in the midst
of everyday life and his grasp of the language, Malinowski was able to observe
and record life 'through the 24 hours of an ordinary working day', something
'no European had ever done' (Malinowski quoted in Stocking 1996: 256). His
periods in Kiriwina provided the basis for a series of monographs on the trade
cycle of the *kula* ring (Malinowski 1922), still one of the most famous of all
anthropological case studies, crime and social transgression (Malinowski
1926), sexual life (Malinowski 1929) and issues of subsistence and land tenure
(Malinowski 1935). The first of these volumes, entitled *The Argonauts of the
Western Pacific*, had a tremendous impact when it was published within academic circles and beyond and helped secure the notion of the benefits accruing
from fieldwork. The opening pages still convey a sense of immediacy and
excitement, as well as indicating the strength of Malinowski's urge to convince
others of the benefits of his enterprise.

However, we now read the *Argonauts* with the knowledge that it contains a
partly fictionalised account of Malinowski's method of working. The publication of his diary in 1967, written for himself and not for public view
(Malinowski 1967), showed that he in fact spent days in his tent reading novels, drank whisky regularly with his friend Billy Hancock, a local trader, and
exhibited bouts of hatred for the Kiriwinans, of whom he often used the term
'nigger'. It is the taint of racism that has done most to change Malinowski's
reputation and precipitate much soul-searching about the nature of his fieldwork method, of which more below.

The re-evaluation of Malinowski's work is not just due to the lack of sympathy with the Kiriwinians (which it is easy to overstate – like many fieldworkers Malinowski probably had both strong positive and negative ties with
local people), but is due to the hyperbole of some of his statements, particularly the notion that the form of fieldwork for which he proselytised, involving participant observation, was something 'no European had ever done'. In
order to see why this claim does not hold up, we need to step further back
into the history of anthropology and consider fieldwork before Malinowski.

The major history of early fieldwork happened in North America. In
Washington, DC, in 1879, the Bureau of American Ethnology (BAE) was set
up under the directorship of John Wesley Powell (Table 3.1). The BAE was
established together with the Geological Survey and placed within the
Smithsonian Museum, so that it carried with it a survey and mapping tradition necessitating fieldwork (Hinsley 1983: 54). The express aim of the BAE
was to document as much of the remaining traditional ways of life amongst
Native American groups as possible, who had suffered terribly as the frontier
of white settlement advanced westward in the middle of the century, and who
continued to be displaced and moved on to reservations. The BAE was thus
engaged in salvage ethnography on a massive scale and compiled huge

amounts of information. Tylor visited in 1884 and was much impressed by the level of organisation, which he compared to the Jesuits (Mark 1980: 145). However, in its years of decline, early this century the BAE was accused of producing too little, too late and of having not enough central focus. There is much that could be and has been said about the characters involved in the BAE (see Hinsley 1981 and Mark 1980 for fuller accounts). I shall concentrate here on the most colourful of all the members of the BAE, Frank Hamilton Cushing (1857–1900).

Cushing spent an unusual childhood, with little formal schooling, but much time spent wandering the woods of New York State, during which time he learned to recognise old Indian settlements and taught himself a series of arts and crafts, including stone tool manufacture, basketry, pottery making and copper embossing so as to produce imitations of Indian artefacts. In 1875 he became an assistant in ethnology at the Smithsonian and the next year, at the age of 19, he became Curator (Mark 1980: 97). In 1879 he travelled to the southwest of the USA on a collecting expedition amongst the Zuñi and the Hopi, accompanying amongst others, James and Matilda Stevenson who also subsequently became famous for their work in the area (Figure 3.1). On arrival in the Zuñi area Cushing started to wander round the pueblo taking notes and making sketches, but experienced considerable hostility. This increased when he moved, uninvited, into the house of the governor of the pueblo, Palowahtiwa. From there tension escalated and came to a head at a ceremony when Cushing was threatened at knife point and might have been killed had he not brandished his own knife and the sketch book which was the cause of much of the trouble. This show of courage won the protection of Palowahtiwa and when the rest of the expedition returned to Washington Cushing stayed on, adopted Zuñi dress, had his ears pierced in a special cere-mony and was given the name Té-na-tsa-li (Medicine Flower). Cushing stayed for four and a half years in all at Zuñi and was initiated into the lowest rank in the society of the Priesthood of the Bow, which marked his shift from being an outsider. From this point on he gained increasing insights into Zuñi life, although always realising that he could never become fully Zuñi. He saw his method as a reciprocal one in which he gave the Zuñi information about his life, in the same way as they taught him about theirs. Cushing and several Zuñi friends travelled east in 1882, partly so that Cushing could show them his world and return their hospitality (Mark 1980: 103). White America was somewhat unprepared for Cushing and his methods, and fears were expressed both about his moral welfare and his habit of appearing in Zuñi dress.

Like many great fieldworkers subsequently, Cushing's work in the field was not matched by similar productivity in publication and Cushing only wrote general accounts for popular periodicals like *Century Magazine*, the Indianopolis grain trade journal *Millstone* or brief accounts of specific aspects of Zuñi life, such as pottery making. It is worth noting that his method of pre-senting his information was very different from Malinowski's. Cushing's accounts did not purport to be objective accounts, but very much his view of

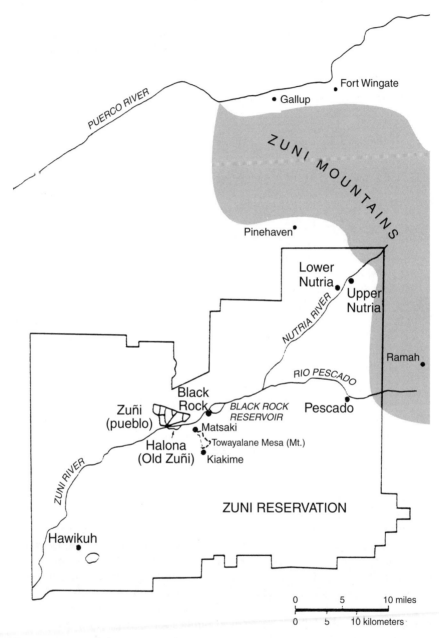

Figure 3.1 Map of the sites visited by Cushing in Zuñi (Aston J. Green (ed.) (1979) *Zuñi:* Map1)

Zuñi life. In adopting what is now known as a reflexive style, putting himself and his concerns in the picture, Cushing was a hundred years ahead of his time, anticipating recent subjective accounts of the fieldwork experience. The other point to make about Cushing's publication is that it was as much for a general audience as a specialist one, indicating that this was still an early stage in the professionalisation of anthropology with few specialist journals and much less concern to address a purely academic audience. It should also be noted that Cushing wanted to raise money from his publications to support the expenses of long-term fieldwork.

One further relevant point about Cushing is that he was not just an anthropologist, but he also excavated in order to probe the Zuñi past. Financed by Mrs Mary Hemenway, a Boston philanthropist in 1886, he led the Hemenway Southwestern Archaeological expedition, the first major piece of archaeological research in the American southwest. Excavating sites that we now know as of the Hohokam complex, Cushing and the team uncovered large settlements and irrigation systems, which obviously had links to state formations in Mexico. Cushing suffered periodic illnesses, was erratic in his handling of people and his recording of the sites, and was replaced as leader in 1888, the expedition continuing until Mrs Hemenway's death in 1894. The expedition is often considered a failure due to the lack of publication and the tensions that wracked the team. But on the other hand it showed the rich nature of the archaeological evidence from an area which is now one of the best archaeologically researched areas in the world. Cushing was also to excavate in Florida where he recovered a remarkable set of wooden artefacts from water-logged deposits. And he died in 1900, choking on a fish bone, on a new expedition to excavate shell middens in Maine at the age of 43.

Cushing and other members of the BAE have only really been rediscovered in recent years and their contributions to both anthropology and archaeology recognised. This is due in part to the writing of history by Boas and his followers. Boas (1858–1941) had a role very similar to that of Malinowski in Britain, in that he is often seen as the founder of anthropology in North America. To promote this myth he systematically wrote members of the BAE out of his accounts of the growth of anthropology and this was not just because he had a difficult relationship with many of them. Boas is best known for his antipathy to evolutionary thought and in America evolutionary notions were most connected to the work of Morgan (see pp. 63–4). Morgan's had been the guiding theory behind the work of the BAE through his influence on Powell. Boas was a complex man with enormous energy and the will to impose his views on the academic community at large. Trained as a physicist in his home country of Germany, he subsequently came under the influence of Bastian who was interested in the way in which what he took to be general human tendencies were given local form through the influences of history and geography. It was this detailed documentation of local areas of life through observation and recording that most influenced Boas, who throughout his life was suspicious of larger bodies of theory and emphasised well-trained and directed induction. Boas carried out fieldwork amongst Inuit groups on Baffin Island (Figure 3.2) in 1883–4 and came to realise the importance of the people's cultural perceptions of the world in which they lived and the history of the cultures that framed those perceptions. These are ideas that he carried with him to subsequent work on the Northwest Coast (Figure 3.3) and meant that he had no place for a theory of evolution in which everyone in the world was supposed to move through the same set of stages.

We shall come back to these points below, but what is crucial here is Boas's role in the professionalisation of the discipline. Boas is unusual in that he worked both in museums and universities, gaining a lectureship in Columbia in 1896, having previously been employed at the Royal Ethnographic Museum of Berlin, helped set up the collections in the Field Museum in Chicago, and

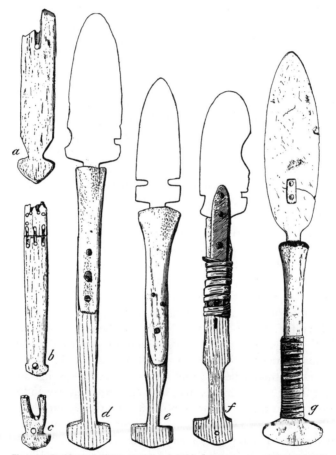

Fig. 202.   Double-edged Knives. *a* ($\frac{50}{3\times7}$), *b* ($\frac{50}{3\times8}$), Length 19 cm.; *c* ($\frac{50}{3\times8}$), Netchillik, length 6.1 cm.; *d* ($\frac{50}{3\times9}$), *e* ($\frac{50}{3\times9}$), Kinipetu, length 49 cm., 43 cm.; *f* ($\frac{50}{3\times9}$), Sauniktu, length 41 cm.; *g* ($\frac{50}{3\times2}$), Copper knife from the region west of King William Land, length 47 cm.

Figure 3.2 Knives from Baffin Island illustrated by Boas (1907). Bulletin of the American Museum of Natural History: Figure 202

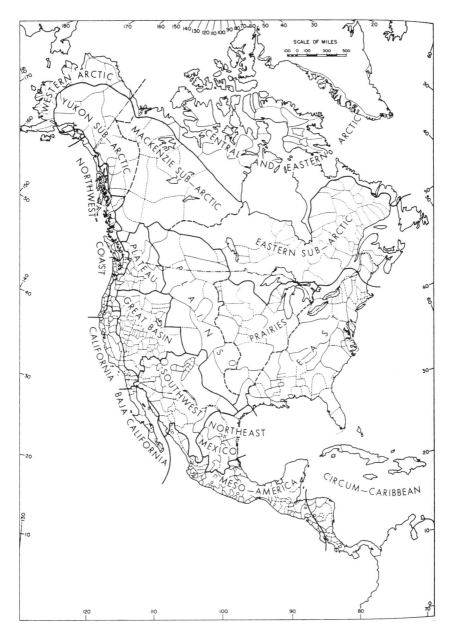

Figure 3.3 Culture areas of North America, including the Northwest Coast (after Driver (1969), *Indians of North America*: Map 2)

the National Museum in New York from which he finally resigned in 1905 (Jacknis 1985). It was from his base in Columbia that Boas had most influence, setting up the American Folk-Lore Society in 1888, modernizing the *American Anthropologist* in 1898, founding the American Anthropological Society in 1900 and reinvigorating the American Ethnological Society in the same year. His students included almost all of the most influential figures intellectually and institutionally in the first half of this century in the USA: Benedict, Herskovits, Kroeber, Lesser, Lowie, Mead, Sapir and Wissler to name just some, who set up departments in Berkeley, Chicago and Northwestern universities.

However, a crucial difference from Britain was the breadth of Boas's interests which included not only social anthropology, but also linguistics, physical anthropology and archaeology. He directed a project of excavation in the Valley of Mexico in 1911 in collaboration with Manuel Gamio in which the latter was influential in furthering stratigraphic excavation in that region. Thus a crucial element of the professionalisation of anthropology in the USA, through the efforts of Boas, was that it did not involve a split with archaeology, due to Boas's general interest in the importance of history. Although Boas rejected evolutionism, as did Malinowski, his notions of culture and cultural change were artefact-focused and looked at both past and present. This interest has been reflected in the position of anthropology in North America to this day, where general Departments of Anthropology are found in the USA encompassing the so-called four fields of the subject: linguistics, prehistory, social and physical anthropology.

Thus we can see that Malinowski's claim to be the first fieldworker ignores the whole early history of the subject in North America. We need also to look briefly at Malinowski's antecedents in Britain, as this reflects upon the nature of his claim. The first point to make is that there was nothing like the BAE in Britain and this was because most of British colonialism operated at a distance, so that there were no native peoples on whom to practise rescue ethnography (although Tylor did set up an ethnographic survey of the British Isles through the British Association for the Advancement of Science). Thus fieldwork was carried out in the colonies with Australia and Papua New Guinea, both important early centres well before Malinowski. One important piece of such work was the collaboration of that rather odd pairing of Spencer (1860–1929) and Gillen (1855–1912). Spencer came from a middle-class family, pursued an academic career and, amongst other things, helped transfer the Pitt Rivers collection to its new museum in Oxford. In 1886 Spencer took up a newly established chair in Biology at Melbourne and in 1894 became the expedition zoologist on the Horn Expedition, which involved a 2,000-mile camel trek into the central Australian desert. In Alice Springs he encountered Frank Gillen, an Australian of Irish stock who had managed the telegraph station for twenty years. Gillen had collected much ethnographic information and contributed twenty-five pages of notes on the local Arunta (now Arrente) to the Horn final report. He and Spencer got on well, despite differences of politics and background; kept in contact and decided together the sorts of information Gillen should collect. In November 1896 Gillen arranged to have a large initiation ceremony held in Alice Springs, during Spencer's long vacation, by agreeing to supply the food for all who attended. Gillen was already seen by the Arunta as a member of the witchetty grub totem and Spencer was able to attend the ceremony as his younger brother. Over a period of three months Spencer and Gillen recorded detailed information on ritual and cultural life, through using pidgin and some Arunta. They published their personal observations and elicitations in 1899 as *The Native Tribes of Central Australia* which contained information of the ceremonies they had witnessed, plus more general background material, which was filled out in subsequent publications. Their work had a major impact on anthropologists and sociologists alike, including a considerable effect on Durkheim's work on the relationship between religion and society, through the subject of totemism. Malinowski wrote in 1913 that half the theoretical works written since Spencer and Gillen's book had been based on it and nine-tenths affected or modified by it (Stocking 1996: 96). However, in Stocking's words, 'Spencer died, however, without leaving academic ethnographic progeny' (1996: 95). The University of Melbourne did not set up teaching in anthropology before his retirement in 1919, so that the University of Sydney in 1926 under Radcliffe-Brown was the first anthropology department in Australia.

One of the people most influential in setting up the Sydney chair from his power base in Cambridge was A. C. Haddon (1855–1939). Haddon's career has parallels to Spencer's in that he started his academic career as a zoologist and competed unsuccessfully for the chair of zoology which Spencer was awarded. Haddon undertook his first piece of fieldwork on the structure and mode of formation of the coral reefs of the Torres Strait in 1888, taking with him a copy of *Notes and Queries*. Indeed he may have been the first anthropologist to use the term 'fieldwork', its origin a reflection of his own scientific background and its rapid acceptance demonstrating the desire anthropologists felt to be seen as engaged in scientific work. His natural sensitivity led him to attempt an understanding of the lives of local people and, unusually both for the time and subsequently, the colonial situation in which they lived. And his socialism led him to a more general awareness of the fact that the map of the world was covered with 'the red paint of British aggression' (Stocking 1996: 102).

Haddon returned to Europe and a chair in zoology in Dublin, but after considerable effort was able to establish himself in Cambridge and from there planned a larger expedition to return to the Torres Straits, which he did in 1898. Haddon's aim was to set up a multi-disciplinary expedition to look at a range of aspects of the human personality through psychology, linguistics, physical anthropology and social anthropology. The members of the expedition appear to have been a most attractive and interesting group: Myers, McDougall and Rivers were three physiologists/psychologists, Ray was a specialist in Melanesian languages, Wilkin a student of anthropology and Seligman a medical pathologist. The expedition was later termed a survey, never staying in one place for more than a few weeks and interviews were not conducted in local languages, but rather in pidgin English. Nevertheless, the Torres Strait expedition is seen as a turning point in British anthropology. First of all, new media were used to record information, including wax cylinder sound-recording, photography and cinematography (4 minutes of film still survive). Here the scientific pretensions of the expedition show through, as these were all seen as forms of realistic recording of information, sceptical though we may be of such a claim today (Edwards 1992). But probably the most important innovation was Rivers development of the so-called 'genealogical method'.

Rivers was not the first to collect genealogical information, but was pioneering in understanding the centrality of kinship to all other aspects of life. He realised that the Islanders memories went back three to five generations and their kinship links represented the framework in which all members of the group could be located. Knowledge of kinship allowed the investigator to order data on residence, clan membership, totems, biography, demography, physical anthropology, migrations, linguistics and group history. The structure of relationships allowed the investigator to lay bare both the social laws of the group and how far these laws were followed in practice. This methodological breakthrough was probably the major result of the expedition which had an immediate impact, but the actual results were less impressive and had nothing like the same influence as Spencer and Gillen's *The Tribes of Central Australia*. But the other crucial result was in institutionalisation, with Rivers, Seligman and Haddon (who formed a central and tight-knit group as a result of their field experiences), having an enormous influence back in Britain. As a result of the expedition's success and the lobbying of James Frazer (author of the *Golden Bough*) and William Ridgeway (Disney Professor of Archaeology) Haddon was appointed University Lecturer in Ethnology. The Board of Anthropological Studies was established and in 1908 it was possible to take a Diploma in Anthropology, the first qualification in the subject at Cambridge, following the institution of a similar Diploma at Oxford in 1906 (Stocking 1996: 116). In the following year Haddon was made a Reader. Rivers held a lectureship in physiological and experimental psychology, but carried out further field research on another two trips to Melanesia and among the Todas of India, and gradually shifted his interests and made major contributions to the origins of psychology and anthropology, as well as treating shell-shock victims, such as Siegfried Sassoon and Wilfred Owen, in the First World War. (It is worth mentioning in passing Pat Barker's novels which have Rivers as a central figure, known as the *Regeneration* trilogy.) Together he and Haddon were responsible for the 'Cambridge School' and trained Radcliffe-Brown, Hocart and Layard amongst many others. Seligman returned to England to work as a pathologist, but then took up further fieldwork in Ceylon (Sri Lanka), Melanesia and the Sudan. In 1910 he was appointed Professor in Ethnology at the London School of Economics from where he directed Malinowski's early training and advised him to carry out fieldwork in Melanesia.

We have thus come full circle, arriving back with Malinowski, and can further evaluate both his and Boas's influence on either side of the Atlantic. The point is neither to bury Malinowski and Boas nor to praise them, but to set their contribution in a more realistic perspective. Malinowski's claim to have moved anthropological fieldwork from the verandah into the village has considerable truth to it, even if this is not the whole truth. There is much more continuity between himself and his predecessors than Malinowski allowed for, particularly in the use of Rivers' genealogical method. It was the systematic nature of the information Malinowski collected that was crucial to him and he saw the need to base anthropology on 'objectively acquired knowledge', not just on 'subjectively formed notions' (Stocking 1992: 51). The revelations of his diary, which show Malinowski in the throes of a complex series of passions concerning career and love which helped structure his perception of Kiriwina, have subsequently thrown doubt on the objective nature of fieldwork. If his myth as the originator of fieldwork is so difficult to believe now, why was it so accepted at the time?

The answer lies in the position Malinowski achieved in 1927 as Professor of Anthropology at the London School of Economics (having been appointed as Lecturer in 1924), plus his political astuteness in using his notion of fieldwork as providing the basis for a new and separate discipline of social anthropology. As Stocking points out, of all the members of Malinowski's generation who carried out extensive fieldwork, only Malinowski and Radcliffe-Brown achieved positions of influence. The crucial element in the argument to establish social anthropology as a separate and viable subject of study was that participant observation was unique to anthropology and could provide reliable information about non-western societies. Malinowski's pupils at the LSE, Montagu, Evans-Pritchard and Raymond Firth for example, carried this argument abroad and were themselves extremely important to the expansion of professional, academic anthropology. In terms of the theories of the formations of disciplines Malinowski's influence was crucial in setting up the first vibrant academic department, with large numbers of students, who had both methods and theories to work with and could perceive a career path before them. Malinowski was incorrect to say that he invented the fieldwork method. However, it is correct to say that he used his conception of fieldwork to help institutionalise social anthropology and in this sense his work built the foundation of the modern discipline.

It is especially interesting in terms of the topic of this book that Malinowski's creation of social anthropology saw the demise of the old Victorian evolutionary approaches which combined ethnography, prehistory and physical anthropology. At the LSE Malinowski and Seligman (Professor of Ethnography) had a prolonged dispute over whether Malinowski's students should attend lectures in technology, prehistory and racial theory as well as social anthropology. It is symbolic that Seligman lost the argument when ill health forced his retirement in 1934 (Stocking 1996: 297). The establishment of the new discipline, with its own methodology and wealth of new facts to be synthesised, caused a split between archaeology and anthropology which in Britain is only now being bridged.

Neither Boas nor Malinowski cynically took and developed a set of ideas they thought would best help establish their discipline. Instead they developed theoretical frameworks which they believed in and used these as the basis of the iv strategies to found the discipline. The differences in the ideas employed on either side of the Atlantic led to varying outcomes, which have affected the whole history of the two disciplines of archaeology and anthropology until present. We shall come back to this point, but first will look briefly at the history of archaeology.

Instituting archaeology

Archaeology has woven a more tangled web on both sides of the Atlantic so that it is more difficult to present a neat history of the discipline and also to see a small number of figures as foundational. An inability to identify mythical founders of archaeology undoubtedly leads to a more realistic perspective, but also provides an insight into the discipline which is useful in itself.

British archaeology owes its genesis to a number of different figures. Field methods were pioneered by Pitt Rivers and those who worked with him, such as H. S. Gray, from the 1870s to 1890s and laid down many of the basic techniques of stratigraphic excavation and recording still in use today. These methods were refined and consolidated in the twentieth century by Mortimer Wheeler (1890–1976). However, none of these people can claim to have made great theoretical breakthroughs which allowed them to present a well-worked package of method and theory as Malinowski had done. The major theoretical advances came from Vere Gordon Childe (1893–1957). There is an interesting contrast between Childe and Malinowski, so that whereas the latter's reputation as the self-styled originator of social anthropology has fallen in the last thirty years, Childe's has risen continuously such that most strands of archaeology attempt to claim him as an ancestor (Harris 1994).

Childe was born in Sydney and became interested in the origins of the Indo-Europeans from a philological perspective. He studied in Oxford during the First World War with people like J. L. Myres and began to see the potential of archaeology. After a brief career in left-wing politics back in Australia he returned to England in 1921, amassed an encyclopaedic knowledge of European prehistory from the Neolithic onwards and published *The Dawn of European Prehistory* in 1925 and other major works, such as *The Danube in Prehistory* (1929). These works represented several major advances. The first was the concept of culture, defined as 'certain types of remains – pots, implements, ornaments, burial rites, house forms – constantly recurring together' (1929: v–vi). He saw Europe as a mosaic of different cultures, which may originally have had their own sets of customs, kinship patterns, rituals and forms of trade, differences represented in the archaeological evidence through variability in artefacts over time and space (Figure 3.4). Not that all artefacts told archaeologists the same things: locally made pottery, ornaments and rites of burying the dead reflected local and conservative patterns of life and were most indicative of ethnic differences. Useful tools, weapons and other elements of technology would diffuse rapidly from one group to another, either through trade or copying. Items which spread rapidly were useful for establishing contemporaneity between different areas, something which was vital in the days before radiocarbon dating (Childe 1929: viii). Much invention occurred in the Near East and thence spread west across Europe to be deployed in new ways by the energetic barbarian cultures.

Childe's picture of European prehistory was a dynamic one, containing both the first real synthesis of the mass of archaeological information available from the continent and a model of the social process. This had a very Boasian look to it and in this stage of his career Childe was also critical of general evolutionary schemes, preferring to emphasise local diversity and creativity. His view stressed change caused by technological innovation in tune with his Marxist background, and with sensitivity to what variations in artefacts meant in social terms, attempting to supply both names and personalities to the variability he perceived. Childe's work was a revelation for many and became a model throughout Europe and North America, not just through the comprehensive nature of his synthesis, but also as an indication of the possibilities inherent in archaeological material. It might seem surprising that this sense of excitement did not trigger some interest amongst the social anthropologists, but then most anthropology was done outside Europe, whereas most British-based archaeological work was carried out within the continent. Also, the structural-functionalism of the anthropologists in Britain, which we shall explore below, gave them little sympathy for the diffusionist and historically oriented work of Childe.

Childe was also one of the two crucial figures in the institutionalisation of the discipline in Britain, the other being Graham Clark. In 1926, the year after he published *The Dawn*, Childe became the first Abercromby Professor in Edinburgh and thus the first person to teach prehistoric archaeology as it is recognisable today, although it had been possible to take a Diploma of Archaeology in Oxford since 1906 and the Institute of Archaeology in Liverpool had been set up in 1904. Childe then took up the first full-time Directorship of the Institute of Archaeology in 1946, Mortimer Wheeler having been temporary Director in 1937. At Cambridge the Disney professorship had been set up in 1851, but only became a properly salaried post in 1927.

Clark became a lecturer at Cambridge in 1935 and held functionalist views very similar to those of Malinowski and Radcliffe-Brown (Trigger 1989: 264). This led to a stress on people's physical needs and therefore their relationship to the environment, as he felt that most cultures were influenced to some degree by ecological constraints. The close interactions Clark had with people like Godwin, the Cambridge scientist who introduced pollen analysis into Britain, led him to abandon a typological view that looked mainly at the distribution of different types of artefacts across Britain and to concentrate instead on the changes through time evidenced in the stratigraphy of the Fens. Clark's key role in the development of the Fenland Research Committee, saw him collaborate with geologists, palynologists and palaeontolgists to reconstruct the history of the Fenland and its human occupation from the late Glacial onward (Smith 1997). Drawing the notion of dynamic succession from ecology, allied to an understanding of the stratigraphy of the Fenland deposits, Clark felt that he could get a real understanding of change from the Mesolithic to the Bronze Age and beyond. Not only was the reconstruction of past environments important for understanding sequence and change, the environment was also a vital element in structuring the nature of life, as Clark was to demonstrate most famously in his work at Star Carr (Clark 1954). Cambridge was the major centre for training undergraduates before the Second World War and this continued after the war when Clark became Disney Professor. Clark's view of culture as a response to the environment left little for links with contemporary British anthropology, although there was some mutual influence between Clark and Leslie White after the war. The stress on ecology became even more marked in the work of Higgs, in the British Academy-funded project investigating the origins of agriculture, set up initially by Clark. For Higgs and his team, archaeology, approached the study of long-term ethology, with people viewed as just another element of dynamic ecosystems, which left little room for any analysis of social forces (Higgs 1972, Higgs and Jarman 1969). This element of the New Archaeology in Britain took the discipline some considerable distance from any contact with anthropology.

The United States was the only country outside Europe which had an indigenous tradition of archaeological research prior to the late nineteenth century (Trigger 1989: 104) and although there were some influences from Europe these were few. In North America the intellectual landscape was very different and archaeology from its inception was much more closely tied to anthropology. There are a number of reasons for this, both institutional and intellectual. Institutionally, archaeology grew up as part of broader surveys, such as those carried out by the BAE, or in universities with their own museums. Intellectually, the climate favoured emphasis on connections between past and present Native American groups, so that ethnology was seen as the key to archaeology, a notion reinforced by the feeling that North American prehistory was short and static.

The BAE had a Division of Mound Exploration, founded in 1882, with Cyrus Thomas at its head, and the US Congress insisted that $5,000 was spent annually on mound studies, reflecting the centrality of mounds in debates about the nation's past. As Europeans moved westwards from the 1780s onwards, crossing the Appalachian Mountains, they found a whole series of mounds and earthworks along the Ohio and Mississippi Rivers which we now know under the names of Hopewell and Adena cultures. They contained artefacts of pottery, shell and native copper of sophisticated manufacture. This sparked a long debate, only resolved a century later, as to whether these had been constructed by groups ancestral to living Native Americans or by Vikings, Mesoamericans or the Welsh (Trigger 1989: 104) who had been dispossessed by incoming Native American groups. For a colonising power, busy dispossessing in their own right, there were obvious advantages in stressing that the group whose land they were taking had recently done the same to others. However, the work of Cyrus at the BAE and others firmly established a Native American origin for the mounds through stratigraphic excavation and a comparison of artefacts with more recent material culture from the same area (Willey and Sabloff 1980: 42). In doing so they reaffirmed the links between archaeology and ethnography.

On the other hand, the BAE as a whole was strongly influenced by the evolutionism of Morgan, who felt that there had been little cultural development within the Americas, and that the supposed sophistication of the Aztecs and the Inkas had been exaggerated (Trigger 1989: 120–1). Although direct connections were perceived between past and present, there was thought to be little change in either and not much to compare with the developments of states in Eurasia. The other on-going argument about the nature and degree of change was that over the antiquity of human settlement, an argument which still rages today (Meltzer *et al.* 1994). One of the major believers in considerable time-depth was Frederic Putnam (1839–1915), who was also crucial in institutionalising the discipline. Putnam became the second Curator of the Peabody Museum at Harvard in 1875, which had been set up in 1866 as the result of a gift by George Peabody. He subsequently became the first Peabody Professor of American Archaeology and Ethnology in 1887 and his title is obviously a significant one in the context of my present discussion. Putnam was no theorist but he was a great fieldworker and organiser. As well as making the Peabody Museum one of the leading institutions in the country, he was also responsible for setting up the Anthropology Exhibit at the 1892 Exposition in Chicago, helping to found the Field Museum of Natural History in Chicago, the Department of Anthropology at Berkeley and the Anthropology Department of the American Museum of Natural History. He was Secretary for the American Association for the Advancement of Science for twenty-five years (Willey and Sabloff 1980: 45). The first doctorate in prehistoric archaeology in the United States was awarded at Harvard to George Dorsey, a student of Boas, in 1894 (Hinsley 1985: 72). Putnam carried out fieldwork in thirty-seven states, plus Mexico and Central America (Mark 1980: 54). Although he was never able to establish Palaeolithic human settlement, Putnam did much else in setting up archaeology, but this was never at the expense of its links with ethnography and the lack of evidence for peopling during the Pleistocene reinforced these links.

Like many others, Putnam had an uneasy relationship with Boas being at first a sponsor and supporter, but then tension entered the relationship around Boas's views on the lack of theory behind Putnam's museum arrangements (Mark 1980: 48–9). Gradually the breach between them was healed, but Boas's emphasis on using material culture to delineate culture areas and local cultural histories came to dominate. North America was divided into areas on the basis of material culture (Figure 3.3) with the implication that little had changed through time and any change was generally ascribed to migration of people or ideas (Trigger 1980: 123–4). Here was a profound difference with Europe, where from the mid-nineteenth century onwards archaeologists attempted to grapple with the enormous and unknown time-depth of prehistory. This, of itself, caused some split with anthropology, in that ideas about ways of life in the present may have little relevance to Ice Age peoples sharing the continent with mammoths and woolly rhinoceroses for which there were no recent analogies. The apparent lack of time-depth in North America helped join the two disciplines and make the methodological differences between them less relevant.

For example, Kroeber, a student of Boas, undertook considerable amounts of archaeological work. In 1915 Kroeber was engaged in ethnological work in Zuñi pueblos, in the same area in which Cushing had worked. On his afternoon walks around the area he discovered eighteen ruined pueblos and became interested in the history of the area. He started surface collections on the abandoned sites and recovered different pottery types. From written histories he realised that red and black-on-red pots had been used until the Spanish arrived, but that the white and black-on-white pottery he recovered was unknown. He thus made the reasonable inference that these latter styles must be earlier than the arrival of the Spanish and he came up with a seriation of the sites with six periods based on the proportions of different pot types. This he saw as evidence for continuity of local tradition and use, a conclusion backed up by the fact that a single corrugated pot type was found throughout, albeit in declining numbers (Kroeber 1916). Such continuity in pottery types was obviously indicative of cultural continuity, an idea reinforced by the excavations of Spier (1917) which confirmed the broad outline of Kroeber's conclusions. These works not only represent some of the first seriations in American archaeology which subsequently became standard in many areas (Willey and Sabloff 1980: 97), they also helped to reinforce the links between past and present.

With the Depression came massive Federal Relief programmes designed to give people work, and archaeology was funded on such a scale as to make possible large open-area excavations. These provided detailed evidence of settlements and areas, allowing the first real attempts to correlate the distribution of artefacts with features such as houses, hearths and pits. Not only did this shift interest away from chronology as such, it also fitted in with the functionalism of the time (looked at in more detail in the next chapter) which in anthropology had come to view cultures as integrated wholes. Archaeologists' attempts to fit together individual elements of sites were patterned on the notion that sites were the structured outcomes of cultural action. This growing concern culminated in Taylor's 1948 critique of archaeology, which he felt had not been concerned with culture as an integrated system and had ignored vast bodies of potential evidence contained in unrecovered bones and plant remains, but also had not taken the complexity and potential of archaeological sites seriously enough. Taylor wanted detailed intra-site analysis of all the evidence, which could then make sites the building blocks to be assembled into regional syntheses. This would eventually allow a detailed understanding of sites and regions analogous to ethnologists' pictures of living cultures.

Taylor's main call was for better methodology in the recovery and analysis of archaeological material and for a bigger picture within which to frame the results of these analyses. His main theoretical stance was drawn from anthropology, which he saw as a scientific discipline, in contrast to history which was particularistic in his view and could only give anecdotal and idiosyncratic accounts. Generalisations about human action were only possible through functionalist anthropology and successful generalisation was the hallmark of science. Taylor's polemic was not well received at the time, but has come to be seen as one of the ultimate inspirations for the New Archaeology of the 1960s (Willey and Sabloff 1980: 139). Not only is New Archaeology associated with attempts to provide generalisations about human action, it is rightly credited with a much deeper concern for the unusual nature of archaeological evidence. Archaeological evidence accumulates over long periods of time and is thus subject to decay, disturbance and destruction; it is also indirect evidence of human life, unlike anthropology, which is based on participant observation, or history, which derives its evidence from written accounts from human actors. This dual realisation led to two sets of archaeological research from the 1960s onwards. The first, which often goes under the name of ethnoarchaeology, was the study of living peoples' use of artefacts and living space in order to create links between how objects and sites were used and the sorts of residues they might leave behind on archaeological sites. Studies such as Binford's on Inuit hunter-gatherers (Binford 1978) or Rathje's of present-day rubbish disposal in Tucson (Rathje 1974) derived from a feeling that anthropologists were no longer interested in material things and were not providing the relevant sorts of information. The second study was of how archaeological evidence might be discarded and preserved, plus how it is recovered through archaeological excavation and survey. Here David Clarke's (1968) theoretical statements on the need for depositional and post-depositional theory spurred much thought and Schiffer's *Behavioral Archaeology* (1976) promoted considerable analytical work on what sorts of transformations archaeological materials undergo after being used.

Since the 1960s complicating developments have taken place in both disciplines to change their relationship either side of the Atlantic; all of these are in areas of theory and will be considered in more detail in the following chapters. In the 1970s an interest in trade and exchange as a means for understanding social structure became prevalent throughout the English-speaking world and utilised many forms of economic anthropology (Renfrew 1975). These influences in combination with various forms of Marxism were also the basis for models of change still influential today (Friedman and Rowlands 1978). In Britain these moves were followed by a general opening up of theory to new possibilities and an increasing convergence between archaeology and anthropology from the late 1970s. In the United States there has been much less convergence of either method or theory. Although most archaeological teaching and research is done within overall departments of anthropology rather than in separate archaeology departments there is little real harmony of interests between archaeologists and social anthropologists, except in the area of historical archaeology. Lack of harmony is partly due to the continuing insistence on methodological rigour and the uniqueness of archaeology, but also the fact that much American archaeology is still pursued within an evolutionary framework, at odds with the current stress on culture on the part of anthropologists. Conversely the British convergence results from a re-evaluation of the nature and worth of fieldwork amongst anthropologists, which was the aspect of their work used by Malinowski and Radcliffe-Brown to institutionalise the discipline as a separate entity. It should also be noted that archaeologists are now starting to critique the nature of their fieldwork as well (Hodder 1997). It is to present-day views of anthropological fieldwork that we now turn.

Doubts about anthropological fieldwork

As you will remember, the main use Malinowski made of fieldwork was as a source of objective and replicable facts which could provide a solid and distinctive empirical basis for anthropology, so that a set of facts created by one fieldworker could be replicated by another in the same field situation with only minor discrepancies. As Stocking (1992: 51) says, Malinowski's aim was to show that ethnographic information was 'objectively acquired knowledge' and not 'subjectively formed notions'. This view was accepted with only minor dissent until the publication of Malinowski's diaries of his experience in Kiriwina showed that not only had he misrepresented his fieldwork methods to some extent, by being less purely a part of the village community than he had claimed, but also that his own overwhelming preoccupations and state of mind must have had a considerable effect on what he saw and the sense he made of it. The diary sparked reflections on the ethics of fieldwork and how far colonial or post-colonial Caucasians had a right to pronounce on forms of life in other parts of the world. It also brought into question the basis for ethnographic authority: if fieldwork did not result in objective accounts, what sorts of knowledge did it create and what forms of self-criticism were needed to understand the point of view from which the information was generated? And if the edifice of anthropological knowledge rested on material gathered in fieldwork, what implications did this have for anthropology as a whole? What might have seemed initially like a relatively technical doubt about method has sparked a debate calling into question the whole of anthropological practice (Stocking 1992: 15).

It was not, of course, Malinowski's diaries that really caused the debate; these were catalyst at most. Deeper changes include the decline in the belief in objective knowledge, so much a part of all the social sciences until the middle of this century. I am sure this decline is linked with the end of colonialism. As an unconscious feeling of superiority on the part of Europeans started to wane, so too did the feeling that they might have a privileged and more secure view of the world which could create incontrovertible knowledge. If not possessed of a superior road to truth, in what way were European accounts superior to people's accounts of themselves, which must, at least, be based on real insider knowledge? This is a question which still unsettles anthropologists today and to which there are a number of answers rather than any single one.

Malinowskian fieldwork had brought together two elements of anthropology which had remained separate in much of nineteenth-century practice: the gathering of basic information, often in the colonies, and armchair theorising and synthesis in the metropolitan centres. Now one person did both, with the added element that the period in the field, with all its physical discomforts and psychological and cultural disorientations, acted as something of a rite of passage, providing the basis for a PhD, the main means of entry into the profession. The complex and messy process of fieldwork had to be compressed into a monograph, which inevitably stripped down the experience into a linear form and gave the authors varying degrees of visibility. But as Clifford (1988: 22) says '[t]he predominant mode of modern fieldwork authority is signalled "You are there . . . because I was there"'. The canonical texts were also used for teaching and many generations of students have worked their way through *The Argonauts*, *The Nuer* or *Growing Up in New Guinea*, bringing new views to them to be sure, but also, on some level, absorbing them as models.

The rise of interpretive or symbolic anthropology in the 1960s questioned what it meant to elicit the 'native point of view'. Under the influence of a number of currents of thought we shall consider later, social life had come to be seen as a negotiation of meanings. If this was true for life as a whole, it must also hold for the anthropological process of eliciting information, and it became inconceivable that one side of a discussion (the anthropologist) could present his or her view as sole truth. At the least there had to be some account of the process of dialogue during fieldwork through which meanings had been arrived at. In the most sophisticated accounts, from the 1960s on, this derived from a consideration of the epistemology of both parties, the basis for their knowledge. This made the anthropologist almost as much a subject of the research as the people being studied, as well as enhancing anthropology's power to throw new light on western ways of thought. Rather than interviewing informants, anthropologists started engaging in dialogue, a two-way process at least, which brought about some joint understanding. Clifford (1988: 36) has described fieldwork as 'living one's way into an alien expressive universe' until various stable forms of knowledge are reached to which understanding can return. Geertz's division between experience-near and experience-far concepts is also useful: the former deriving from the lived experience of social negotiation in the field and the latter to do with both the taken-for-granteds of the culture from which the fieldworker comes and the specific anthropological ideas they bring with them into the field. It is also Geertz

(1973b) who popularised the notion of cultures as texts to read and re-read as new interpretations become available.

Now that fieldwork is seen as negotiation and dialogue, it is also possible to see that local people have considerable ability to control the information coming to the anthropologist and to impress new themes and thoughts on them. Rosaldo (1980) describes how he arrived in the Philippine Highlands determined to make a study of present-day social structure, but was forced to listen to, and write down, long accounts of local history, which he thought he would ignore when he got home. But once he was home, and having given the subject considerable thought, he realised that these texts represented a fascinating body of material on Ilongot views of history, and this became the subject of his final text. It is Clifford (1988: 45) who asks the question – if all this was written against his will, who is actually the author of the field notes? We could also ask about the motives of the Ilongot in telling so much of their history.

Questions of authorship, considered at length in Clifford and Marcus (1986), have led to experimentation with new forms of expression better suited to the more complex conceptions of fieldwork. Texts like Bateson's *Naven* are seen as honourable precursors to present trends, as he wrote about a single New Guinea ceremony from three different points of view (Bateson 1936). Recent texts take a number of different forms. These range from edited self-accounts of people, such as Shostak's (1981) *Nisa: The Life and Words of a !Kung woman* and Strathern's (1979) *Ongka: A Self-account by a New Guinea Big-Man*, to explorations of the process of fieldwork, like that of Rosaldo mentioned above and include hybrids such as Crapanzano's (1980) *Tuhami: Portrait of a Moroccan* which tries to do both. Marcus and Fischer (1986: 42) see experimentation as a tool to develop theory in exploring the potentials and limits of interpretation and feel that they would like to see texts which explore both the larger political and historical situations in which people live in the present, together with the fine details of people's lives and experience.

Anthropologists feel much more ambiguous about fieldwork than they did, but it is still a central point of discussion within the discipline. And in some ways things have not changed. The fieldwork-based PhD is still the major, although not exclusive, means of entering academic anthropology. However, the subject matter of field research has shifted enormously. No longer does the researcher seek out a tribe living in their pristine state on the margins of the colonial world, but will rather look at the local group's relationship to the national and transnational forces of capitalism. This may take the form of focusing on Australian Aboriginal struggles for land (Povinelli 1993), or use of the media, or relationships with mining companies, the development of western business elites (Marcus 1983) or rural communities in France (Favret-Saada 1980). This concentration on the position of small communities within late capitalist global structures has necessarily given much work a political and ethical edge and has often made anthropologists spokespeople for their group (see chap. 6 for further discussion). As such fieldwork has come a long way from disinterested, distanced and objective research.

The more complex and, it must be said, realistic view of fieldwork is of necessity both baffling and challenging. It is not clear any more what role field-work can and should play within anthropology, but it is also clear that anthropology cannot live without some form of face-to-face contact with, and personal involvement in, the world being studied. In terms of my broader argument about field methods and methodology generally being the point of division between archaeology and anthropology, the present uncertainty about basic forms of gathering information has contributed to the erosion of a feeling of the uniqueness of anthropology. I argued in the first half of the chapter that fieldwork gave anthropology its own unique set of evidence and that this was used within universities to create anthropology as a separate sub-ject. It is worth raising the question whether the decline in the old concept of fieldwork lies at the root of changes within the discipline? The exploration of landscape, material culture and forms of representation, such as photograph and film have all called for new methodologies different from, or complemen-tary to, participant observation based on a grasp of the language and requiring extended periods in the field. Field sites of anthropologists have also changed to include shopping centres, museums and offices. It is fairly obvious that the conception of subject matters of archaeology and anthropology have con-verged over the last twenty years. But perhaps re-evaluation of the basic methodologies of the subjects have also broken down barriers and eroded claims to uniqueness? No subject is structured solely by its methodologies, however, and theory is always important. It is to theoretical questions that we shall turn in the next two chapters.

4   Evolutionary, social and cultural anthropologies

In this chapter I shall attempt to survey the main theories employed by anthropologists, and to some extent by archaeologists, between roughly the late nineteenth century and the Second World War, together with a sketch of the groupings and institutions to which they belonged. In terms of ideas this survey will take us from Victorian formulations of the evolution of human societies to the heyday of structural-functionalism. But I shall also outline the changing ways in which key concepts were developed and used, prime amongst these being 'society' and 'culture'. In Britain in this period we can see a move from an emphasis on culture by the evolutionist Tylor to a concentration on society by structural-functionalists such as Malinowski and Radcliffe-Brown. In the United States something of a move in the opposite direction is clear, although this is less obvious, from the social structure of Morgan to the centrality of the idea of culture in the work of Boas. A further crucial touchstone of difference on either side of the Atlantic was varying attitudes to history.

Ideas cannot be considered in isolation from their social context, '[b]ecause intellectual groupings bear some analogy to the lineage groups studied by modern social anthropology' (Stocking 1987: 305). Adherence to a group meant continuous contact with other members of that group, which tended to reinforce joint views of the world, although familiarity could also breed dissent. The nature of these groups changed over the period of interest here, from the enthusiastic amateurs, members of the Anthropological Society of Britain and Ireland or the American Ethnological Society, to university departments with their more formalised and prescriptive modes of entry. Writing of the short period of study necessary for a PhD at Columbia, Kroeber wrote that Boas was mainly concerned that students should have an adherence to his values and they could learn what they needed to know of the details of anthropology later (Kroeber 1959, quoted in Mark 1980: 52). It may also be that the tightest groupings were those that proselytised most strongly for new approaches, such as the Boasian view in the United States and the structural-functionalists led by Malinowski in Britain and Radcliffe-Brown in other parts of the world.

The evolutionists: Morgan and Tylor

Let us turn first to evolutionist views, as these came first historically. These, though diverse, had core notions in common. First, and maybe the most important, of these was the comparative method. In the eighteenth century Turgot had held that the present state of the world contains all the past stages of humanity and the key to history lay in the systematic comparison and ordering of societies in the present. In the nineteenth century we have only to look at the full title of Lubbock's bestselling work on prehistory – *Prehistoric Times, as Illustrated by Ancient Remains, and the Manners and Customs of Modern Savages* (1912) – to see that comparisons of ancient and modern were the way to understanding the former. The logic of this argument was that all ancient times from the Palaeolithic (a term coined by Lubbock) onwards could be illuminated through modern-day groups at the same stage of development. A further premise was that present-day diversity arose out of initial unity. Locke's statement, that in the beginning all the world was America, had been replaced by the feeling that Tasmanian aboriginal groups with their supposed simplicity of material culture represented the Lower Palaeolithic of the northern hemisphere. These ideas were developed to oppose the degenerationist view that so-called primitive races had declined from a civilised state through wandering to the margins of the world, away from the centre of civilisation in Eurasia. One further commonality of the evolutionists, but by no means restricted to them alone, is the stress on positivism, which held that the truths of science rest on the evidence of the senses. Consequently, trained observation could yield the building blocks for a comparativist and scientific view of humanity past and present.

Morgan is of particular importance as he developed an historical scheme which paid most attention to the organisation of society as we understand the term today and, indeed, many of the issues he highlighted are still discussed at present. It is thus worth dwelling on his scheme.

Morgan, in his most general work, *Ancient Society* (1985, first published 1877), presented an historical scheme for social change which ran from savagery to civilisation. He divided this history into two lines: that of inventions and discoveries, which was a cumulative history, each age building on the last; and that of institutions, in which change unfolded rather than accumulated. These two lines of history were linked and mutually supporting. As far as institutions were concerned Morgan made another twofold division between the *gens* in which personal ties of blood and marriage predominated and political society which was founded on territory and property rather than on personal relations. This division between kinship and civil society provides a framework for understanding change to this day and much recent discussion of the growth of the state focuses on the breakdown of kin-based society.

Morgan combined information from ethnography and historical sources to come up with a global scheme of human change, based on the notion that so-called savage groups around the world preserved in their social forms previous stages in the progressive history of humanity. The very earliest stages of people's spread across the globe were not thought to be preserved today, but there were many examples of a savage way of life. Savages lacked pottery and by implication the settled village life which brought progress in the simple arts. Australian aborigines or Athapascan tribes around Hudson's Bay formed examples of this stage of life and were people who also lacked sophisticated forms of marriage, brothers and sisters often marrying each other. Three stages of barbarism spanned the invention of pottery, the domestication of animals and development of metal working. The upper barbarians were known from the earliest historical sources which gave details of the Greek tribes at the time of Homer or the Italians before the founding of Rome. These groups mark the boundary of kinship society which had been transcended by the 'Semitic' civilisations of the Near East and subsequently the Aryan city states and empires of Greece and Rome. These ancient civilisations still contained survivals of kinship, particularly in the form of the *gens* which could be discerned even within the city of Imperial Rome.

The fact that all the peoples of the earth exemplify these stages demonstrated the unity of origins of humanity. Progression up these stages was powered by technical inventions. Here the barbarian ages were the most important for subsequent progress with their development of the domestication of plants and animals, which secured the food supply, and the eventual mastery of metals. 'Furnished with iron tools . . . mankind was certain of attaining to civilisation' (Morgan 1985: 43). This in turn caused the eventual move from kin to civil society and the parallel changes in family type from the consanguine to the monogamous family. Central to all these moves was the developing notion of private property and once this concept had become a 'controlling passion' civilisation had begun.

The comprehensive nature of Morgan's scheme, which tied in technical change with familial and group forms of organisation, made it impressive to contemporaries such as Marx and Engels, as well as people like Leslie White in the subsequent century. Not only was Morgan's scheme influential but he also mentioned an extra problem which confronted all subsequent investigators into social change: what sort of evidence can we expect to find of different forms of society? Here his concentration on technical change provided part of the answer. People like Lubbock (1912) had taken the classification of artefacts produced by Thomsen, Montelius and Worsaae into stone, bronze and iron and used it as evidence of progressive stages in human history. What Lubbock provided was a systematic historical scheme in the same manner as Morgan had done, although stressing changes in religious sentiment more than the older man. However, the combination of the classification and implied dating of artefacts which had been carried out in Europe together with Morgan's scheme made possible the empirical investigation of social forms through archaeological evidence, which set a direction and standard for all subsequent research.

Tylor breathed in this general ether of ideas and was able to come up with some of its most telling general statements and to show how broad theoretical precepts could lead to systematic research. Tylor and others felt that present institutions could only be understood from the study of the past. Because he subscribed to the basic Darwinian premise that historical processes did not make leaps but operated in slow continuous manner he could also say that past and present held the clues to the future. He was determined to set this study on a scientific footing, demonstrating that the comparative method would convince those engaged in 'mathematics, physics, chemistry, biology to admit that the problems of anthropology are amenable to scientific treatment' (Tylor 1888: 245). Through proper and consistent observation and comparison of information from around the globe it should be possible to show:

> that the institutions of man are as distinctively stratified as the earth on which he lives. They succeed each other in series substantially uniform over the globe . . . shaped by similar human nature acting through successively changed conditions in savage, barbaric and civilised life.
>
> (Tylor 1888: 269)

Tylor's central concept was that of culture, which he presented in a formulation that has had vast influence since it was put forward in his best-known work, *Primitive Culture*, in 1871. Culture is 'that complex whole which includes knowledge, belief, art, morals, law, custom, and other capabilities and habits acquired by man as a member of society' (Tylor 1871: 1). Tylor believed in the psychic unity of humanity, for, despite apparent differences, we all have the same mental apparatus, although social conditions have led to different levels of rational development. With an ethnocentrism that now takes our breath away, Tylor saw Europe and America as the standard for the rest of the world to reach and thought it possible to rank other societies in an ascending order below these – Australian, Tahitian, Aztec, Chinese, Italian, to use an example Tylor cited – that no one could dispute.

In its overall structure Tylor's scheme parallels Morgan's with its movement from savagery to barbarism and then civilisation. In Tylor's view of the world, rational and moral development were linked in a move from primordial chaos to the order, goodness and happiness of the civilised state. The earliest groups were matriarchal, as lack of biological knowledge meant that no fixed role was ascribed to the father and it was only the link between mother and child that could provide the basis for ordering kin groups. Lack of biological knowledge was part of a wider lack of understanding in which the savage saw the natural world as animated by spirits and random forces. A systematic understanding of cause and effect were established in the modern world through the rise of science, leading to the technological power of Victorian England, as shown by the Great Exhibition. With the growth of knowledge of paternity came kin reckoning in both lines and the development of exogamy, which saw regularised marriage exchanges between groups to their mutual benefit. A more rounded understanding of kinship relations within groups led to classificatory systems of status: for example, all women of one generation within a settlement might be called 'mother' by all members of the next. It was only with the rise of individualistic civil societies that roles adhered to individual actors.

The monogamous family was the eventual result of a greater biological and social understanding, and this was sanctioned by religious law as the moral element of marriage was seen to be crucial. The weight of moral responsibility fell to the father who shouldered the task of both providing for the family physically and protecting its moral welfare. Savages lived by hunting, fishing or gathering wild plants and had no concept of property, or of cultivation, and therefore little reason to improve their lot. Pastoralists and agriculturalists did have a notion of private property and also some division of labour which, because of greater specialisation, had a propensity to produce a surplus. Surplus, in turn, became the basis for increasing levels of material production through deepening specialisation and heightened forms of social stratification. Political leaders were needed to rationally co-ordinate different economic and social functions and so the civil state was born. All these factors helped fashion sovereign individuals differentiated in terms of tasks and status from their fellows and needing to develop their rational powers to perceive and pursue their own interests.

It is easy to ridicule attitudes of social superiority and patriarchy that lie behind Tylor's scheme, but much more salutary to realise that almost identical schemes rose again to prominence in the middle of this century and are still prominent in some forms of archaeology, masked slightly by the dropping of more offensive forms of terminology, such as savagery and barbarism.

The years of change: Haddon and Rivers

Tylor's views arose at the apogee of Victorian self-confidence but even by the 1890s were being nuanced by the views of others with different experiences. One of these was Haddon who, influenced by his early career as a biologist, assumed a Darwinian perspective. But his work in one relatively small region, that of the Torres Strait, meant that he became interested in localised evolution as a complement to global trends and in an attempt to define local artistic provinces in the borderland between Australia and Melanesia. Importantly, Haddon also felt that the comparative method could only be used when historical studies had shown whether the cases being compared were truly independent or had a linked genesis, a point that became a major part of Boas' criticisms. Haddon's interests linked into older forms of diffusionism, which looked at the movement of traits from one area to another. Although diffusionism is often seen as antithetical to evolutionary ideas, Stocking has shown that it remained as a complement to the mainstream interest in global evolution (Stocking 1996: 106, 181–2) and always remained as a possibility for explaining individual resemblances. Tylor's original interests were in diffusion of cultural traits and this was overlain by the new evolutionary framework, rather than replaced by it.

Another person with a complex relationship to both evolutionism and diffusionism was Rivers. Rivers' career is a most varied and interesting one. Starting his professional life as medical doctor, he became interested in neurological and psychiatric problems. After reading Herbert Spencer on mental evolution Rivers became interested in grounding evolution in empirical research on the working of the nervous system and perception. He felt that mental evolution took place at a level below that of linguistic concepts and sensory perceptions. In discussing an experiment which looked at how his friend Henry Head's arm regained feeling after nerves had been severed, Rivers and Head mentioned the implications this might have for the developmental history of the nervous system (Stocking 1996: 187). However, it is not for these strands of his work that he is best known today. As we saw in the last chapter Rivers' major methodological advance was in developing means of collecting genealogies which in turn could be used as the framework for understanding almost all aspects of a group's life in a systematic manner. Rivers was to return to Morgan in order to give his kinship information relevance to broader questions of evolution.

In discussing the kinship systems of the people of Mabuiag in the Torres Strait, Rivers produced the first kinship diagrams and referred to Morgan on terms of classificatory kinship (Figure 4.1). He then applied his genealogical method to the Todas of southern India in 1901–2 and the resulting monograph (Rivers 1906) was seen as a massive step forward in making anthropology a science. Amongst the Todas, a woman ideally had several husbands (often brothers) and it was impossible on biological grounds to know who was the father of a child. Ritual means were found to give one man paternity, until either he died or another could push his claim. It was cases such as this that broadened Rivers' interest in the classificatory nature of kinship. In Rivers' reuse of Morgan's *Ancient Society* he felt that present-day familial and kinship relations could only be understood through the evolution of such relationships in the past. Rivers set up an evolutionary scheme of marriage types which, while based on that of Morgan, differed from it in details and this saw a move from Australian Aboriginal forms of marriage, to that in Mabiuag, the

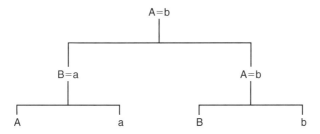

Figure 4.1 Marriage across moieties (Rivers (1914), *Kinship and Social Organisation*: Diagram 3)

Murray Islands (also in the Torres Strait), to Hawaii with an elimination of the distinction between cross-cousins (where a woman's children marry those of her brother) and parallel cousins (where the children of two sisters or two brothers marry). He also saw that marriage groups could often be divided into moieties (that is two out-marrying groups within the tribe) so that all the women from one half of the group sought husbands from men in the other half. This also meant that kinship terminologies were divided into two halves so that a child would call all the people from their mother's side by terms relating to their mother (mother's father, mother's brother, mother's brother's daughter, etc.) and the same for the father's side. People act according to these statuses, entering avoidance, closeness or joking relations with particular rela tives and whilst some of the people in the other moiety would have a known biological relationship to an individual in the opposite moiety, those who did not would be fitted into a status equivalent to a kinship niche. Thus all relationships in such societies worked through the idiom of kinship, with right and wrong action determined by actual or fictive kin relations. Furthermore such sets of relationships could be seen to have an evolution of their own. Kinship and its terminologies came to be seen as a means of mapping the social world and the bounds of that world in terms of permitted action. Kinship influenced economic action through who worked and exchanged with whom, plus also marriage, ritual groupings and day-to-day patterns of talk and avoidance.

Kinship is now seen as fundamental to many aspects of life in vast numbers of societies and this is partly due to the work of Rivers, who saw it both as deriving from social forces and acting to shape those social forces. Morgan was important to Rivers as he indicated that the study of social organisation could be a scientific one (Stocking 1996: 199). It is somewhat ironic that in his home country of the United States, Morgan was eclipsed by the influence of Boas, whereas in Britain he had a long influence as a result of Rivers. A further paradox is that after rediscovering Morgan, Rivers distanced himself from an evolutionary approach, marking his change of view in a paper in 1911 (Rivers 1926) where he spoke of his 'conversion' from evolutionism to diffusionism, feeling that before it was possible to find general laws of evolutionary development there must be detailed historical analysis of actual contemporary cultures. He did not give up evolutionary goals so much as postpone them, and tended to see cultural forms in stratigraphic terms, preserving previous substrates of life into the present. Such an idea was prominent in his major work (Rivers 1914) where he saw Melanesian society in the present as being the result of a mixture from three or four waves of immigration and diffusion, each bringing its own sets of customs and material culture, such as *kava* or betel nut. Rivers came to emphasise the complexity of culture and included contemporary colonialism as one of the major effects on life in the western Pacific.

Rivers' diffusionism fractured what had been a more holistic view of culture into various component parts in order to look at the influx and combination of individual elements. Using modern colonial contacts as a starting point he saw the introduction of new elements of material culture (such as iron tools in the contemporary case) as relatively unimportant alterations; as were changes in language and religion with people taking up Christianity and various forms of pidgin with relative ease. But it was the social structure that provided the basic fabric of Melanesian society (or any other) and this had remained essentially unchanged through European incursions and depredations. As in the present, so in the past, and Rivers saw social structure as the integrating force which brought together all aspects of life, many of which, such as the movements of material culture, were due to the accidents of diffusion and contact. The first volume of *The History of Melanesian Society* (1914) contained a morphological study of the social system of different groups based on the idea that social institutions only arise in response to definite social needs. In positing a central integrating core of society and linking this to the needs of the group, Rivers clearly anticipated many of the main tenets of functionalism (Stocking 1996: 207), as we shall see.

Rivers' work set the basis for social anthropology in Britain through concentrating on social roles and obligations structured through the relations of kinship. These sets of social relations were crucial to the contemporary life of the society and to their history. Even in his later diffusionist phase, where material culture became more important, Melanesian societies were said to have kinship at the core. The stress on social relations, as continued in the work of Malinowski and Radcliffe-Brown, became the key feature of British social anthropology, remaining so until the last twenty years.

Rivers' work had multiple historical effects, however, due to his wide-ranging interests and the number of different theoretical positions he explored during his life. His 'genealogical method' had an immediate and obvious effect and has been used and refined by all subsequent anthropologists interested in kinship (and there have not been many that were not). His explorations of both evolution and diffusion, plus his reflections on the nature of history deriving from both positions, had complex influences on Malinowski and the hyper-diffusionists such as Grafton Elliott Smith. Rivers' concern about colonial impacts, his use of the colonial situation as a model for understanding past forms of contact and his notion of cultures as hybrids anticipate many similar discussions today. Lastly, as we have just seen, his later ideas, focusing on the integration of social forms and their attempts to supply basic needs flowed through into functionalism. Finally his psychological and physiological concerns were a direct influence on Malinowski's psychologism. He lectured to, and greatly influenced, Malinowski (who called Rivers 'my patron saint of fieldwork' (Stocking 1996: 235)) and Radcliffe-Brown, who was taught by Rivers and saw himself as a disciple of the early Rivers, before turning away later in life. It is symbolic of the changes taking place in anthropology that Rivers' sudden death in 1922 coincided with the first publication of Malinowski's and Radcliffe-Brown's mature works, which were to lay the basis for functionalism (Malinowski 1922, Radcliffe-Brown 1922). The relative lack of acknowledgement of Rivers after his death was due to a series of factors: the relative marginality of Cambridge anthropology between the wars; his movement towards diffusionism later in his life, which associated him in some minds with the excesses of Grafton Elliott Smith (who became his literary executor) and the fact that in founding a new anthropology on the basis of systematic fieldwork and functionalism both Malinowski and Radcliffe-Brown tended to play down, although not deny, earlier influences of which Rivers may been seen as the chief.

Boas, relativism and culture history

Attempts to rewrite the history of anthropology were even more marked in the United States, through Boas' (1858–1942) attempts to define himself as the founding culture hero of the discipline. Many people have noted Boas' systematic disregard for earlier anthropology in the United States, even though he had close contacts in his early years with the Bureau of American Ethnology, and especially with Putnam who helped establish him in American anthropology (Mark 1980: 173). Boas was crucial in establishing cultural anthropology in the United States, which had quite a different set of interests to Rivers' social anthropology in Britain. Boas focused much less on kinship, but more on the sets of beliefs and customs of the societies he studied, integrating a concern for material culture, art and local history into his analyses. It has been said, with some truth, that Tylor could be seen as a major inspiration for American cultural anthropology, whereas Morgan became the model for British social anthropology.

Boas' early training in Germany, as with many others of that period, was in science, studying first physics and then moving to geography. He came under the influence of the ethnologist Ratzel who stressed the importance of diffusion and attempted to show that items such as the bow and arrow and the blowpipe had been invented only once in the world and then diffused to other groups. Although the diffusion of different traits was an accidental and random process it did result in culture areas, where similar sets of traits were grouped together on the earth's surface. These ideas had a profound effect on Boas, staying with him for the rest of his life. Boas' innovation, however, was to stress the profundity of the difference between various cultures. In an early paper (1889), Boas looked at the categorisation of sound. He argued that the inability of some groups to make the same sorts of sound distinctions as Europeans was not due to primitiveness, but rather to differences in sense perception and categorisation (Boas 1982). This insight opened up the possibility of whole different worlds of experience and certainly of basic variations in rendering experience in words. Differences between groups would not be of a superficial kind, but at the level of experience and speech so that there were new worlds to be explored through the process of anthropology.

Such a view differs vastly from the broad comparative projects of Morgan and Tylor. A stress on such deep otherness poses questions for the project of anthropology: how far can one culture ever understand another? This is a question we are still grappling with today. For Boas, part of the answer to this question lay in a more systematic study of cultural difference and particular cultural areas. Boas found American anthropology to be a mess. In his obituary his student Ruth Benedict said famously of him 'Boas found anthropology a collection of wild guesses and a happy hunting ground for the romantic lover of primitive things; he left it a discipline in which theories could be tested' (Benedict 1943: 61), thus participating in the denigration of any prior anthropological study. Boas is most famous for his fieldwork amongst Inuit groups and the Kwakiutl of the Northwest Coast, but had anthropological and archaeological interests as far away as Mexico. Boas was to document groups, especially those of the Northwest, in unprecedented detail. However, as the wheel of history turned, he was to be criticised for the fact that the detail was at the expense of a synthesising structure, making it almost impossible for the reader to grasp an overall structure behind the 10,000 pages of Kwakiutl ethnography (White 1963: 55).

It is worth looking at Kwakiutl ethnography (or Kwakaka'waka as they are now known) to see both the nature of Boas' achievement and the criticisms of it. The Kwakiutl, studied by Boas for over forty-five years from 1886 onwards, lived in an area of enormous ecological variety on and around Vancouver Island. This region had large rivers, temperate rainforests and abundant marine resources of fish, seals and whales. They are renowned partly for living in large, settled villages of several hundred people in the absence of any form of agriculture. The Japan current brings warm water from the southern Pacific northward along these shores, helping to moderate the cold of the climate somewhat. It also brings halibut, cod, herring and five species of salmon. The salmon run up the rivers to lay their eggs and could be caught by net, spear or trap (nowadays over-fishing, dams and pollution have drastically reduced numbers). Elaborate technologies were developed for exploiting the sea, with large canoes from which nets, harpoons and lines could be used. Fish and other products could be dried or smoked in times of abundance to provide food throughout the year. The people of this coast created a remarkable art in carved totem poles, canoes and other objects (Figure 4.2).

According to Boas (1897) the Kwakiutl lived in groups of matrilineal descent known as *numaym*. 'Here the woman brings as a dower her father's position and privileges to her husband, who however is not allowed to use them himself, but acquires them for the use of his son' (Boas 1897: 334–5). Delving into the history of the group, Boas felt that there had been a movement from a prior patrilineal state to the present matrilineal one, exactly the opposite move posited by Tylor and Morgan within their evolutionary schemes. This became a test case for Boas and his students to show that on a central point evolutionary theory was wrong and further examples were sought throughout the Americas (Harris 1968: 305). Subsequent workers have interpreted the *numaym* as a cognatic group, one that derives from both the maternal and paternal lines, although a far more radical overhaul of views on anthropology and history from this part of North America has since been undertaken.

Figure 4.2 Art of the Northwest Coast (Royal Anthropological Institute (RAI 2075))

Even more important than the debates over descent was Boas' discussion of the potlatch. This was a set of ceremonies revolving around the destruction of material goods: copper vessels were smashed or thrown into rivers, blankets ripped to shreds, slaves thrown into the sea to drown and, in the most extreme cases, whole villages were burned down. The aim of these ostentatious and incredible destructions of wealth was seen to be the aggrandisement of the local chief, whose status was based on the amount of wealth he could afford to throw away. In a competition between two chiefs, it was the person who could give or destroy the most wealth that was deemed the victor and socially superior to his rival. The potlatch was viewed by Boas and others, such as Benedict, as a form of social pathology in which the totality of social effort ultimately went to feed the destructive urges of the chief. Potlatches were further argument by example against evolutionary views and said to confound any notion of the growth of western economic rationality, because they give evidence for an 'irrational' use of surplus.

As with all the best known anthropological case studies the potlatch has been interpreted and reinterpreted ever since Boas. For instance, Harris (1968: 306–10) has tried to supply an economic and evolutionary viewpoint of the potlatch. His starting point, as that of most other critics, is that Boas ignored a very specific history in his work: colonialism. Since the first voyage by a European into the Northwest Coast – Cook in 1778 – local groups had suffered massively from introduced diseases, changes in warfare due to muskets, the British Columbian gold-rush of 1858, logging and fur trading. There had been a massive population decline all along this Northwest Coast and changes of settlement pattern and social organisation due to demographic collapse and trade with Europeans. Harris sees these factors as creating an imbalance between the population and the relatively rich environment so that high levels of competition were possible, but also that in its food-sharing, rather than its destructive aspect, potlatch helped even out local and temporary inequalities in the distribution of resources.

However, all this was in the future as far as Boas was concerned. His chief aims were to provide a model for the careful documentation of one exceptionally rich region and to demonstrate, through looking at a number of different elements of life, the local peculiarity of the cultures of the Northwest. His students followed suit. Kroeber spent an academic lifetime, from 1901 on, setting up the Department of Anthropology at Berkeley. He engaged in detailed documentation of Californian and other groups of the southwest, complementing studies of contemporary societies with archaeology, as we have seen. He attacked Morgan's views of classificatory kinship on the grounds that some of the features Morgan saw as sequential were in fact found together in the same culture. Kroeber became interested in the nature of history, such as the history of western fashion and came to the conclusion that culture was an organism of its own, obeying its own laws beyond the scope of its individual carriers and that each particular culture, whether in Mesopotamia or China, followed its own laws of change (Kroeber 1944). Such views led to an eventual falling out with Boas, who saw this as over-generalising, even if the general statement asserted that there were no global laws of history or development.

Boas is weakest in his refusal to generalise or to provide a theoretical framework beyond the idea of cultural specificity and the importance of local histories. There is nothing in his work to provide a theoretical justification for the ways in which different elements of culture were sewn together. Indeed, his insistence that cultures were made up of accidental borrowings alone renders such a general theory impossible. Boas' real contribution was to set up a rounded cultural anthropology, quite different from British social anthropology. He did this partly by example, through the close documentation of particular cultures, especially those of the Northwest coast. Art and material culture were central aspects of anthropology for Boas, through his joint experience of working in museums and universities. Indeed, it was not only through his ideas that he was influential, but also through his institutionalisation of the discipline in the United States.

The hyper-diffusionists

Before leaving the subject of diffusionism we must once again cross the Atlantic and consider the most extreme form of the idea as developed by

Grafton Elliott Smith and Perry in London. It is ironical that the last time that archaeology, physical anthropology and social anthropology were brought together in Britain was in the service of the thoroughly discredited idea of hyper-diffusionism. For Tylor the notion of independent invention was crucial to his evolutionary theory, as it demonstrated that the human mind worked to the same laws everywhere, coming up with identical solutions to social needs in unconnected places. His prime example of independent invention was the pyramid, found in both Egypt and Mesoamerica. Tylor chose this example, not at random, but with the refutation of an early nineteenth-century diffusionism at the back of his mind, which had seen Egypt 'as a center of . . . civilizational advance' (Stocking 1996: 208).

These views were to return with a vengeance through Grafton Elliott Smith, an Australian anatomist. Smith studied in Sydney and then worked in Cambridge where he must have met Rivers. In 1900 he was offered the first pro-fessorship of anatomy at the Government School of Medicine in Cairo. Whilst in Egypt Elliott Smith carried out comparative work on mummies' brains and other skeletal remains. Although initially an evolutionist, he soon became con-vinced of the blending of cultures and races and, in particular, the influence that Egypt had had upon Europe. The Egyptians had introduced metallurgy to Europe and the megaliths of the Mediterranean and the Atlantic were 'crude copies' of the monumental pyramids, a theory that was only finally dispatched through radiocarbon dating which showed the megaliths to be earlier than the pyramids (Renfrew 1973a). On the basis of perceived similarities of skulls in Oceania to those in Eurasia and the existence of megalithic monuments there, Elliott Smith proposed a broader diffusionary spread, which also included America. Back in Sydney on a visit Smith discovered two mummies from the Torres Strait, which he felt were the result of identical techniques to those used in Egyptian mummification. Smith then proposed a 'heliocentric' culture com-plex composed amongst other things of megaliths, sun and snake worship, swastikas, mummification and the birth of the chosen people from an incestu-ous union. The origin point was, of course, Egypt and after 900 BC heliocentric culture was spread to most other parts of the globe. Elliott Smith's ideas were systematised and taken further by Perry (a student of Rivers) and they both taught together in the Department of Anatomy, University College London in the 1920s. Perry's major work, *The Children of the Sun* (1923), was published in the year Tutankhamun's tomb was discovered and was immensely popular with general audiences. It was much less so amongst the academic community, being roundly attacked by Haddon, for instance. What is surprising is that Rivers supported the theory and even came to see *The History of Melanesian Society* as a limited exemplification of a broader trend of diffusions, which the hyper-diffusionists took as important support for their views. Of more historical moment was opposition to the theory on the part of the functional-ists, who developed their ideas on the importance of synchronic studies of soci-ety as much in response to the hyper-diffusionists as an attack on evolutionary theory.

Functionalism: Durkheim, Malinowski and Radcliffe-Brown

It is often felt that functionalism, which later became hyphenated to structural-functionalism, was developed mainly in reaction to evolutionism. But when Malinowski was developing his own point of view at the London School of Economics the major rival school was that of Smith and Perry at University College London. Malinowski described his proposed treatment of 'Smith, Perry & Co. like a basketfull of rotten eggs; with the greatest care and consideration, not to say respect' (quoted in Stocking 1996: 275). At the same time he was careful to define his position so as to differentiate it most clearly from the 'sun-mania'.

In developing the position which became known as functionalism, Malinowski and Radcliffe-Brown drew on the resources of the wider European intellectual tradition, employing the ideas of Freud, but more particularly those of Durkheim. It is impossible to comprehend the development of functionalism within anthropology without some understanding of Durkheim.

Durkheim (1858–1917) was the crucial figure in the creation of sociology, which he consciously tried to professionalise both by providing a theoretical basis and institutional support. Intellectually he was deeply concerned about the nature of modernity, as were Marx and Weber, particularly the industrial, individualistic society in Europe. Much of his attempt to come to terms with anthropology was to provide a historical perspective on European changes. Durkheim had an interesting reciprocal relationship with anthropology, the full story of which has not yet been told, and read much British anthropology from the 1890s onwards. In turn he was to become the major intellectual influence on British anthropology, through the advocacy of Radcliffe-Brown, from just before the First World War to around 1945, having a second wave of influence in the last forty years due to Evans-Pritchard.

Durkheim was a positivist, as were all later functionalist anthropologists, and wanted to establish sociology on a sound empirical basis around the notion of social facts. Social facts were elements of social action that could be studied with the same rigour and results as chemical reactions or photosynthesis. He also accepted a broad evolutionary scheme for human society, in which human history had seen a succession of different social forms, as different from each other as biological species. More importantly the simpler, early social forms held in embryo many of the major characteristics of later complicated societies and therefore represented the opportunity to study basic facets of life in a setting uncluttered by later complexity. This was not to say that nothing had changed; in fact major alterations had come about in the arrangements of human societies, especially over the last few hundred years. Through studying the changing structure of social solidarity and the sources and nature of moral authority much could be learned about recent developments, principally the rise of modern individualism. Durkheim saw the emerging study of sociology as the new centre for the social sciences, throwing fresh light on problems of history, philosophy and economics. In this he was followed later by Radcliffe-Brown, who saw anthropology as a part of a comparative sociology.

There is considerable continuity in the themes and approach of Durkheim's work from his earliest major publication *The Division of Labour in Society* (1893) through *The Rules of Sociological Method* (1895) and *Suicide: A Study in Sociology* (1897) to *The Elementary Forms of the Religious Life* (1912). During this period he went from being a lecturer in social science and education at Bordeaux to a position in education at the Sorbonne in 1902, becoming Professor of Education there in 1906 and managing to change the title of the chair to Education and Sociology in 1913. In 1897 he established the journal *L'Année Sociologique* which did more than anything else to concretise his influence into a school. He also gathered round him some of the luminaries of French social science, many of whom were killed during the Great War, setting back French anthropology, among other disciplines, at least a decade. In the event his most famous and influential intellectual descendant was his nephew, Marcel Mauss.

In *The Division of Labour* Durkheim laid out his historical scheme for social change which centred around the move from what he called 'mechanical' to 'organic' solidarity. In the simplest societies, characterised by mechanical solidarity, the group was made up of a series of identical units, just like organisms formed of colonies of identical cells. Over time these start to segment into kinship groups, or clans, but still exhibit little individuality because each person is subordinate to the *conscience collective*. The former term can only be translated into English by combining the notions of conscience and consciousness. Continuing segmentation eventually transforms mechanical into organic solidarity, found in societies ordered like the human body, so that there are organs with different functions (heart, liver, lungs, etc.) combining to support the complex whole. There is now a complex division of labour in which economic tasks are no longer embedded in the family unit and power becomes concentrated in the hands of some central agency (either monarch or state). Legal codes are now centred on respect for the autonomy, dignity and freedom of the individual. It is vital to Durkheim's argument that individual freedom is not a personal characteristic or God-given right, as in the American Constitution or the broader utilitarian theory from which it derives, but a social product. Individualism is historically peculiar, developing as an aspect of societies organised on the basis of organic solidarity in which there is 'a cult of the individual', to use Durkheim's famous phrase. Such societies are said to have arisen in Europe with the breakdown of the feudal system some 500 years ago. No analysis can start on the basis of the autonomous individual as people do not belong to themselves but are always enmeshed in broader social forces. Just as none of us creates the language we speak, we are also tied into broader social demands and norms through moral codes and law.

In order to look at the relationship of individual to group in a formulation most influential in anthropology we need to move to Durkheim's last work *The Elementary Forms of the Religious Life* (1965). As mentioned above, during the 1890s Durkheim read British anthropologists such as Tylor, Frazer and Robertson-Smith. From the last of these he derived the idea that periodic forms of ceremony were vital in sustaining the individual's commitment to the community. In 1900 he reviewed Spencer and Gillen's newly published *The Native Tribes of Central Australia* (1899) and came to see this as the vital documentation of the most primitive forms of religion, from which all others could be understood. Groups like the Aranda (today known as the Arunta or Arrente), which Durkheim took to be indicative of the state of society in all Australian Aboriginal groups, were divided into clans who considered themselves related through blood or marriage. Each clan identified itself with a totem, a class of objects (often plants or animals) seen to have sacred properties. In connection with this totem the universe is considered to be divided into sacred and profane things, a division Durkheim thought ran throughout all human societies. The sacred nature of the totem carries through to its image in body or sand painting, rock art or artefacts. Furthermore, all members of the clan are felt to partake of the sacred properties of the totem; this is in distinction to later religions where only a special group of people, such as priests, are felt to be set apart by their sacredness.

People, objects and the totems themselves are all intermingled in a complex cosmology which makes no distinction between culture (people and material culture) or nature (the plant or animal totem). At definite periods of the year scattered groups will congregate together in both public and private ceremonials, which are of an intense and emotional character. In everyday life, where people are pursuing their own ends, the hold of the group over the individual may weaken, but the intensity of ceremonies binds people back into the group. Such binding functions can be very important in mourning rituals, where the group is threatened by the loss of one of its members. Through ceremony the continuity of the group is reaffirmed in the face of the transitory nature of individuals, subject to birth and death. Totemism also produces veneration of the ancestors of the group as the ultimate source of the group and its religiosity, so that over time these can become depersonalised and approach the status of gods.

Cosmologies by definition describe the ordering principle for the whole cosmos, providing a classification of the world and a set of prescriptions for correct action towards the world in both its human and non-human elements. A work written with Mauss in 1902 (Durkheim and Mauss 1963) generalised the idea that religion was the basis for classification, seeing the Greek gods, for example, as individually representing different principles of nature and human existence so that the pantheon as a whole provided an understanding of relationships and hierarchy within the human and natural worlds. They went on to say that scientific classification had an ultimate basis in these religious forms. Such a scheme, which saw the ordering of experience as based on the nature of social and religious life, went counter to Kant's influential view

that basic categories of experience such as time and space were universal properties of the human mind. For Durkheim, time and space were social cre-
ations, as could be seen from the fact that many Australian groups saw space
as describing a huge circle, mirroring their circular encampments.

There is much that could be criticised from a present-day perspective in
Durkheim's views. In defining totemism he used a single Aboriginal group to
stand for the whole, masking much diversity, as Spencer and Gillen themselves
realised. The division between sacred and profane does not stand up as a
binary opposite in many groups, including the worlds of Aboriginal people
for whom the two elements mingled constantly in everyday and ceremonial
life. At a more abstract level, Durkheim never systematically analysed the
working of power, or of conflict arising from power struggles within society.
Furthermore, there is a considerable difference between Durkheim's statement
that 'no religion can be false', by which he meant that they all reflected the
nature of society in which they arose and Marx's view that 'religion was the
opium of the masses'. Nor did he exercise any self-criticism about the categories he brought to his study, seeing social facts as self-evidently discrete
rather than chunks of life artificially isolated from the flux of daily experience
by a particular set of analytical tools.

Having said all that, Durkheim was vastly influential in viewing societies as
integrated wholes, which change in evolutionary sequence from single-celled
to multi-cellular organisms, but each having within them some of the same
mechanisms for creating social and moral order. This was a set of ideas which
appeared to have immense power for understanding the ordering and
functioning of many non-western societies and providing the basis for
systematically integrating the mass of detail gathered in fieldwork into a
whole. Indeed, Marcus and Fischer (1986: 19) feel that anthropological
functionalism was a general means of ordering the results of in-depth fieldwork, as much as a theory, so as to produce an account of how the component
parts of a society fitted together into an integrated whole.

Marcus and Fischer's remarks are very apposite for Malinowski for whom
fieldwork was primary, but less so for Radcliffe-Brown who was convinced by
functionalism as an idea in itself. Malinowski, in the years after his Trobriands
fieldwork, was certainly preoccupied with how to transform the mass of
detailed material in his notebooks into a convincing synthesis of Trobriand
life. His general premise was that culture was the means by which people ful-
filled their needs and his view shifted from early in the century when these
needs were seen mainly in psychological terms, following Freud, to a greater
emphasis on physical need. Eventually he was able to synthesise the two positions on the basis that people everywhere represented a 'biopsychic unity,
based in instinct and passion, but expressed in pragmatic, instrumental behavior directed toward adaptive ends', in Stocking's (1996: 287) words. In developing his views on the integrated state of Trobriand society, Malinowski did
not reject evolutionism, but felt that only through a detailed understanding of
present-day processes would we have a real basis for understanding historical

change. He did, however, reject possible real connections with neighbouring disciplines, feeling that anthropology should slough off 'the purely Antiquarian associations with Archaeology and even pre-history' (Malinowski to Seligman quoted in Stocking 1996: 291).

Given the diffuse nature of Malinowski's theoretical statements we can do no better than exemplify his ideas through reference to the Trobriand Islands. What follows is my highly compressed account of the Trobriands as Malinowski saw them and it must be noted that there has been much subsequent disagreement with him over the nature of Trobriand life (see Leach and Leach 1983 for an overview of work within the *kula* area as a whole).

The Trobriand Islands consist of one main raised coral island of Kiriwina and several smaller islands. The Trobrianders lived in roughly circular villages, with an outer ring of family houses at the circumference of the circle, yam storage houses in the inner circle, with the chief's hut, the main yam storage house, the ancestral burial ground and dancing areas in the centre (Figure 4.3). There is some opposition expressed here between the female, profane outer portions of the circle and the male, sacred inner part. Socially, villages were made up of one sub-clan, or a number of them, usually with one dominant. Each sub-clan would have houses on one portion of the circle. The main base

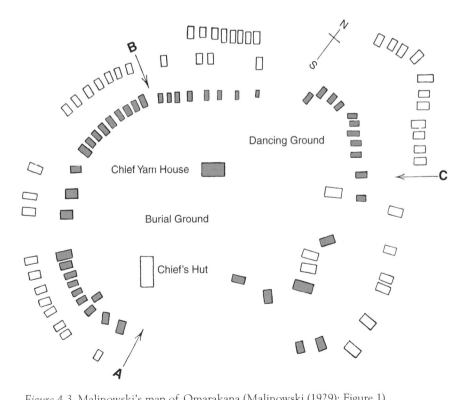

Figure 4.3 Malinowski's map of Omarakana (Malinowski (1929): Figure 1)

of subsistence is swidden gardening and, prior to white contact, the major crop was the yam, with some taro, although today many introduced crops are grown. Gardening is structured around the wet and dry seasons, with the bulk of the work done in the latter period. The ground for a new garden is cleared by the village as a whole and all work is done under the direction of someone specialising in garden magic. The garden is divided into squares using trees cleared from the area and each household has several of these; men plant and women weed; both undertake the harvest.

The yams produced are of a prodigious size and are grown in far larger numbers than needed to supply the nutritional requirements of the household. The largest and best yams are given away to households of the husband's sister and to the leader of the village, through so-called *urigubu* payments and many of these yams are never consumed but rot. *Urigubu* payments are seen as recompense to the women of the clan, who, having married out of the clan, still have claim to some of its produce. This claim is especially strong as the Trobrianders reckon descent matrilineally. Each clan area has an origin place from which an ancestress emerged to give rise to the sub-clan or *dala*, and each child born is seen as the reincarnation of an ancestor. The *dala* is composed of men related through their mothers, mothers' mothers and so on, the sisters of these men and the children of these women (although not the children of the men). The sub-clan is exogamous and the women marry out, with adolescent boys moving to the village of their own sub-clan in adolescence. From the point of view of the men, a man's sons leave him and he takes responsibility for his sisters' sons. Thus within a village one sub-clan will be made up of the men and adolescent boys of the sub-clan, their wives from different sub-clans and the young children and unmarried daughters of the sub-clan. In actual fact the composition of the village or sub-clan is rarely that simple, being subject to fluctuations of population size and subject to marriage strategies where men marry a number of women from different sub-clans (this is a polygamous system) to give themselves a foothold in different villages.

The *urigubu* payments, on one level, seem to act to reinforce the integrity of the clan, through maintaining links between brothers and sisters. But there is also an element of subordination involved in such payments. They reinforce the dominance of the givers' sub-clan, because Trobriand society is ranked into chiefly and commoner sub-clans. Chiefly men are more able to contract marriages than commoners and thus receive *urigubu* yams from all the sub-clans linked through marriage. If all these sub-clans are lower ranked than the husband's, the *urigubu* payments take on the form of tribute and these yams can be redistributed to others to reinforce links of dependency and indebtedness. A leader who is high-ranking through birth and adept at manipulating local flows of yams, valuables and people in marriage and conducting war (before this was outlawed) could come to dominate a cluster of villages, a position he holds not by right, but as a result of his personal qualities. Rank is maintained by a mixture of inheritance and action.

Of course there is an extra and most important arena for seeking prestige and this is the inter-island exchange known as *kula*. The Trobriands are one group in a series of islands within what is today the Massim Province of Papua New Guinea, and these islands can be conceived of as a ring (Figure 4.4). The ring of islands is joined by the movement of valuables known collectively as *vaygu'a* and these are divided into two types. *Soulava* are long necklaces of shell disks which move round the islands in a clockwise direction. *Mwali*, white armshells, move anti-clockwise. At the level of the individual transaction this means that an armshell can only be exchanged for a necklace. Exchanges take place between partners, who may sometimes be related by marriage. Exchanges are not immediate. An armshell given now may be reciprocated by a necklace some years hence and part of the art of *kula* is not just to exchange items of similar value, but at the right time and with the proper sense of occasion and style.

A quote from Malinowski will give a sense of both *kula* and also his narrative style.

> Let us suppose that I, a Sinaketa man, am in possession of a pair of big armshells. An overseas expedition from Dobu, in the D'Entrecasteaux Archipelago, arrives in my village. Blowing a conch shell, I take my armshell pair and offer them to my overseas partner, with some such words, 'This is a *vaga* [initial gift] – in due time thou returnest to me a big *soulava* for it!' Next year, when I visit my partner's village, he either is in possession of an *equivalent* necklace, and this he gives to me as *yotile* [restoration gift], or he has not a necklace good enough to repay my last gift. In this case he will give me a smaller necklace – avowedly not equivalent to my gift – and will give it me as *basi* [intermediate gift]. This means that the main gift will have to be repaid on a future occasion. . . . The final gift, which will be given to me to clinch the whole transaction, would then be called *kudu* [equivalent gift].
>
> (Malinowski 1922: 99)

We get a glimpse here of Malinowski's attempt to make the reader present at the scene of the action, a narrative device aimed at verisimilitude, and we also get some hint of both the theatre and complexity of transactions and stratagems involved in *kula*. The main rules are those of reciprocity and equivalence of value: once a man has been given a gift he has to repay with something deemed by both parties to be of the same value. Most men take part in *kula*, although no women, but men of the highest rank exchange with each other only using the oldest and most famous valuables. Such exchanges represent the highest level in the political sphere within the Massim and only those of considerable local standing find partners of high rank. Success in *kula* increases a man's standing at home. As part of any *kula* expedition there was also *gimwali* trade, carried out through haggling, which involved fish, vegetables and useful artefacts so that the high-level *kula* expeditions had the side-effect of benefiting many people.

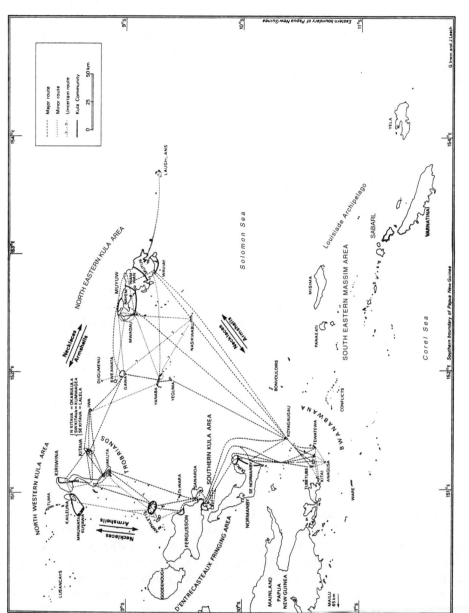

Figure 4.4 The *kula* ring (Leach and Leach (1988): Map 1)

There is much more that could be said about the Trobriands on the basis of Malinowski's accounts and I have not touched on sex, crime or the sea, all of which had monographs dedicated to them. However, I hope that enough has been said to show that Malinowski presented the life of the Trobrianders as an integrated whole, where local production, kinship and political life inter-meshed with the broader sphere of *kula* and inter-island relationships, so that decisions made in one area of life flowed through to others. For instance, in planting a garden a family would take into account not just their own needs in food, but also their local kinship obligations in *urigubu* and the possibility of *gimwali* trade as a by-product of a future *kula* expedition. Malinowski's pre-sentation was very different from the 'shreds-and-patches' approach of the Boasian trait diffusion analysis, or Tylor's attempts to see particular groups as exemplifying a stage of development. It was the coherence and roundedness of Malinowski's pictures of the Trobrianders that made them so convincing and the model for many that followed him.

More of an emphasis on theory and less on fieldwork is found in the work of Radcliffe-Brown (1881–1955) which was eventually to give rise to the term structural-functionalism. Radcliffe-Brown (who was, in fact, plain Brown until 1926 when he changed his name by deed poll) had a most chequered career and was influential in setting up anthropology departments in several parts of the world. He initially studied Mental and Moral Sciences at Cambridge, fell under the spell of Rivers and became his first pupil in anthropology. Radcliffe-Brown carried out fieldwork in the Andaman Islands between 1906 and 1908. He used a fellowship at Trinity College, Cambridge 1908–14 to start writing up his material, but also carried out fieldwork in Australia. It was dur-ing this time that he started to see the possibilities in Durkheim's work. The attractions of Durkheim included 'scientific method, the conviction that social life was orderly and susceptible to rigorous analysis, a certain detach-ment from individual passions, and a fashionable French panache' (Kuper 1996: 37–8). In 1914 he became a schoolmaster in Sydney and from 1916 to 1919 was Director of Education in Tonga, an experience of very little benefit to anthropology. Here he became ill and was advised to leave so joined his brother who lived in Johannesburg. He held a number of minor museum jobs but, in 1921, Haddon's intercession brought a breakthrough when he was requested to set up a new Department of Anthropology at Cape Town. After this time he did no more fieldwork, but was to make a major institutional and theoretical contribution.

During his stay in South Africa he taught administrators about the people they governed, but he also attempted to collate as much as possible of the existing anthropology on southern Africa. In 1926 Radcliffe-Brown returned to Sydney to take up the first chair in anthropology to be established in Australia. Here he set up an undergraduate programme, got the journal *Oceania* off the ground and made another attempt at collating the Australian anthropological information. To say that he was not an easy man to deal with is an obvious understatement; his relations with others in the department were poor and within the university as a whole they were disastrous. Radcliffe-Brown appointed Firth who, together with Elkin, managed to regenerate the department after Radcliffe-Brown's departure. Meanwhile, Radcliffe-Brown was in Chicago where he arrived in 1931. Here he encountered an existing anthropological tradition for the first time and his functionalism provided a coherent alternative to Boasian approaches, now on the wane, which some were glad to take up. Even those such as Margaret Mead, who was beginning to explore the links between psychology and culture, were influenced positively by Radcliffe-Brown. In 1937 Radcliffe-Brown was appointed to the first established chair of anthropology at Oxford, where he was in the company of Evans-Pritchard and Meyer Fortes. After his formal retirement in 1946, Radcliffe-Brown taught in Cambridge, London, Manchester, Grahamstown in South Africa and Alexandria in Egypt. There have been few academic lives so full of travel as Radcliffe-Brown's and not many have had so much of an impact on one discipline in so many parts of the world.

In some ways Radcliffe-Brown's institutional legacy has been more long-lasting than his theoretical one. Having said that, he was the major theorist either side of the Second World War in South Africa and Australia and had a considerable impact in the United States and Britain. At the core of Radcliffe-Brown's endeavours was an attempt to make anthropology scientific on the model of a natural science, in a positivist pursuit of laws of social life. The laws he found were distinctly underwhelming:

> Any human social life requires the establishment of a social structure consisting of a network of relations between individuals and groups of individuals. These relations all involve certain rights and duties which can be defined in such a way that conflicts of rights can be resolved without destroying the structure.
>
> (Radcliffe-Brown 1952: 43–4)

Fortunately, the insights he provided in actual analysis compensated for the blandness of some of the theoretical prescriptions. The real subject of study was the set of social relations which structured actions, rights and duties: the social structure. There was little room for a concept of culture, which Radcliffe-Brown saw as learnt ways of thinking, feeling and behaving, all of which derived from the social structure. Once a stripped-down model of the social structure had been arrived at, it was possible to proceed to comparison and classification of social forms. This would ultimately tell us how many different societies exist, in what respects they differ from each other and, equally importantly, what sorts of features they all share. It might be possible to construct an evolutionary scheme of societies, but much more, and more reliable, historical information would be needed before this could take place.

Some of his analyses, such as those of Aboriginal totemism, indicated the importance of a notion of structure. In looking at totemism Radcliffe-Brown wanted to answer a question that Durkheim had neglected: why are particular animals and plants chosen as totems? His main answer is that the choice derives from the manner in which species symbolise group relationships. In a famous example, many groups in New South Wales were divided into exogamous moieties, named eaglehawk and crow, where eaglehawk women marry crow men and vice versa. The two birds are often linked in myths and their relationship is seen to be one of dual similarity and opposition. Both are meat-eaters and compete for food and in myths both are seen as opponents in various struggles, an opposition brought about by their similar natures. This parallels the blend of rivalry and alliance found between the moieties named after the two birds, which have both joint and individual interests, which are sometimes in harmony and sometimes clash. Radcliffe-Brown generalised out from this instance as was his wont:

> The Australian idea of what is here called 'opposition' is a particular fea-
> ture of that association by contrariety that is a universal feature of human
> thinking, so that we think by pairs of contraries, upwards and down-
> wards, strong and weak, black and white.
>
> (Radcliffe-Brown 1958: 118)

In statements such as these Radcliffe-Brown was moving from structural to structuralist analysis, and may have predisposed British anthropology to this new French theory which it would start to embrace in the post-war period.

Through combining the various strands of discussion in this chapter we can see the growth of social anthropology institutionally in Britain, Australia and South Africa and theoretically from Rivers' stress on genealogy to Malinowski's and Radcliffe-Brown's functionalism. Malinowski saw society as being animated to meet social needs. Radcliffe-Brown viewed social anthropology as a branch of a broader comparative sociology, which would embrace all human societies. Boas had no time for broad comparison and put much less stress on social structures, concentrating instead on the local histories of cultural forms. Both social and cultural anthropology made their breaks with evolutionism and hyper-diffusionism. However, evolutionary theory was to make a return after the last war and played its part in creating a much more complex theoretical landscape. It is to this we shall now turn.

5 The post-war picture
Neo-evolution, Marxism and structuralism

The history of anthropology has been one of varying closeness to historical approaches. Each time anthropology developed an interest in history it was also brought into proximity with archaeology. The evolutionary interests of the nineteenth century made little real distinction between archaeology and anthropology in their covering rubric of ethnology. The same was true of Boasian culture history, although it employed a very different view of the nature of the historical process, emphasising the local and not global comparisons. Functionalism, by contrast, with its attempt to stop the clock and consider the integration of a system at one moment, usually the moment described in a period of anthropological fieldwork, down-played evolutionary interests and created distance between social anthropologists and archaeologists. This was as much disciplinary strategy, as deeply held antipathy to evolution, in an attempt to develop social anthropology in a form most obviously distinct from prehistory or evolutionary ethnography. The rhetoric, at least, of Malinowski and Radcliffe-Brown was that concerns of evolution and change could be returned to once the discipline had developed a sufficient grasp of social processes in the present.

This return occurred in the 1940s and 1950s with the rediscovery of Morgan in the United States, which set up a new strand of anthropology alongside the existing concerns of psychology and culture developed out of Boas' ideas by Benedict and Mead. In Britain there were moves in the opposite direction. Although Evans-Pritchard returned to history in a conscious reaction against Radcliffe-Brown's synchronic analysis, there were also important moves towards structuralism, another form of synchronic analysis to which some in Britain were predisposed by Radcliffe-Brown's later ideas. Structuralist approaches, developed in France by Lévi-Strauss, fed into broader symbolic and interpretive forms of anthropology which increased in popularity through the 1960s. Another strand in this increasingly complex web of schools of thought, is a return to Marxism, which brought anthropology back to history by a different route. And although there was overlap between neo-evolutionary views and Marxism, partly deriving from the influence Morgan had on Marx and Engels, the two strands remained mainly separate, employing different ideas and terminology and existing in separate social networks.

One important element to bear in mind is the link between the increased complexity of the theoretical landscape and the growth in the numbers of people involved in the discipline of anthropology. Kuper (1996: 67) estimates that there were only around twenty professional anthropologists in the British Commonwealth in 1939 and the London School of Economics was by far the dominant British institution until the Second World War. I have no figures for North America, but numbers were very small by present-day standards, and centres of research and teaching very few. Three men (reflecting the gender bias of the discipline) had a predominant influence on anthropology world-wide: Boas, Malinowski and Radcliffe-Brown. After the war the situation changed dramatically: by 1953 there were twelve universities offering instruction in anthropology in British Universities and some thirty-eight teachers of anthropology. As a result there were 160 people studying social anthropology, half of them at the postgraduate level (Kuper 1996: 116, citing a survey by Forde). Even larger growth occurred on the other side of the Atlantic and in South Africa, Australia and New Zealand new institutions and courses were begun. New funds for research also became available, either from government sources or foundations, many of the latter being based in the United States. The speed of change increased again from the 1960s onwards to create an academic world unrecognisable to that which existed twenty years earlier.

The broader world had also changed as a massive phase of decolonisation started, initiated by India's independence in 1947. Newly independent countries set up their own university systems, many of which had anthropology and archaeology departments, initially staffed by Caucasians. Increasingly, however, students were natives of the countries concerned, so that local traditions of anthropology grew up which were often critical of ideas coming from the older metropolitan centres and especially of the colonial milieu from which anthropology had uncritically taken many of its assumptions of progress and European superiority.

The main point to be made here is that many aspects of anthropology that we take for granted today arose in the post-war period, both in terms of the larger and more dense nature of the academic community and the changes in basic assumptions about what the subject was and should become. The history of anthropology, from its inception, is never a simple one to tell. Unfortunately drastic simplification increases as we get nearer to the present and this is not just because we are more immediately aware of the subtlety and ambiguity of recent concerns, but also due to the greater complexity and variability in the discipline as a whole.

This chapter chops the complex story into three parts. In the first we shall consider the return to evolutionary theory which flowed through, and partially united, archaeology and anthropology. We shall then turn to the related, but separate story, of Marxism, still very much a contemporary influence. Lastly we shall look at structuralist and symbolic approaches, which overlapped with Marxism to some extent, but maintained a decent distance from evolutionary schemes of global history. Again both symbolic approaches and evolutionism are alive and well in various parts of the two disciplines of archaeology and anthropology, or, in the case of symbolic anthropology, are directly antecedent to many of the dominant approaches.

Neo-evolutionism

In the United States neo-evolutionary ideas had a considerable impact on anthropology from the 1940s onwards and on archaeology from the late 1950s. In Britain, the influence on archaeology was contemporary with the US, but neo-evolutionary ideas never had much impact on British anthropology. Two figures are crucial in the early history of neo-evolutionism: Leslie White and Julian Steward; and although there were many arguments between proponents of various forms of evolutionism, certain consistent features stand out, partially overriding the differences. On the one hand, Trigger (1989: 289) has credited the post-war economic prosperity in North America with providing the broader context for belief in human progress propelled by material and technical forces. By contrast, Willey and Sabloff (1980: 184) believe that the taint of Marxism which hung around any materialist theory in the days of McCarthyism gradually receded allowing evolutionism to seem more mainstream.

Leslie White (1900–75) was crucial in the initial re-introduction of evolutionary ideas. He certainly saw himself as the direct heir of Morgan and Tylor, an opinion with which others concur. Harris (1968: 640) felt that White's most influential book *The Evolution of Culture* (1959) was an up-dated version of Morgan's *Ancient Society*. White started academic life as a Boasian, training in both New York and Chicago, but then had a conversion experience through reading Morgan after getting a job at the University of Buffalo and starting research into the local Iroquois, on whom Morgan was one of the earliest writers. White went to the Soviet Union in 1929, an unusual move for the time and became acquainted with Marx and Engels' work, although this never had much influence on his own. He returned to the University of Michigan in which he succeeded in setting up one of the country's most flourishing centres of anthropology.

Although White and others have seen his work as a return to the themes of Morgan and Tylor, there are significant differences. One crucial area of divergence was the stress on thermodynamics – 'Other factors remaining constant, culture evolves as the amount of energy per capita per year is increased, or as the efficiency of the means of putting the energy to work is increased' (White 1959: 368–9). The centrality of energy to White's thinking was noted by all commentators, positive and critical. As Meggers wrote in her contribution to White's *Festschrift*:

> The law of energy and cultural evolution was set forth by White in 1943. . . . This law was based on the recognition that cultures are composed of three general classes of phenomena: technology, social organiza-

tion, and philosophy. Of these, technology is primary and determines the content and form of the other two components.

(Meggers 1960: 302–3)

White's approach was essentially global. He was laying the basis for understanding General Evolution (in which the capital letters were significant) as a process which lay behind the broad sweep of human history from the earliest hominids to the twentieth century. White was less worried about the details of individual cultures and quite willing to concede that some were sadly lacking in their energy-processing capacities, but these exceptions simply made the achievements of the technological west more remarkable.

As the quotation from Meggers brings out, White viewed the technical-economic realm as the cutting edge of culture, the point at which energy was gathered and fed into the system, with all other elements of social life ordered around the energy-processing units. Some have seen this scheme as a reflection of a Marxist stress on the forces of production, whereas most Marxists view White's work as the worst sort of vulgar materialism and lacking any analysis of the social relations in which the processes of production, distribution and consumption are embedded.

Julian Steward's (1902–72) work is always discussed together with White's because it is similar, but different. The major difference was a stress on divergence on the part of Steward, who saw general evolutionary processes as lying behind all human history, but was in fact much more concerned with the directions local sequences take under the influence of regional conditions. Steward's multi-linear evolution came about because he was much more of an ethnographer than White, being the general editor of a six volume *Handbook of South American Indians* and carrying out research in both the Midwest and southwest of the United States. His early training in Berkeley under Kroeber and Lowie, where he was awarded a PhD in 1931, gave him a good grounding in the analysis of specific aspects of cultures. A further influence was Steward's combination of archaeological and anthropological research in almost equal measure in his search to understand long sequences of change.

Steward believed that similar natural settings would produce similar cultural responses, and cultures could be seen as clustered around sets of core features, deriving from the nature of subsistence activities, but involving economic, political and religious patterns. His methods became known as 'cultural ecology', focusing on the web of interconnections between a culture and its ecosystem. These ideas had enormous influence on archaeology on both sides of the Atlantic, through Graham Clark in Britain and Binford, Flannery and others in the United States. Steward also made comparisons between cultures he considered to be at the same level of evolutionary development, juxtaposing the emerging sequences from northern Peru and the Valley of Mexico on the one hand with Mesopotamia, Egypt and northern China on the other. His schemes stress the importance of the American evidence for these broad comparative projects. Once hyper-diffusionism was rejected, moves towards agriculture and state forms of organization within the Americas could only be seen as independent from the Eurasian examples and thus indicative of general processes of change inherent in all societies, which could form the basis for broad-scale generalisations about human capabilities and their historical manifestations. The broad comparisons that Steward was one of the first to make are still with us today and formed the basis for New Archaeology's comparative approaches.

Equally influential for archaeology were the formulations of the next generation of evolutionists, prime amongst whom were Sahlins and Service. Sahlins wrote a PhD on comparisons within Polynesia of different levels of chiefly social organisation and their correlations with the local ecology, coming to the conclusion that the largest islands with the richest and most varied ecosystems, like Hawai'i and Tonga, were able to support the most highly stratified societies (Sahlins 1958). His ideas have gone through a complex evolution of their own and we shall meet him again in a number of guises. Service, it is fair to say, is best known for generalising works on evolution (e.g. Service 1962). One contribution Sahlins and Service made, important at the time but less so in hindsight, was to attempt an accommodation between White's emphasis on general evolution, which they saw as an overall progressive movement underlying human history and influencing all human societies, and specific evolution, deriving from Steward's work which analysed the adaptation to the local environment in which a group lived. Sahlins and Service felt that general and specific forms of evolution were mutually compatible, whereas White and Steward tried to present them as alternatives, deriving from different scales of analysis of the global situation in the former case and the local in the latter.

By far the most important contribution Sahlins and Service made was to distinguish different forms of society and create an evolutionary sequence, seeing human history as the movement from band to tribe to chiefdom and finally the state. This terminology has been vital to evolutionary anthropology and archaeology since its formulation in the early 1960s and is still very much with us today. The idea of band societies derives from a generalisation Steward (1936) made from the work of Radcliffe-Brown on Australian Aboriginal groups and a number of surveys of the Americas. Band societies, in Sahlins' and Service's formulation of them, have existed for most of human history, certainly since the development of fully modern behaviour and are still with us today in the form of hunter-gatherers, such as Australian Aborigines, Inuit or Bushmen. Band societies gather wild plant foods and hunt non-domesticated animals, they generally have a restricted range of material culture and an egalitarian social structure with institutionalised levelling mechanisms to guard against the accumulation of material wealth which might lead to personal aggrandisement. Tribes are also relatively egalitarian, with the only positions of power and influence deriving from people's deeds in their lifetime; personal standing dies with the individual rather than being inherited from one generation to the next. The New Guinea bigman forms the quintessential example of such a social category (Sahlins 1963). Tribal societies do have an agricultural subsistence base, together with a set of reciprocal exchange links, as is known from the kula and many other examples.

The main difference between tribes and chiefdoms is in the degree of institutionalisation of inequality: chiefs are born to their rank, this being ascribed, in contrast to the achieved status of bigmen. The basis for chiefly and other forms of rank, such as specialist religious leaders and craftspeople, is redistribution on the part of the chief. The economic historian Polanyi (1957) recognised that in many societies the mass of the people were obliged to give a proportion of all the food they grew, plus sometimes also craft products, to the chiefs. The chiefs would then redistribute materials back to the people, but not before creaming off a proportion which could be used to support themselves and craft or religious specialists without the need to engage in agricultural labour (Sahlins 1958; Figure 5.1). In the evolutionist view this had two advantages: regulation at the centre of the economy could lead to greater

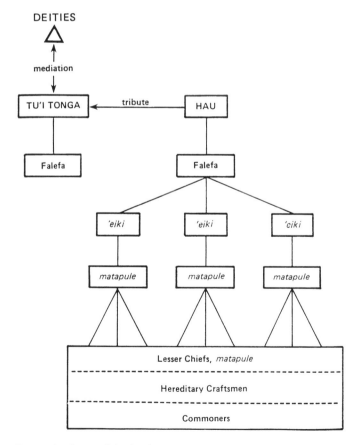

Figure 5.1 Pyramidal chiefly structure (after Kurch (1989), *The Evolution of Polynesian Chiefdoms*: Figure 75)

co-ordination of decision-making, innovation and possible intensification; greater specialisation in the division of labour brought about by the existence of directed flows of agricultural surplus could lead to increased efficiency and sophistication in craft-production. The existence of a set of decision-makers in the heart of the economy differentiated chiefdoms from acephalous tribes (although to the critic this looked rather like a modern managerial structure). On the other hand, tribes and chiefs were similar to each as both were regulated through the ties of kinship – the chiefs were related genealogically to the people at the base of the social pyramid. Kinship obligations ensured that chiefs had to treat people decently according to local norms, thus constraining chiefly power.

Kinship ties were broken as civil society and the state developed, removing such restrictions. Separate social classes formed and were defined by their ownership of land and means of craft or industrial production. The aristocracy owned land, the middle classes, where they existed, based their power on production or trade, and the working classes were just that, the people who did the work but enjoyed few of the products due to their lack of ownership of land or the instruments of production. States centralised decision-making to a much greater degree than chiefdoms through the existence of a class of specialist bureaucrats using writing and other forms of notation to keep a track of produce, trade and people. The state also had a monopoly on the use of legitimate violence through the deployment of armed forces and a penal legal code. States were seen to have existed for many thousands of years in Mesopotamia, Mexico and China, for instance, and are the social formations we still live in today, having been translated into nation states over the last few centuries.

Band, tribe, chiefdom and state together cover the whole of human history from the Palaeolithic to the present, for those who believe in these categories, and form the basis for recent comparative work within the evolutionary framework and beyond. As a brief example of the sort of work produced within such a framework, plus a demonstration that it contained within it many elements of functionalism, we can take Service's (1971: chap. 8) analysis of the so-called 'section system' among Australian aboriginal groups. Based on the work of Radcliffe-Brown (1930–1) and others who had identified differing numbers of divisions within Australian aboriginal groups, Service came up with a developmental sequence for these differing sectional systems and their relationship to the environment. Amongst Aboriginal groups there have been identified the so-called two-, four- and eight-class systems. Two-class systems come about when society is divided into two moieties who always take their marriage partners from the opposing moiety. Four-class systems make a distinction between adjacent generations within each moiety, so that children are automatically in a different group from the parents, in effect putting them in the same group as their grandparents. Eight-class systems derive from an added distinction between parallel and cross-cousins within each generation. The complexity generated by eight-class systems is legendary and has led to complex kinship analyses on the part of anthropologists over the last century. Service (1971: 132, footnote 5) acknowledges that this complexity has been seen by some as a contradiction within evolutionary theory, which posits that simple social relations will be found where there is a simple technology. His response is that the section system is, in fact, a codification and simplification of kinship links through boxing them into broad categories. Apparent complexity hides the real simplicity of social relations deriving from the fact that 'Australian society is a very primitive one . . .' (Service 1971: 118), the quote highlighting the inherently derogatory and judgmental nature of many evolutionary statements.

Some, such as Morgan, have seen the Aboriginal section system as primarily regulating marriage. However, Service follows Radcliffe-Brown's view that the sections order social behaviour by laying down rules as to how any individual should behave towards all others. This is especially important in being able to relate to strangers, who, once they have been placed in a relation of kinship to a group they are visiting can be treated with the appropriate degrees of hospitality, respect or avoidance. Service says fine categorisations are much less important to people within a group who have known and ongoing relationships. Service goes on to look at the distribution of section systems across Australia (Figure 5.2), noting that around the coast there are accounts of one- class systems, that is people who make no distinction as to sections at all. Also, on the coast and some inland areas there are two-section systems; with four- and eight-class systems found predominantly in the centre and the north of the continent. Service relates this distribution to the nature of resources and differences in population densities. The richest areas of the coasts and the southeast and southwest held the most dense populations (before their annihilation by white settlement, a point Service neglects to mention), whereas the deserts were always sparsely populated. Here the relatively separated groups often encountered each other as strangers. Such encounters were either accidental or in large periodic ceremonial gatherings characteristic of all areas of the continent. However the encounters take place, it is likely that in the desert areas people will most frequently meet others that they do not know. Thus in the relatively empty desert areas there is the greatest need for a set of categories laying down social conduct prior to any individual meetings. It is no surprise, following this logic, that the most complicated distinctions are made in the deserts and the least complex on the coast. There may also be a temporal development as well, with a stratigraphic layer of different complexities of system (Figure 5.2, top), as the moiety divisions developed from a situation where no distinctions were needed, with the four- and eight-section systems developing from the initial binary division.

Service's argument neatly links ecology, population and the social organisation, with the last seen as a direct outcome of the first two factors. Such a functionalist approach would have been applauded by Radcliffe-Brown as a neat appreciation of the function social organisation plays in coping with environmental conditions, although it is quite likely that he would have seen the

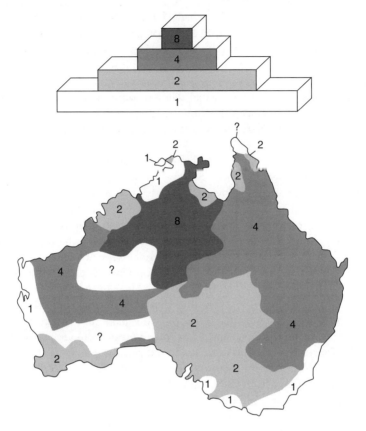

Figure 5.2 The section systems of Australia (after Service (1971): Map 2)

argument about the development of more complex systems from simpler ones as a piece of conjectural history.

Unkind critics, some of whom may even be within the discipline, see archaeology as always being conjectural history. Much of the effort in the New Archaeology was to move archaeology away from historical particularism, often associated with the work of Boas and White's criticisms of that work. Figure 5.3, taken from Willey and Sabloff's history of American archaeology provides a genealogy, which can read partly as the movement away from the categorising and structuring of regional sequences towards attempts to generalise about society as a whole, with White and Binford crucial to these later moves. In helping establish the New Archaeology, Binford's influence from White took a number of forms. The most important of these was the dual attempt to reconfigure archaeology as a nomothetic discipline, searching for laws of human behaviour by focusing on the use of the environment and capture of energy. Binford's distinction between technomic,

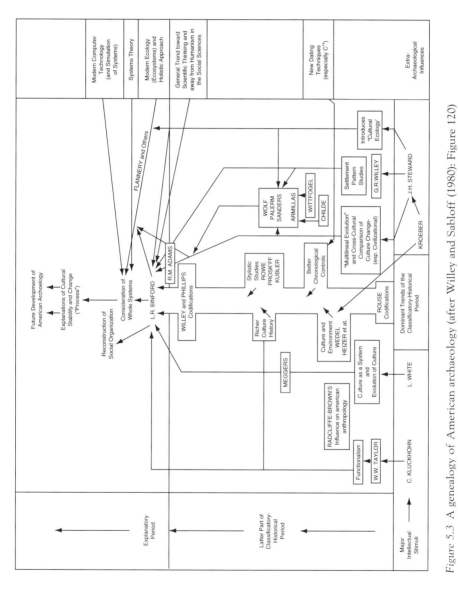

Figure 5.3 A genealogy of American archaeology (after Willey and Sabloff (1980): Figure 120)

sociotechnic and idiotechnic was both an attempt at a holistic archaeology, which linked together all aspects of life, and a reaffirmation of technological determinism, where culture is really an extension of human muscles and limbs to enable greater amounts of resources to be captured from the environment. Binford's view is a possibilitist one in which people are able to invent the technologies, social forms or religious systems they need to adapt the group to a new situation (Trigger 1989: 296).

Binford's global hunter-gatherer model is one of his most influential attempts to develop generalisations about the structure of people's environment, particularly focusing on stress, and the nature of sedentism and social organisation. The global nature of the model comes from the differential distribution of energy throughout the world's ecosystems. Terrestrial ecosystems decrease in productivity with distance from the equator, whereas the reverse holds true for the oceans. Lee (1968a) has shown that gathering plant foods amongst hunter-gatherer groups is most important in all areas except for high latitudes where the lack of plants means that hunting and fishing take over as dominant modes of subsistence (Table 5.1). Binford (1980) has used Murdock's measure of effective temperature to make systematic comparisons between storage and settlement systems, as this can stand as a proxy for the length of the growing season and the period annually that various resources will be available (Figure 5.4). Again the high latitudes, which have short periods of availability of resources support human groups who have developed sophisticated forms of storage to get them through the lean times of the year. Mobility presents a slightly different pattern, being high in tropical rainforest environments with rich but dispersed resources and also in high latitudes with low overall productivity. Sedentism is most likely in boreal and temperate forest regions where overall productivity is high for much of the year (Table 5.2). Such approaches have been given broader application by Kelly (1995). Global models have also been criticised on the details of their appreciation of the environment (see Foley 1982 on Lee's work). They could also be criticised for an ahistorical view of hunter-gatherers (as we shall see) and the assumption that ecosystems will be determinant.

Table 5.1 Primary subsistence source by latitude (from Lee 1968a: Table 6)

Degrees from the equator	Primary subsistence source			
	Gathering	Hunting	Fishing	Total
More than 60°	—	6	2	8
50°–59°	—	1	9	10
40°–49°	4	3	5	12
30°–39°	9	—	—	9
20°–29°	7	—	1	8
10°–19°	5	—	1	6
0°–9°	4	1	—	5
World	29	11	18	58

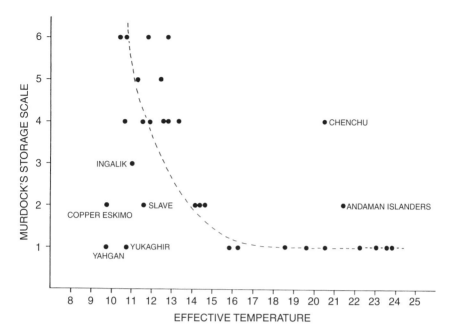

Figure 5.4 How effective temperature is seen to affect storage and settlement (from Binford (1980): Figure 4)

A rather different aspect of the New Archaeology is demonstrated by the work of Longacre, Hill, Leone and others on the pueblos of the southwest of the United States. In this work anthropology acts as both an orienting goal, in that archaeology is trying to produce results of similar type to those of ethnologists, and also a means to that end. Hill (1968) attempted to identify rooms and other features with particular functions through combining all the evidence available, on pottery, other artefacts and pollen, using statistical analyses. Hill also used historical and ethnographic data from the Hopi and Zuñi to show that the largest rooms had the greatest range of artefacts, reflecting their wide range of functions, whereas smaller rooms showed greater storage and processing of plant foods. He also used deviations from the expected patterns to show that the sites and features within them had changed over their thousand-year occupation. Longacre (1968) examined pottery production and use, through making a number of ethnographically derived assumptions, such as that women made pots. Using this assumption he argued for the existence of matrilocal clans and the movement from small single-kin unit communities to larger groups which had aggregated due to adverse climatic change. Finally, Leone (1968) looked at relations between sites and attempted to come up with generalisations good both for the southwest and for farming communities more generally. Leone's proposition was that increasing dependence on agriculture led to greater economic autonomy for each community

Table 5.2 Settlement modes in hunter–gatherers on a global scale (from Binford (1980): Table 2)

Effective temperature	Fully nomadic (1)	Semi-nomadic (2)	Semi-sedentary (3)	Sedentary (4)	Total	Index value
25	2	0	0	0	2	
24	1	0	1	0	2	
23	3	1	0	0	4	
22	2	0	0	0	2	
21	1	1	0	0	2	
Sub-total	9 (75.0%)	2 (16.7%)	1 (8.3%)	0	12	1.33
20	1	1	1	0	3	
19	3	1	0	0	4	
18	2	1	0	0	3	
17	1	0	0	0	1	
16	2	1	0	0	3	
Sub-total	9 (64.2%)	4 (28.5%)	1 (7.1%)	0	14	1.42
15	2	11	2	0	15	
14	1	10	1	5	17	
Sub-total	3 (9.3%)	21 (65.6%)	3 (9.3%)	5 (15.6%)	32	2.31
13	3	17	4	4	28	
12	1	15	8	1	25	
Sub-total	4 (7.5%)	32 (60.3%)	12 (22.6%)	5 (9.4%)	53	2.33
11	2	15	9	3	29	
10	3	6	3	4	16	
Sub-total	5 (11.1%)	21 (46.6%)	12 (26.6%)	7 (15.4%)	45	2.46
9	5	3	1	1	10	
8	0	1	1	0	2	
Sub-total	5 (41.6%)	4 (33.3%)	2 (16.6%)	1 (8.3%)	12	1.91
Grand total	35 (20.8%)	84 (50.0%)	31 (18.4%)	18 (10.7%)	168	

and more social distance between them. Greater variability in basic tool types was seen to be a measure of the dependence on agriculture; social distance derived from greater endogamy within the village, the archaeological indicator of which was more localised attributes of form and colour in the decoration of pottery. Leone found a positive correlation between an increase in agricultural tool types and the differentiation of pottery by community. He further suggested that similar patterns might be found in Neolithic communities elsewhere.

These studies together show a concern for relatively fine-grained analysis of kinship, settlement structure and interconnections between sites, all of which are understood through a combination of ethnographically derived hypotheses and archaeological analyses. They all show social changes as ultimately depending on the environment or technology of the group, following a basically functionalist premise. The studies also demonstrate an awareness of long-term change and the desire to use local results to feed into debates about the links between economy, settlement and society globally. These were ambitious and exciting programmes for the time, made possible by a long tradition of ethnographic and archaeological work in the southwest deriving from Cushing and the Stevensons and they were to spawn considerable emulation elsewhere, where often the evidence was less good.

On the other side of the Atlantic the New Archaeology took different forms, but again inspired anthropologically based generalisations. One of the most influential bodies of work was that of Renfrew, who attempted to use the categories of band, tribe, chiefdom and state to understand the prehistoric sequence in Europe, the Near East and globally. Renfrew took as a basic structuring assumption the notion that all sequences could be understood as progressing through the stages from band to state (although not all areas of the world made it to the top of the evolutionary ladder). In some works Renfrew attempted an holistic analysis of all the salient features of a form of organisation that can be derived from the archaeological evidence, especially when looking at states (Renfrew 1984, Renfrew and Cherry 1986). In other pieces of work, Renfrew sought archaeological measures of different social forms, focusing especially on trade and exchange (Renfrew 1975).

In his work on trade and exchange Renfrew used the generalisations of Polanyi and Sahlins to make links between the distribution of archaeological materials and the forms of society moving these materials. The division between band societies ordered through reciprocity and egalitarian relationships, tribes with reciprocal relations but with attempts to control flows of materials to personal advantage, chiefdoms ordered through redistribution and states with markets was seen to form a typology which could be distinguished archaeologically. Renfrew felt that, all other things being equal, there would be a regular fall-off in the amounts of materials at archaeological sites with increasing distance from source. Deviations from this expected pattern might indicate social processes such as boundaries between different groups or the existence of centralising mechanisms like a redistributive chief (Figures 5.5, 5.6). Such a set of models took archaeology's new ability to chemically

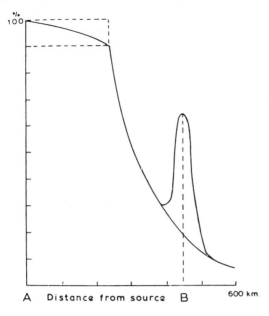

Figure 5.5 Renfrew's generalised model of distance-decay. (The square at the top shows a contact zone and the peak a point of redistribution.) (From Renfrew (1975): Figure 10)

source items like obsidian or pottery, undertake statistical analyses of graphs of fall-off patterns and combine them with anthropological generalisations in a manner many found compelling. Renfrew's work on trade and exchange raised the possibility of understanding what happened in a local case, like the production of Neolithic pottery in Britain, but also of combining a series of individual cases into a generalising scheme potentially covering the whole of human history.

Revisionist histories

Of the many criticisms that could be raised against the New Archaeology's generalising use of anthropology on both sides of the Atlantic, I would like to concentrate on the lack of interest in two sets of history: that of colonialism and the local histories of the areas from which anthropological exemplars were drawn. To take the impact of colonialism first. Thought on hunter-gatherers has changed continuously over the last 150 years, one of the most famous changes being occasioned by the 1966 *Man the Hunter* conference (Lee and DeVore 1968). This conference not only showed the importance of plant-gathering rather than hunting in many groups, thus contradicting the title of the conference. It also purported to show that hunter-gatherers did not need to work hard in order to supply their needs. Sahlins (1972: chap. 1) charac-terised hunter-gatherers as the 'original affluent society' whose needs were

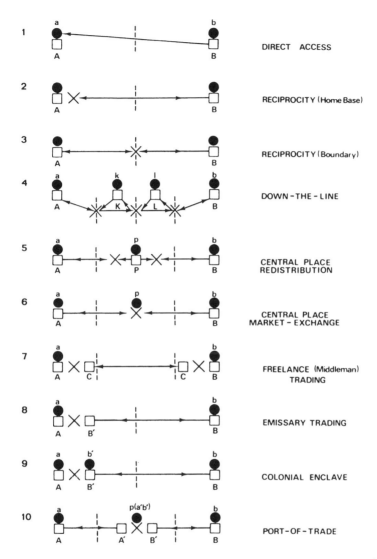

Figure 5.6 Different modes of trade and their spatial implications. (Circles A and B represent the source and destination of an item; squares A and B the person at the source and the recipient. Circle P is a central place, square P is a central person. Exchange transactions are indicated by a cross and territorial boundaries by a broken line.) (From Renfrew (1975): Figure 12)

easily satisfied because they were few. Sahlins' reappraisal of the imperative to work has stayed on the collective academic consciousness, even though it has been shown that the evidence on which it was based was inadequate or wrong, with many hunter-gatherer groups having to work an approximation of our eight-hour day (Kelly 1995: Table 1–1). However, there is a point made at the end of Sahlins' essay which has come to recent attention.

> I must raise the possibility that the ethnography of hunters and gatherers is largely a record of incomplete cultures. Fragile cycles of ritual and exchange may have disappeared without trace, lost in the early stages of colonialism, when the intergroup relations they mediated were attacked and confounded. If so, the 'original' affluent society will have to be rethought again for its originality, and the evolutionary schemes once more revised.
>
> (Sahlins 1972: 38–9)

The possibility that present-day hunter-gatherers may not be representative of Palaeolithic groups was a radical departure from trends of thought dating back to Morgan and before. Many have now amplified Sahlins' point that colonialism cannot be ignored. Whereas in the period before the creation of farming, some 14,000 years ago, it might be assumed that the world was populated by hunter-gatherers who shared many common characteristics, all hunter-gatherer groups today live in close proximity to, and contact with, social forms unlike themselves. In Africa, Bushmen have been pressed into military service because of their knowledge of how to operate in the bush and have moved in and out of pastoralist, agricultural and foraging ways of life for centuries (Gordon 1992, Wilmsen 1992, Wilmsen and Denbow 1990). Many groups in Southeast Asia only survive through long-standing trade contacts with agriculturalists and some of these connections now feed rainforest products onto the world market (Hoffman 1984). In North America and Australia there has been massive dispossession and death through disease and now many groups live on a combination of the dole, the proceeds of sales of art and artefacts, and hunting and gathering (Morphy 1991). Within life today foraging may be as much an affirmation of self-worth as a source of food, with Aboriginal groups emphasising cosmological links to the land, which in turn are central to their own identity, through the food quest (Povinelli 1992, 1993).

The so-called hunter-gatherer revisionist debate has led to a general reassessment of the possibility of using present-day groups as the model for the past, with some questioning the possibility and utility of making links between past and present groups (Hall 1988), while others reassert the influence of ecology as the vital factor structuring life and overwhelming the influence of the modern world (Kelly 1995: 35–7).

The realisation of the impact of colonialism is not new. Malinowski, late in his career, came to realise the loss of power of many of his analyses through his blindness to the changes brought about by colonialism. He felt that 'the most serious shortcoming of my whole anthropological research in Melanesia' had been the failure to acknowledge the 'decay of custom under European influence'. This was because he was 'still mainly interested in the "real savage" as representative of the stone age' (Malinowski 1935 I: 479–81).

These realisations came to Malinowski after a trip to South Africa in 1934, during which time he experienced the reality of racial segregation and the true conditions in which the black population lived (Stocking 1996: 413–15).

Similar arguments can and have been made about other groups used to underpin general categories, such as the New Guinea bigman. Bigmen, through the work of Sahlins (1963), have come to stand for a state of society in which relations of reciprocity in trade and exchange are manipulated by individuals so as to achieve superior personal standing within their lifetimes. The bigman turns from human individual to category of society, embodying the heart of tribal societies in the evolutionary writings from Sahlins and Service (1960) to Renfrew (1975) and beyond. However, closer attention to historical detail in Papua New Guinea shows that bigmen may not be a social category that can be universalised, but the product of a recent set of historical interactions. Golson (1982) has combined historical ethnography and archaeology in looking at the intersection of agricultural intensification and white contact in the Wahgi Valley in the Highlands (Figure 5.7). Drawing on accounts of missionaries who entered the Wahgi soon after the first European contact in 1934, Golson describes a society with inherited, not achieved, status. Vital in creating and maintaining status were marine shells, exchanged from group to group between the coast and the Highlands. In the pre-contact period, links were so attenuated and difficult that few shells made it through into the western Highlands and only people with high rank had the trade connections necessary to achieve a steady supply. Shells were vital to wealth payments in many areas of life, including initiation, marriage and mortuary ceremonies and the bulk of the population was dependent on those with access to shells in order to make the right types and amounts of payments.

When the first gold miners entered the area after 1934 they flew in several million shells from the coast in order to pay their workers. Suddenly all ranks of people had direct access to shells in some number, causing the collapse of the hierarchical social structure and its replacement by a set of exchange relations between relative equals. These were the bigmen documented by the first intensive ethnographies in the New Guinea Highlands from the 1950s onwards, the results of which flowed into generalising works, such as those by Sahlins and Service by the 1960s. If we follow Golson's argument we must accept that the western Highlands bigman is not the essential feature of egalitarian relations past and present, but the product of colonial relations reified into a static social category by an ethnography structured around the myth of the ethnographic present. Change is not a product of colonialism alone and Golson goes on to show that the introduction of the sweet potato, either 1,200 hundred years ago or in the last few centuries, may have caused a similar democratisation to that brought about by the introduction of large numbers of shells in the 1930s. The sweet potato can be grown in poorer soils and at higher altitudes than taro, the previous dominant crop. Prior to its introduction, people with access to swamp lands in valley bottoms could have

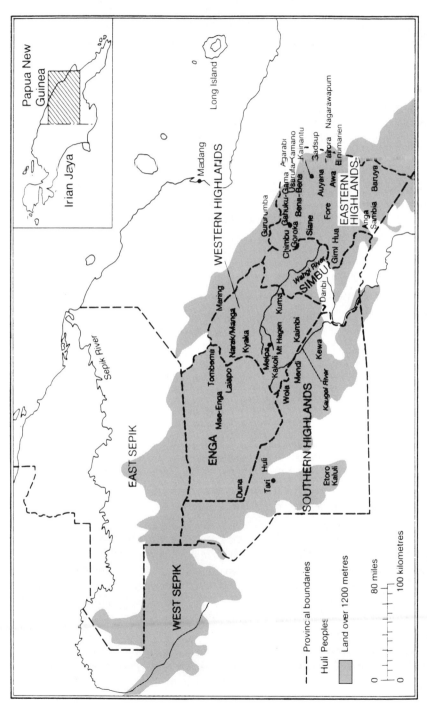

Figure 5.7 Map of Papua New Guinea Highlands (from Feil (1987) *The Evolution of Highland Papua New Guinea Societies: Figure 2*)

grown sufficient taro in wetland conditions to allow them to keep large pig herds. This fact has also been vital to exchange systems, as those with the most pigs could always dominate others in regional exchange systems. The coming of the sweet potato changed this differential ability to support exchange and those who had been previously disadvantaged could manage higher levels of production once they could grow sweet potato on their poorer soils or in higher and colder gardens. This and much other evidence showed a dynamic and changeable relationship between society and exchange, which could not be simply glossed into a static category of bigman.

These two examples can be taken as a part standing for a larger whole: the major point being that each area and group of people have their own history, extending over many thousands of years and their own sets of contacts with colonialism. Colonialism is a long and complex process but one that has been systematically filtered out of much anthropology, where the search for pristine exemplars of various states of society or history has been paramount. To take a series of the best-known ethnographic examples, which can be used to come up with generalised categories, such as band, chiefdom and state and to then combine these into a scheme for understanding history on a world scale must be suspect. For good reasons, many such generalised schemes of history, so-called grand narratives, are falling into disrepute. Whether this means we cannot generalise at all about human society past and present is an on-going question. A further attempt to understand history within a general theoretical framework is Marxism, to which we now turn.

Marxism

The figures of Marx and Engels have been absent from this story until now, which may seem surprising given their general influence on modern thought. However, it is amazing how little academic influence they had in the late nineteenth and early twentieth centuries in the west (in areas like Russia, influence was crucial and early). This general lack of influence also makes more striking the Marxist thought of Gordon Childe, the only major figure in either discipline in the English-speaking world to be a self-professed Marxist.

As is well known, Marx himself took an historical view of human society, holding that no point in time could be understood without looking at the social forces which led up to that point. However, this was a different history from the progressivist views of other nineteenth-century thinkers, in that Marx saw contemporary Europe as an ultimate contradiction, a time of huge wealth and grinding poverty, unparalleled possibilities for the expansion of the human spirit caged by the miserly mentality of capitalism. Marx came upon anthropology late in life and his only serious earlier influence of this kind was Malthus, who used the work of missionaries and explorers from around the world to construct his theory that population growth will inevitably outstrip human attempts to increase food production, a view Marx reviled (Spriggs 1997: 188). By far the major influence on both Marx and

Engels was Morgan's *Ancient Society*, which Marx only read two or three years before his death (Krader 1972: 86–9), and it was left to Engels (1884) in *The Origins of the Family, Private Property and the State* to connect Morgan's ideas with those of Marx and his own in anything like a systematic manner. In this work pre-class societies were divided into pre-clan, matriarchal clan, patriarchal clan and terminal clan stages, followed by three forms of class societies – slave, feudal and capitalist, with history terminating in future socialist and communist systems. Much of Engels' view of clan societies was derived from Australian Aboriginal examples and, as Spriggs has noted, it is surprising how much the views of people in Europe were shaped through a few key synthesising works, like Morgan's, when there had been an explosion of information about Aboriginal groups published in the 1870s and 1880s (Spriggs 1997: 207).

The relative poverty of writings by both Marx and Engels on anthropological topics, in terms of both their numbers and scope, has left Marxist anthropologists and archaeologists with a series of basic principles pertaining to the process of labour and the social and ideological relations resulting from that process, but little in the way of specific models to apply to non-capitalist societies. Also, over the century since Marx died there have been subtle currents within Marxist thought which have subjected principles drawn from Marx to constant criticism and revision. We can artificially separate two elements of Marx's thought which have been influential in anthropology in different ways: his general philosophical approach and his historical scheme of social change.

Marx took much of his theoretical underpinning from Hegel. Hegel's thought was dialectical, centred around the view that an idea can only be really understood in the context of its contrary and ultimately through the synthesis of thesis and antithesis. Marx believed this to be the best mode of philosophising, but he also applied the dialectic to social change, saying that societies were made up of a mass of internal contradictions, which were the cause of major change. Capitalist societies were riven by contradictions and conflicts of class which could be overcome through moving to socialism and communism, with the latter being unique in that it was characterised by an absence of such conflicts. However, communism exists purely in the imagination and in all social analysis up until now there is a parallel between a dialectical mode of thought and a dialectical movement of society, making the one better suited to understand the other than any other form of analysis. Not only would dialectical thought bring about a better grasp of social reality than any previous approach, Marx believed, but also people learnt about the world through working with it. Marx's theory is often seen as primarily an economic one. However, his concept of labour shows that this is not the case. Labour not only transforms the world and makes useful things for people to live on, it is a two-way process which shapes people through their productive action. Engels made the same point when looking at the evolution of the human hand: the hand was the product of millennia of human practical action as well as the instrument responsible for productive action. Life is partly a story of self-creation through action and it was the tragedy of all forms of society that they had put such constraints on the realisation of human potential. The locus for these constraints lay in the productive process, understood through the notion of the means of production.

Marx developed a generalised history of modes of production from primitive communism to present-day capitalism. Marx's view of a mode of production was that it was made up of the forces of production, which were the technological means by which society produced the goods it wanted, and the relations of production, which specified the relations between people pertaining to both the division of labour and the division of the items produced. As a generalisation, it is possible to say that early in this century there was a tendency to economic and technological determinism on the part of Marxist thinkers. Here the division between base and superstructure in society has been vital. The base is seen to be composed of the economic forces of society: the forces and relations of production. These influence the superstructure of society, made up of the social divisions into kin groups or classes and the ideological apparatus or worldview of the group (Figure 5.8). Those holding to a strict division between base and superstructure see cause flowing in one direction from the forces of production, such that once one can understand these forces all other elements of society become clear. These views bring them close to those of Leslie White, who saw the energy-processing capacity of society as crucial.

While by no means a rigid economic determinist it is possible to see in the later writings of Childe just such an approach. In his view, it was the relatively flexible position that Bronze Age smiths held in Europe which led to their inventiveness and the growth of the individual spirit characterising Europe. Similarly, the economic revolution brought about by the Neolithic sowed the seeds for the eventual birth of the modern Industrial Revolution. Criticisms

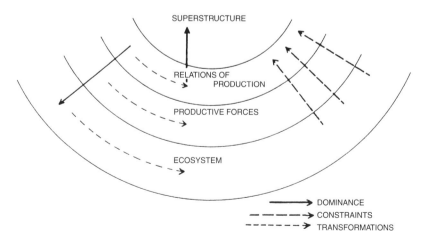

Figure 5.8 Friedman and Rowlands' (1978) view of the relationship between base and superstructure: Figure 1

of this view reassert the balance between the economy and the rest of society, such that the superstructure is seen to influence the economic structure. Thus the economy can be seen as first amongst equal sets of causes, rather than as a prime mover. In broad terms, the move away from economic determinism was instituted by people like the critical theorists of the Frankfurt School, who saw twentieth-century capitalism as moved by ideological forces ranging from Nazi propaganda to advertising campaigns designed to foster mass consumption (Held 1980). Through these influences Marxism has come to be interested in structures of power, class and gender as well as the symbolic systems maintaining social forms and inequalities.

In America and Britain there were moves towards Marxism from the 1950s onwards. Some self-proclaimed Marxists, especially Marvin Harris, have been seen by many as more like standard evolutionists due to their rejection of dialectics and many other key elements of Marxism (Bloch 1984: 133–5). The acknowledgement that capitalism is vital in shaping societies studied by anthropologists has brought many to Marxism, prominent amongst whom are Mintz (1974) and Wolf (1971) who look at how the peasantry in the Caribbean and elsewhere are enmeshed in the workings of the world system. Wolf (1982) has gone on to look at the implications that the creation of the modern economic system over the last 500 years has had for anthropology. 'British anthropology in the period of its strength and its glory, 1920–1960, almost entirely ignored Marxism' (Bloch 1984: 145). What cognisance of Marx there has been in subsequent years, as in the United States, has often been linked to a growing acknowledgement of colonialism. Worsley's (1957) pioneering work on cargo cults in Papua New Guinea saw these as a local response to the material wealth of Europeans who colonised the western Pacific and fought using such extravagant amounts of material in the last war. Talal Asad's (1973) innovative work also took some inspiration from Marx, although other currents of thought were at work, and continue to be, as interest in colonialism has strengthened, as we shall see.

In France the strength of the Communist Party was a paradoxical constraint on the entry of Marxist ideas into anthropology. Party discipline meant that it was difficult to criticise unilineal schemes of historical change emanating from the Soviet Union. However, after the Soviet invasion of Hungary in 1957 many left the Party and the Communist Party itself started to move away from Moscow's influence. Godelier (1977) and others were able to say that not all of Marx and Engel's work was of equal usefulness in the present, limited by their lack of exposure to anthropology and their major concern for the history of Europe. Althusser (Althusser and Balibar 1970) and others have combined structuralist ideas, common in French intellectual life, with Marxism to show that there may be different speeds in the development of the forces and relations of production, plus more than one mode of production present in any one social formation (Hindness and Hirst 1975). A renewed acknowledgement of complexity has led to the use of an analogy of society as a series of intricately interrelated structures. Structural Marxism, as this trend is known, has had considerable influence on Marxist approaches in both archaeology and anthropology. This is found in the works of anthropologists inspired by Althusser, who gathered empirical evidence of a variety of non-capitalist social forms. Writers such as Meillassoux (1981), Terray (1975) and Godelier (1977) tackled a particular aspect of the base–superstructure problem: what sorts of relations of production are exercised in the absence of classes and how is the control over production translated into social power and standing? One answer given to this problem was that direct control was not exercised over production at all, but that power derived from the control of the movement of high-ranking items of exchange. These in turn were used to control the flow of people in marriage, which had important consequences for the demographic strength of a group. In societies dominated by kinship the conclusion consequently was that the relations of reproduction were central to the social process, rather than the relations of production.

These ideas had a direct impact on archaeology in the form of the prestige goods model put forward by Frankenstein and Rowlands (1978) and given more general features by Friedman and Rowlands (1978). The former paper looks at the development of chiefdom structures in Europe north of the Alps under the influence of trade from the Mediterranean. Greek and Etruscan items were incorporated into the exchange networks to the north such that the flow of artefacts could be used to control both the movement of locally produced items and of marriage partners. Here, again, direct control over agricultural or craft production is seen to be less important than the flow of people in marriage (Figure 5.9). The Frankenstein and Rowlands paper also fits in with a further strand of Marxist thought which is the spatial structure of economic units within a larger whole or 'world system'. This influence derives from the work of Wallerstein (1974, 1980), whose interest was in the growth of capitalism. Wallerstein's main point was that it is impossible to understand the development of capitalism by focusing just on Europe, as many historians had done, while ignoring the rest of the world which contributed raw materials, labour and precious metals to the industrial process. In his view Europe and the rest of the world were involved in one set of relations which could not be analysed piecemeal, but had to be seen as a global whole, with Europe forming the centre of the world economy and the rest of the world a periphery. Through the 1970s archaeologists have struggled to reconcile an interest in local development, which had arisen to replace diffusionism, with an interest in trade and exchange as both an indicator and cause of particular social structures. Wallerstein's ideas are attractive in that they allow one to set local sequences of change in a broader social perspective, which includes links between regions through the movement of materials and people. His influence has thus spurred a number of studies of various archaeological periods and places (Rowlands *et al.* 1987). It is instructive to note in passing the difference between the spatial analyses carried out by processual archaeologists and those with Marxist leanings. Whereas the former tend to fix upon the increased efficiencies brought about by centralised co-ordination, the latter

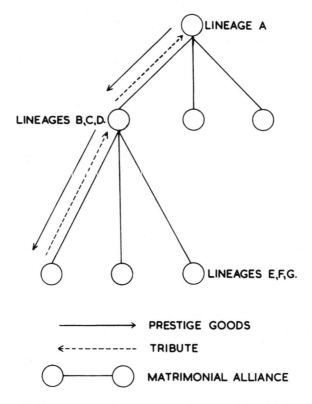

Figure 5.9 The structure of a prestige goods system (after Friedman and Rowlands (1978): Figure 5)

look at the structures of power and the benefits accruing from being in the centre of a world system rather than on the periphery.

Over the past fifteen years Marxism has opened up archaeological debate to theory and data from outside the discipline, particularly from Marxist anthropology (see Spriggs 1984). In doing so it has countered the implication underlying much of the work in processual archaeology that social formations are benign, operating for the general good and able to supply society's wants with increased efficiency and on a larger scale as time goes by. Marxism in both anthropology and archaeology has had to struggle to re-apply theory developed mainly to understand class-based societies to kin ordered groups. Such a re-application has focused on the reproduction of people, as crucial to the social process as the production of things. The application of Marxist theories to archaeology has not always been successful and this is in part because of the relatively limited range of anthropological models drawn upon. Many of these stem from African anthropological case studies concerned with the nature of lineages and closed spheres of exchange. Such cases provide a rather slender basis for global models applicable to kin-based societies everywhere, although they do often include the influence of colonialism on the historical process (Ekholm 1972).

As well as a concern for social reproduction, Marxists have also given much thought to practical action. A concentration on practice derives, for the Marxist, from a general materialist orientation, whereby it is felt that action shapes the world and creates human beings and their modes of experience at the same time. For those with a more hermeneutic viewpoint practical consciousness intersects with discursive consciousness through which the group makes sense of the world. Both Marxists and symbolic anthropologists share an interest in discursive and practical consciousness. However, the former would tend to stress the practical as the place to start in generating understanding, whereas the latter emphasise that the world must be conceived of symbolically before it can be acted upon practically. Many have noted the parallels between Marx's thought and that of Lévi-Strauss, and much French Marxist anthropology has borrowed the notion of structure. However, similarities should not be over-stressed and the differences are important enough to create the basis for elements of anthropology quite at odds with Marxism.

Structuralist and symbolic anthropologies

In the middle of the century, starting in France, but moving into the English-speaking world in the 1950s and 1960s, came a stress on meaning which promoted both a revolution in anthropology, partly through a return to older forms of thought, especially those of Boas and Durkheim. Lévi-Strauss's structuralism was an eclectic mix, but with a considerable coherence to it. We have encountered some of these elements before; others are new. From Durkheim Lévi-Strauss took an interest in how societies are integrated, the differences in the mode of integration and the fact that ideas, such as totemism, matter. From Mauss's *The Gift* came a very specific principle of integration for classless societies: reciprocity. Generalising from Malinowski and other writers on gift exchange, Mauss saw that there is an obligation to receive a gift (refusal is often unacceptable) and an obligation to repay what has been received. These two seemingly simple obligations together create a web of connections between people, binding them into larger wholes through the creation of relationships out of the flow of gifts.

In his first major work, *The Elementary Structures of Kinship* Lévi-Strauss (1969a) looked at how the principle of reciprocity worked itself out in the movements of people in marriage. He made a distinction between simple systems of exchange, in which it was precisely specified who each individual should marry (a mother's brother's daughter, for example), and complex systems in which there was merely a prohibition on whom an individual could not marry. Prohibitions led to much more complex and strategic choices of partner and the obligations which would flow from marriage. So-called simple societies, like the Bushmen, had complex forms of marriage, so there was no straightforward link in Lévi-Strauss's mind between simplicity of technological means and marriage arrangements. A further distinction is that between generalised and restricted exchange: in the former system marriage partners move from group A, to B, to C and so on until one group closes the circle by giving people back to A. This is a flexible system, which can be extended if necessary by adding a new group. Restricted exchange occurs between two groups only and is symmetrical, with partners moving back and forward between the two, along the lines of the two-group Australian Aboriginal section system we saw previously. Lévi-Strauss's analysis shows how social order and cohesion can be maintained in, and between, groups with no overarching political structure and he goes into far more detail and distinctions than I am able to follow here. He also attempts to show how underlying the apparent profusion and confusion of kinship links there lie a few simple patterns.

The search for deep structures giving rise to diversity is a theme of all aspects of Lévi-Strauss's work (1966). Of both his kinship work and that on mythology which followed, Lévi-Strauss asked:

> in the presence of the chaos of social practices or religious representations, will we continue to seek partial explanations, different for each case? Or will we try to discover an underlying order, a deep structure whose effect will permit us to account for this apparent diversity and, in a word, to overcome this incoherence?
>
> (Lévi-Strauss and Eribon 1991: 141)

Put like this, the question can only have an affirmative answer which differentiated him somewhat from another major influence, Boas. During the war Lévi-Strauss was rescued from France by a Rockfeller Program to save prominent Jewish intellectuals and he taught at the New School for Social Research in New York between 1941 and 1945. During this period he came into close contact with Boas and was, in fact, present when Boas died. From Boas Lévi-Strauss took the idea that cultures have their own sets of logic and in some ways are sufficient unto themselves. He obviously differed from the older man in seeing order underlying variety, whereas for Boas local variety was all. Lévi-Strauss's intellectual means of grasping underlying structure was through the influence of structural linguistics deriving from Saussure and which Lévi-Strauss first encountered through a meeting with the prominent linguist Roman Jakobson.

Structural linguistics derives from the work of Saussure at the beginning of this century. Rather like functionalism, with which it otherwise had little resemblance, structuralism was interested in how language worked in the present moment, unlike the previous historical linguistics which tried to account for the historical growth and differentiation of languages. Structuralists wanted to know how meaning was created through the use of language and had an internal view of meaning. Meaning derived from a set of relations within language itself rather than from the ways in which words related to the objects, people or emotions they designated. The crucial relationship was between words (the so-called signifiers) and the concepts they referred to (the signified). A word on its own has little or no meaning and it is only in the context of a whole series of other words that it comes to life. 'Cat' as an isolated word means nothing according to the structuralists, whereas the sentence 'The cat sat on the mat' provides a structured set of differences, created by the words themselves (cat, mat and sat all mean different things), but also by the grammar of the sentence. The important element of linguistic structuralism for anthropology is that it showed that languages each had their own internal logic. It was vital to understand how this logic affected the ways in which words were combined in order to understand how meanings were developed and conveyed in a particular tongue.

Structuralism made it possible to probe the workings of individual languages, but made a comparative project difficult unless one posited some more universal structure. Like Chomsky in linguistics, Lévi-Strauss overcame this relativism through finding a commonality in the structure of the human mind. A direct indication of the workings of the mind is contained in myth, the sets of stories, metaphors and images through which a group tries to make sense of the world. Each group classifies their world into categories – flying versus earth-bound creatures, dangerous objects versus safe ones, the dead and the living – and these pairs of oppositions are combined into connections or resemblances, so that the spirits of the dead may fly abroad bringing danger in their wake and the connection between flight and danger may spill over to other flying creatures. Systems of thought operate by analogy, linking like with perceived like and having a logic of their own in doing so. These schemes of opposition come not from the natural features of the world being classified, but from the structure of the system of classification: the same region could be perceived in radically different ways depending on who was perceiving it, as is the case with Aboriginal and non-Aboriginal Australians. For the former the eaglehawk could be a vital element in set of totemic relationships between people and other creatures; for the outback farmer raptors are mainly useful in keeping down pests such as mice.

For Lévi-Strauss cultural schemes of thought and representation were codes to be unscrambled, providing the key to social relations and connections with the phenomenal and spirit worlds. A myth is only superficially about the story it purports to tell. It can be made to reveal a set of underlying analogies and resemblances at the heart of the culture in question: this is the *real* story. Kuper (1996: 161) says that Lévi-Strauss's ideas hit Britain from 1960 onwards with the force of revelation and that the leaders of the new British structuralism, such as Leach, Needham and Mary Douglas, had an almost messianic desire to bring this new vision to their partially sighted anthropological community. As we saw in the last chapter, some pre-adaptation to Lévi-Strauss's ideas had come through the later work of Radcliffe-Brown who tended to slip from structural to structuralist analyses on occasion. But the movement from social relations to systems of thought was a crucial one. Although Lévi-Strauss never combined his earlier work on kinship with his later analyses of myth, he hoped that his contribution would be a 'socio-logical' one, combining structures of society and of thought. In pursuing this desire to ground thought in the actual conditions of the community as well as in the structure of the mind, Lévi-Strauss often cites the influence of Marx. Such an influence became reciprocal and allowed Lévi-Strauss to make a considerable impression on post-war Marxist trends in France which helped create structural Marxism, as we saw above.

A further complex reciprocal influence was with the cultural anthropology in the United States. Kroeber and Kluckhohn (1952) wrote a review of the concept of culture in which they listed 164 definitions of the word, before settling on their own view of culture as an ensemble of 'patterns, explicit and implicit, of and for behavior acquired and transmitted by symbols' (1952: 181). Such a view had striking resonances with that of Lévi-Strauss, without invoking the same set of complex intellectual influences. Clifford Geertz, a student of Kluckhohn's, was to develop this view of culture 'as a system of symbols by which man confers significance on his own experience' (Geertz 1993c: 250). The cultural anthropology of the 1960s and 1970s in the United States was concerned with ideas and values, as these were manifest in symbols. Geertz has described his own approach as anthropology 'From the native's point of view' (Geertz 1983: chap. 3), and, by and large, American cultural anthropology, in tune with Boas, has been more interested in local views than a global scheme to fit them in. Mary Douglas, although much influenced by Lévi-Strauss, criticised him for his intellectualist position and inability to appreciate the emotional force of local contexts of ideas. Douglas concluded, in a review of Victor Turner's demonstration of the importance of ritual to Ndembu life, that 'It should never again be permissible to provide analysis of an interlocking system of categories of thought which has no demonstrable relation to the social life of the people who think in these terms' (Douglas 1970: 303). This is very much the position taken by many symbolic anthropologists in the United States, first on the grounds that we should take other people's worlds of experience seriously and not just as a series of examples contributing to grand intellectual schemes and, secondly, that it is only in the links between symbols, experience and life that any one of these terms can be understood.

Geertz has argued against the use of formal models and for a new ethnography based on 'thick description'. By this Geertz means a detailed and evocative description which mirrors some of the density of real social life. One of the best-known examples of Geertz's approach is his account of a Balinese cockfight he and his wife, Hilda, first witnessed in 1958 (Geertz 1993b). Geertz uses this important element in Balinese life both to reflect on the position of the anthropologist (they were accepted into the community for the first time when they fled from a police raid on the village, as cockfights were illegal) and the set of meanings attached to the fight (see Crapanzano 1986: 68–76 for a critical account of Geertz's account, which is in turn criticised by Boon (1990: 202, n. 11) on the grounds of Crapanzano's lack of understanding of the Balinese context). Geertz's account of the cockfight allows a privileged insight into Balinese life, or rather Balinese male life. Before the invasion of the Dutch in 1908 cockfighting was carried out in the cock-ring (*wantilan*) in the centre of the village, near the council house, origin temple, market place, signal tower and banyan tree, all vital elements of village life. Cockfighting was outlawed by the Dutch and remained illegal under Sukarno, in the latter case because it was considered 'primitive'.

The importance of cockfighting, both to the Balinese and the anthropologist, is due to its multiplicity of links with other aspects of life. For a start it is a male activity and the word 'cock' has the same range of meanings as it does in English, leading to puns and *doubles entendres* about masculinity, and men being attached to their cocks (Geertz 1993b: 417). Cocks, as birds, also represent the power of animality, an inversion of human status and a connection to the powers of darkness. In one aspect a cockfight is seen as a blood sacrifice to animal demons who threaten the world. Most of Geertz's account, however, concerns the manner in which cockfights reflect the hierarchy of Balinese society and its antagonisms. Balinese society has a whole series of groupings ranging from kin groups, villages, irrigation societies, temple congregations and 'castes'. In cockfighting individual fights are not pre-planned but are brought about by negotiations between a mass of men, holding their birds, in the ring before each fight. Contests have varying significance, depending partly on how well the two birds are matched, but more importantly on the social groupings and individuals ranged behind each bird. Social solidarity and stress are both revealed through betting, to which Geertz dedicates much of his discussion.

Two sorts of bets are placed on a fight: the main wager being between the two social groups, one backing the owner of each bird; second, a series of subsidiary bets between individuals. It is the main wager that is socially significant and the 'deepest' contests are between individuals or groups who are opposed to each other through conflict of general interests or a specific grievance. When the two birds are most evenly matched the outcome of the fight is least predictable, betting is high and much rides on the result, both economically and socially. Cockfighting can be seen as 'play' aggression between two groups, which at times comes enticingly close to the real thing. It is also regulated by a mass of rules, passed down from one generation to the next, inscribed on palm-leaf manuscripts. Such fine regulation contrasts with the cockfight itself, as the two birds throw themselves at each other with their 12 cm long razor-sharp spurs and fight to the death. As Geertz (1993b: 424) says it is 'the doubleness of the event, which, taken as an act of nature, is rage un-trammelled and, taken as an act of culture, is form perfected, defines the cockfight as a sociological entity'. Balinese society is dedicated to the cultivation of a polished, smooth existence which hides the mass of emotions lying beneath, but which are, at some level, recognised by all social actors. Cockfighting allows people to reify many of the tensions of clan and hierarchy and is 'a

Balinese reading of Balinese experience, a story they tell about themselves' (Geertz 1993b: 448).

For the anthropologist, cockfighting represents a text to be read and interpreted around its central elements of animal savagery, male narcissism, opponent gambling, status rivalry, mass excitement and blood sacrifice. It is also part of a larger whole. In Geertz's (1993b: 452) famous formulation 'The culture of a people is an ensemble of texts . . . which the anthropologist strains to read over the shoulders of those to whom they properly belong.' There is no standard method that can be used in this reading and no special place to start. One could begin with cockfighting and move to clan and caste or the general theatrical nature of the political process in Bali. Or one could make broader comparisons with other systems of governance which maintain power through theatre, such as the court in Elizabethan England. Geertz's attempts to understand meaning take a very different form from Lévi-Strauss's structuralism, with its unified theoretical structure. Geertz's work brought anthropology close to literary criticism, through his reference to the work of Hayden White (1973, 1978) and others. And in fact his approach to culture is like that of producers of Shakespeare's plays, which can be played 'traditionally' at the reconstructed Globe, in modern dress or any number of myriad ways. There is no one correct approach to *Hamlet*, but this and other plays can be worked and reworked, with the only major guidelines being that the reworkings should be insightful and make us think about the world anew. Hermeneutics, the study of meaning, is vital here and, in fact, a double hermeneutic is necessary so as to understand both the structures of meanings of the Balinese and of the anthropologist reading over the Balinese shoulder, but using their own local intellectual resources.

The work of Geertz was realistic in that it also included history within its descriptions. Bali was not to be understood just in the here and now, but against the background of Dutch colonialism and the contemporary Indonesian state. A realisation of the broader context of post-colonialism is one that has come over anthropology and archaeology as a whole in the last twenty years. It is to this we now turn, moving away from the history of the subjects we have been considering until now and looking instead at contemporary problems and issues.

Part II
The contemporary scene

Introduction to Part II

So far I have concentrated on the history of anthropology and archaeology, trying to bring out some of the mutual influences between the two disciplines. In the second section the focus shifts to contemporary problems and issues in anthropology and archaeology. The role of this brief introduction is to provide a bridge between the two, bringing out some of the salient aspects of the history of the subjects, as some elements of history still structure debates in the present. I shall also argue for a particular viewpoint seeking a conjunction between cultural anthropology and archaeology, around issues of practice and agency in the material world. In arguing from one perspective, I shall try to be as inclusive as possible in discussing other points of view, so that the reader can gain an impression of the present intellectual scene. I feel it more realistic to make a virtue of the fact that I have my own opinion of the issues discussed. To purport to present a bland and balanced overview would be intellectually dishonest. More importantly, I think there are interesting possibilities of synthesis between a variety of ideas within archaeology and anthropology, which indicate new directions for both.

One of the great divides in the history of anthropology is that between social and cultural anthropology. A stress on society goes back to the genealogical method of Rivers, who pointed out that all important roles, duties, customs, rights and access to resources in societies without class structures rested on kinship. Rivers' method of collecting genealogies was taken up by Malinowski and Radcliffe-Brown in their intensive forms of fieldwork to produce large and consistent bodies of data on all areas of social life, with kinship at their core. Social anthropologists stressed social relations and thought that the material settings of action or items exchanged ceremonially were only to be understood starting from the matrix of social relations. Gell, in a recent statement of the centrality of social relations to an anthropological theory of art, has said 'My view is that in so far as anthropology has a specific subject-matter at all, that subject-matter is "social relationships" – relationships between participants in social systems of various kinds' (Gell 1998: 4). He then goes on to say that art should not be viewed as an element of culture, as culture is an abstraction, but rather to look at how art is efficacious in maintaining and altering social relations. Social anthropology is now attempting to incorporate material culture into its analysis of social relations, as Gell's work shows, nevertheless the primacy of the social remains the starting point. A stress on social relations has been partly responsible for an emphasis on the present rather than on change. It has been felt from Malinowski onwards that kin-based societies were so complex in their operation, that it was necessary to document them in the here and now, rather than putting too much energy into understanding change. In the early structural-functionalist analyses this led to the view that eighteen months of fieldwork represented the 'ethnographic present'. More recently, social anthropology has become interested in the time-spans of biographies of people, or the life cycle of the household or kinship groups, incorporating some degree of history, without getting into the complications of great historical depth.

Cultural anthropology, from Boas onwards, has focused on the material and the historical. Culture areas were distinguished by the special set of traits of art or material culture found within them and the manner in which these traits had been put together over time. Social relations were seen to be dependent on the material means through which links between people were maintained. More recently culture has been equated with meaning, either through the structuralism of Lévi-Strauss or the more semiotic orientation of Geertz, who read the texts of cultures.

My viewpoint derives from new forms of cultural anthropology, which emphasise material worlds and meanings as these are worked out through material culture and landscape. The details of these approaches are discussed in the following chapters. I shall bring out just a few points of importance here. I make the opposite statement to that of Gell: there is no such thing as social relations. By this I mean that human relations are never simply between people, they always involve things as well. Relations are always material and social at once, so that material culture is not an added extra in social life, but right at its heart. Once we start to look at the creation of social relations through the medium of material things, then objects become social agents in their own right and their formal properties and their combination into assemblages both become important. The durable nature of material things, especially once landscape is included, makes it difficult to ignore questions of history. People are socialised within material settings, so that the world is an important part of social reproduction, as one generation succeeds the next. Different approaches have various time scales built into them. Classic social anthropology, between the wars, took its eighteen-month span of fieldwork as the only crucial timescale, excising both past and future from the analysis. Current forms of cultural anthropology work with a range of timescales from the biography of the individual or object, to the longer-term histories of colonialism. For archaeology, cultural biographies of things and people would represent the minimum unit of temporal analysis, with the maximum stretching into millions of years.

Cultural anthropology and archaeology overlap in both subject matter and timescale. They also draw on similar theoretical structures as will be detailed in the following chapters. I should like to highlight two different viewpoints, deriving from separate bodies of theory, which can bear further useful development. The first derives from what is called the 'dwelling perspective' to use Ingold's (1993a, 1993b) words. Such a perspective is a reaction to the analytical process which divides up the world into bits called things like technology or society. The idea of dwelling derives from the phenomenology of Heidegger (Gosden 1994). Dwelling tries to approach an appreciation of life as it is lived, as an undifferentiated whole, with people in touch with the world through all their senses and acting using socially inculcated sets of bodily skills and practices. The work of Bourdieu has been crucial in inspiring much practice-based anthropology and archaeology, stressing the importance of the mutual involvement of people, material culture and landscape. I shall present and develop the ideas of Ingold, Bourdieu and others (chaps 6 and 7), but also stress notions of aesthetics and cosmology which can give some overall shape and style to patterns of life.

The second perspective I would like to develop is complementary and even contradictory to the first, in that it is an outsider's analytical viewpoint. This derives from the deconstructionist anthropology of Melanesia, associated with Marilyn Strathern and Roy Wagner. This is a relational view, holding that people and things have no essential properties, but that these properties crystallise out of the relationships within which entities are enmeshed. A person's character in any one situation will depend and derive from the sets of material and social relations that go to make up that situation. Gender, for instance, is not an inherent and invariable property of a person, but rather relations of gender are created and evinced in different ways depending on context. Life as a whole can be seen as a series of transformations, as the relations composing people and things shift. Some of these transformations are regularly occurring ones: we would call these continuity. Some transformations are unexpected and bring about new sets of relations: we would call these change. Whether looking at continuity or change we should never forget that life is always a state of becoming and even a stress on continuity does not mean the social process is static.

A dwelling perspective and a relational view are usefully complementary. The former reminds us that life is lived as an undifferentiated whole, through which we are immersed in the world and work to change it. All analysis does violence to life as it is lived, chopping it into bits because it is impossible to understand the whole simultaneously. A relational view allows us to isolate different contexts of action and causes of change, whilst always keeping in mind the importance of interconnectedness. However, we must constantly beware not to mistake the model of reality for the reality of the model, to repeat Bourdieu's caution (Bourdieu 1990).

An analytical model of relations also allows us to pull back the camera to look at broader relations in time and space; by definition, the dwelling perspective is place-specific and has a tendency to be synchronic. The first benefit of a broad outsider's perspective is to link different domains of transformation into a whole. Such a set of relations between relations can specify the various forms of transformation that people and things undergo in different contexts of life. The total set of transformations might be called the culture. But rather than getting too bound up in defining the broadest field of culture, we must be aware that it is unbounded, there is no neat edge to cultures in space; they are not like nation states. An individual culture area is more like a centre of gravity, where certain special sets of relations between people and things pertain, which are less likely to be found elsewhere. The unboundedness of cultures is all too obvious in the present state of the world, where people and objects can move around the globe on a regular basis. The global nature of culture has created what seems like a new context for anthropology and archaeology. It has also brought a new sense of local lives-experience. It is with concerns about the body that I shall start.

6 Bodily identities
Gender, sexuality and practice

This chapter picks up two themes mentioned in the section introduction: practice-based and relational or transformational views. Approaches which study practice look at how life is learned and lived, through concentrating on embodied skills inculcated through the process of socialisation. Life is not learnt or enacted all of a piece, and different elements of social action are created in and create varying locales of action and efficacy. One very productive application of ideas of practice, drawn from Bourdieu, is in the consideration of ritual. A practice-based theory of ritualisation takes us away from a sterile debate over definitions of ritual, but instead argues that some sets of actions become formalised and repeated through their social value. Why and how certain aspects of practice are picked out and ritualised can only be judged through an overall appreciation of practice and such questions also lead to consideration of the performative aspects of culture in general.

One criticism of the work of Bourdieu and others in considering practice is that although time and change are part of the theory, there is no well-formulated consideration of the multiple influences on any one set of social actions; nor is there a real theory of transformation. The work of Marilyn Strathern within anthropology and Butler within feminist theory stress the fact that no aspect of human life, such as gender or class, can be considered in isolation without our understanding becoming uni-dimensional. All human identity is created through multiple influences. Strathern's ideas are especially useful in her stress on the relational nature of life: all aspects of individual personality and group culture are created through relations with other people and groups. Gender, for instance, is not an invariant aspect of women and men, but something evoked within particular circumstances and situations. People vary through the relationships they enter and create. Each of us is in a permanent state of change and flux, as we move from one situation to another, rather than having core aspects of our personality that we carry with us at all times. Such views see society as in a constant state of becoming and change. They are, however, the views of outsiders: they are analytical, seeing relations as crucial and, in Strathern's case, these relations compose a system of signification rather than connections between flesh and blood people with real material culture.

I shall argue that both points of view, the practice-based and the relational, have their strengths. The former looks at how social skills are inculcated and enacted; the latter at how transformations occur between varying contexts of action. The two views form part of a dialectic, moving us between being and becoming. A further important element, which is not stressed in either view, is the notion of aesthetics. Life is made up of bodily action mediated by material relations which are felt to be appropriate within particular cultural settings. Appropriate actions are those which are efficacious, stylistically pleasing and morally right. Used in this sense aesthetics takes us well beyond considerations of beauty, which adhere to the term in its western usage and towards a understanding of what it is to live well in any one cultural setting. Including aesthetics helps tie the transformational view to the material world, for there can be little discussion of aesthetics without links to artefacts or bodies. It also helps move practice from the purely pragmatic where it has some tendency to linger. It is to theories of practice that I turn first.

Good practice

The roots of modern thought about practice can be traced at least back to Mauss (mentioned in chaps 4 and 5). Mauss's thought and that which has followed reversed the links between biology and culture, where the former was seen as cause and the latter as effect. For instance, Lévi-Strauss notes (1987) in relation to Mauss's work, that racial theories saw people as products of their bodies, but in fact the body can be seen to be produced through different social techniques. This was Mauss's originality to see the forms of bodily action as a social product. Everyday actions, such as walking or swimming, differ between the closely related cultures, such as the Americans, French and British. Mauss came up with the notion of body techniques to look at the manner in which people from different cultural backgrounds used their bodies. Such techniques were transmitted through tradition and learnt unconsciously as part of our basic socialisation, forming the deepest level of social convention on which all else rested. Making the body more central caused a re-evaluation of our understanding of social life – 'Child-rearing is full of what are called details, but they are actually essentials' (Mauss 1979: 108).

A new concept was needed to focus on the ordinary everyday actions which are unnoticed because they are so common and basic to our lives. Habitus played this role and was a term compounded from *habitude* (habit or custom) plus *exis* (acquired ability or facility). The acquisition of basic habits of the body through being socialised into particular social and physical milieux showed that the body was not just our 'first and most natural technical object' (Mauss 1979: 104), but the basis of all social conventions. An holistic anthropology could only start from the body, as perception and psychological dispositions derived from training the body in socially channelled ways. History was composed of such fundamental moments as education in vision, education in walking and education in general bodily composure and comportment. The variety of such educations meant that the concept of self and individuality varied enormously from one society to another.

The focusing of attention on the minutiae of life and their basis in the body are central features of the work of Pierre Bourdieu, whose overall approach might be seen to combine structuralism and Mauss in an unusual French cocktail. Bourdieu started academic life as a structuralist, but gave this up when he moved away from conscious knowledge as found in myths to the need for models of unconscious actions generating practice. A major part of his work concerns the tension between the thought and the unthought, both in academic and daily life. He argues that there has been a downplaying of the active side of human existence in favour of thought and theory from Plato onwards (Bourdieu 1990: 28). For Bourdieu, understanding the difference between thought and action, as quite distinct relationships to the world, is the 'most significant product of my whole undertaking' (Bourdieu 1990: 15). One of the most original aspects of Bourdieu's work is to highlight the links between academic thought and practice, as anthropologists and others tend to ignore the fact that the type of knowledge they produce is abstract, theoretical and the view of outsiders. Bourdieu points out that only strangers to a place need a map to find their way; locals know their terrain and the routes through it. Anthropology is a discipline of map-makers, creating simplified, abstracted two-dimensional views of social space, which leave out the lived dimension. Anthropologists, like all social scientists, are likely to mistake the model of reality for the reality of the model and forget or suppress their view as outsiders (Bourdieu 1990: 14, 27). For our present purposes, Bourdieu's attempt to highlight the link between the practice of anthropology and the types of knowledge it produces is less important than the fact that he sees this link as general in social life. Practical action gives rise to thought and feeling, but a conscious appreciation of the world also affects the way we act, so that there is an important and complex relationship between thought and action. However, given that anthropology has thought so much about thought, then some redress is needed through thought about the body.

Thinking about the body has taken Bourdieu back to Mauss and a reformulation of the concept of habitus. Habitus is still habits which are socially learnt and transmitted, but in his infamous definition becomes:

> systems of durable, transposable dispositions, structured structures predisposed to function as structuring structures, that is as principles which generate and organise practices and representations that can be objectively adapted to their outcomes without presupposing a conscious aiming at ends or an express mastery of the operations necessary to obtain them.
> (Bourdieu 1990: 53)

Habitus is a second nature. People produce thought, perception and action without thinking about how they are doing so, but in a manner which has its own inherent logic. Social life is neither made up of wild and unpredictable improvisation nor the mechanical reproduction of social rules. Habitus is learnt through the process of socialisation: through imitation and encouragement rather than through conscious learning. Young children absorb a whole range of social norms and these become something one is rather than something one knows. We learn not just practical skills, but also a whole range of social distinctions. Gender and class distinctions create the body in different ways: the proper forms of comportment for girls and boys are learnt early and stay with us forever, as do acts of deference or the right to command. A confident upright stance or crouched servility are as much a part of social action as any words spoken, gifts given or violence perpetrated. The injunction to a child to 'sit up straight' contains a whole history of overtones of social norms. Bodily comportment always has an historical element, being transmitted from one generation to the next, giving a local quality to life which the outsider can find shocking or unsettling. While there is definite truth to this, there is also less of a stress on change than is really useful, with slight overtones of social conditioning, a point we shall pick up again below.

Habitus is hard to capture in words. Playing a game is partly about planned tactics and strategy, but also relies on a feel for the game both by individuals and the team as a whole. Such a feel for the game blends the physical and the social: each needs to have the skill to propel the ball, puck or whatever in the right way at the right time, but also needs to know without thinking what their team mates and opponents will be attempting and expecting. Playing a game means adhering to the rules, but also coming up with unexpected and novel moves which opponents cannot counter. Similarly social life is a blend of the physical and the social, which also combines conscious thought with an intuition about situations. Intuition is not mystical, but derives from long familiarity and deep forms of knowledge which are hard to analyse. The difficulty of rendering a feel for a situation in words obviously poses a problem for anthropology and lies partly behind the moves to new experimental forms of writing and representation discussed in previous chapters.

A further difficulty is posed by time and timing. The linear nature of prose makes it ineffective in rendering the complexity of social time where many things generally happen at once and an important element of action is not simply what you do, but when you do it. As Bourdieu (1990: 106) says, gift exchange is fundamentally about when a return is made. To reciprocate too quickly is to belittle the relationship created by the original gift. An immediate return is a form of refusal to be under obligation and an insulting disregard of the other party. Waiting too long to make a return is an embarrassing reflection of lack of social knowledge of the rules or looks like a lack of respect. Timing is integral to social life, but again is not generally taught, but absorbed through the overall process of socialisation. Timing is a core aspect of habitus, but one which is hard for the outsider to capture, so that outsiders' accounts tend to collapse the timing of action, missing any sense of anticipation or suspense inherent in the action itself. In all social formations it is not just what is done that is crucial, but the style with which it is done and style, both ineffable and essential, lies at the heart of social differences.

Lévi-Strauss sought the fundamental structures of the human mind through an analysis of myth and symbols. But if thought arises from contexts of action and action derives from the social worlds into which people are socialised, then each society has its own structure of the mind and this structure is heavily implicated in the actions of the body. Herein lies Bourdieu's break from his immediate, structuralist past: he starts with the body not the mind and emphasises the local not the global. Moreover, his work tries to refuse the division between the body and the mind, looking instead at the complex interweaving of discursive and non-discursive knowledge. And although Bourdieu emphasises local forms of socialisation, bodily action and consciousness he is still seeking to build a general model of habitus and to develop a set of generative schemes from which the logical coherence of practice is generated. There is some tendency to emphasise the nature and creation of social order in Bourdieu's work (see his analysis of Kabyle domestic space for instance, Bourdieu 1990: appendix) within a synchronic framework, perhaps resulting from his structuralist years. Time and timing in social life are embraced, but not fundamental change, a point to which we shall return.

Dwelling

A stress on dwelling is an antidote to what Bourdieu calls the outsider's perspective in anthropology. Dwelling emphasises the full sensuous experience of living in the world, a rounded appreciation of which is lost from most analytical perspectives. There is much overlap between theories of practice and a dwelling perspective and this derives in part from their joint phenomenological heritage (see Gosden 1994). An emphasis on wholeness has led to attempts to overcome divisions into mind and body, subject and object. One domain of discussion in which these divisions are dominant is in the consideration of the evolution of human intelligence and I shall use these discussions as a means of introducing the strengths of the dwelling perspective.

Central to studies of human evolution is the consideration of the origins and development of human intelligence. An older view, which can be traced back to Darwin, is that tools have given hominids a crucial competitive advantage over our competitors and prey and that the intelligence which lay behind the creation of tools has been selected for over millennia and millions of years. Tool use is the main reason for the development of intelligence. In recent years this idea has been countered by the notion that the most complex aspect of any present primates' environment (and the same would be true of our primate ancestors) is the social environment in which they live. Closely knit social groups are necessary for the long period of education of young and within these groups social competition and co-operation is intense. Understanding the motives of others and being able to alter their actions through manipulation or deception has become crucial to the individual.

Deception involves a subtle appreciation of others' thought and action: being able to foresee both what another would do if they were apprised of the true facts and how their actions would be altered if they could be fooled into believing something else. The ability to see alternative futures and to alter the actions of others to bring about one, advantageous, outcome rather than another, shows complex mental processes. The idea that intelligence developed from the intense interactions of the primate group is often known as the Machiavellian intelligence hypothesis, due to its stress on manipulation, and traces its origin back to Humphrey (1976) and the subsequent discussions that it has inspired (Byrne and Whiten 1988, Gibson and Ingold 1993).

The counterposing of technological and social intelligence makes for good debate, but like any argument with two alternatives it may have set up a false dichotomy. This is exactly what Ingold (1993b) has said, advocating instead not so much a middle way, but rather a synthesis of the technological and the social in a manner which redefines intelligence. The image of intelligent action lying behind both these approaches is that it derives from the action of the mind, so that acts of cognition, such as mental representations of physical states of affairs, consideration of alternatives and formulation of plans precede and inform action. The body executes what the mind directs. But Ingold argues that life is not like that and skilled practice represents a unity of thought and action, so that we pay attention to what we are doing with all our senses and action derives as much from the skills of the body as the rationality of the mind. Skilled practice is non-verbal, something that we know physically rather than being able to put into words or other forms of representation. I have said much the same (Gosden 1994: chap. 7), adding that conscious attention only comes into play when things do not work and we then have to work out alternatives. Ingold calls his view a 'dwelling perspective', meaning that we are immersed in the flow of life composed of both social relations and practical actions.

Ingold's dwelling perspective is given a spatial dimension through his image of taskscape, which is seen as an array of related activities spread across the physical landscape (Ingold 1993b: 158). I have come up with a similar notion of activities forming a system of reference, such that an activity carried out in one place refers explicitly or implicitly to a host of others carried out elsewhere (Gosden 1994: 15–20). Making a stone tool is embedded within a system of other purposes, whether it is made to reap or scrape a skin will affect not just how it is made, but when and where. Acts are not isolated, but link into complex chains creating a sense of space and of time and we will return to these points when looking at landscape, in the next chapter. The ideas of taskscape or a system of reference are valuable in keying us into the creation of space through action, but they also help emphasise time. Activities which are separated in space must also be spread out in time and each taskscape has its own temporality, its rhythms of action and of rest.

A dwelling perspective is not just static being in the landscape, but gives a human shape to time through the pattern of activities. However, although a dwelling perspective includes change through time, it is still in a sense syn-chronic in that it does not look at longer sequences of change. This is partly due to its origin within the thought of Heidegger, who stressed a rootedness in the here and now, a more authentic form of being as against the superficial action and change of the modern world. But against this being in the world, we need to consider how the world was created, or rather, how people create worlds for themselves and are in turn shaped by these worlds. A stress on dwelling is a vital corrective to a distanced appreciation of human action, but it is not the whole story, as we shall see later. One extra benefit that can come from theories of practice, is the formalised aspects of action and the struc-tured physical spaces in which rituals are carried out.

Ritualised actions

Many competing definitions of ritual have been offered over the years. For Durkheim, ritual was the means by which collective beliefs were generated and affirmed and the practice of ritual saw the meeting of collective representa-tions and individual experience (Durkheim 1965). Ritual was vital to the group's sense of itself and to bind the individual to the group. Tambiah (1976) saw the timeless and traditional nature of ritual being always opposed to the historical and changing nature of everyday life. Somewhat similarly, Victor Turner (1977) contrasted the unity of the community brought about through the process of ritual with the competitiveness and social friction of everyday life. More recent attempts have focused on how ritual functions versus what it symbolises, reflecting the general division within anthropology between func-tion and meaning. The common element in all these differing definitions was the assumption that there was an essential core to ritual to be found where ever it is practised. Much effort has been expended on defending these differ-ent conceptions of ritual and the division between everyday life and ritual action inherent within them with their echoes in the division between the sacred and the profane.

Quite a different view is constructed by Catherine Bell (1992) which focuses on practice. For Bell ritualisation, not ritual *per se*, should be the focus of examination and we can only understand ritual within the context of other areas of social practice. Because ritual is contextual it is not one thing but many, involving aspects of life which are picked out from the overall flow of life as being particularly important and given a more formalised quality. A focus on ritualisation, rather than ritual, leads us to ask how ritual distin-guishes itself from other practices and what ritual accomplishes in doing so (Bell 1992: 89). All human action, for Bell (1992: 81) is situational and cannot be understood abstracted from its specific context. Following Bourdieu she sees action as regulated improvisation so that practice is strategic, manipula-tive and expedient, but arising from local habitus. Action also unfolds within a context of power relations. Each person operates within their own sense of the possible, the options they have for action and the constraints upon them.

The feel for the social game is made up of the interweaving of possibility and constraint, plus the individuals' sense of themselves within a complex network of relationships. Rituals are often formalised actions, but the degree of formality depends on context. Evangelical churches have ritualised worship, but they see their worship as more authentic by contrast to the formality of services in longer established churches. Rituals and the degree of ritualisation of activities cannot be discussed in the abstract, but only by reference to the specifics of action in a time and a place.

Within the overall warp and weft of actions and relationships are ritualised actions, which have special power and potency. Common to strategies of ritualisation are: the differentiation of action through its formalisation and special periodicity; the centrality of the body; the orchestration of schemes whereby the body defines a set of locales and is defined by those locales; physical and mental mastery of ritual; and a negotiation of power through ritual so as to influence the overall hegemonic order of society. The body is the central feature of ritualisation. Quoting Bourdieu, Bell (1992: 97) says that every group 'entrusts to bodily automatisms' the most basic principles of the organisation and maintenance of the group. The body becomes the locus of all levels of physical, social and cosmological experience. Different arenas of bodily practice become co-ordinated to form a social whole. Ritualized activities become part of the overall panorama of social practice, with effects that extend far beyond ritual itself. The end of ritual is a ritualised body, with a cultivated set of dispositions which echo through the rest of life. Kneeling helps create subordination in the one who kneels and subordination in one context may manifest itself in another (Bell 1992: 98–100). Ritualized actions take place in particular locales, set apart from the daily activities, and which are internalised through ritual action, to be evoked outside the ritualised setting.

To summarise Bell's position we can say that ritual has no final meaning or purpose and it is difficult to find common elements to ritual which run through many different social situations. However, some generalisations can be made. Ritual creates a sense of order through prescribed bodily actions in defined physical settings. Ritual actions have to be mastered, but have the effect of mastering the individual. Rituals are mysterious and ineffable, but they also create a physical experience of order and a fit between taxonomies of order and individual experience. Although ritualised actions are created and carried out in special settings their effects are far-reaching. People carry their ritualised bodies with them everywhere, including their habits of deference or control and the sets of actions appropriate to such feelings. To study ritual is to probe crucial aspects of the society as a whole and an analysis of which actions are ritualised and which not will say a lot about the social process as a whole and its divisions of gender and hierarchy.

A similar approach to Bell's but with some significant additions and differences to her approach is contained in Humphrey and Laidlaw's (1994) account of Jain ritual. They, too, take a practice-based approach, saying that ritualisation is a quality that action can come to have. They look at ritual as a means by which people become committed to meanings through a commitment to the ritual process itself. As ritual acts are in some sense external to the individual actors and are not derived from their individual intentions, then ritual is a means of binding people to broader group meanings. In ritual, individuals both are, and are not, the authors of their own acts and although this could be said of life in general, it is more obvious in formalised activities. Like Bell, they see the possibility for any set of actions becoming ritualised if they are deemed important enough. Humphrey and Laidlaw also make a useful distinction between litany- and performance-based rituals (1994: 8–12), both of which may be found in the same society. Performance-based rituals try to create the conviction that supernatural events happen through ritual: that spirits appear or miracles occur. Performance-based rituals are less ritualised and formalised, more inclined to spontaneity and innovation and may be found in contexts where shamans operate. Litany-based rituals follow a set course with closely prescribed actions, texts and physical settings. Participants in performance rituals ask 'Did it work?', whereas those taking part in rituals with litany at the heart will ask 'Did we get it right?' The stress on correct procedure in the latter case will lead to calls for reform on occasions so as to get to the true meaning of the actions, whereas the former seek an eruption of the supernatural into the everyday and there may be different means of achieving this.

Both Bell and Humphrey and Laidlaw agree that ritual action can only be understood against a background of social activity in general, but also that the consequences of ritual stretch far beyond the ritual itself, helping to engender particular casts of mind and body or to attach people to sets of meanings they then find hard to ignore in all areas of their life. Because rituals create and reinforce core social meanings their analysis can give a privileged insight into society and the social process in general. It also leads us to consider how patterns of action set up in one area of life can transform action in another.

Gender in anthropology

Gender is a perfect area to study transformations, if gender itself is approached from particular points of view. The view I shall develop here is that of gender as transformation, one of the most important of a series of transformations brought about by the sets of relations composing cultural life.

Feminist thought is the main arena within which gender has been tackled, but it is not the only one. So-called masculinist theory (its name echoing feminism) has tried to come to terms with the constructed nature of gender from a male (but not androcentric) perspective (Connell 1995). And inevitably, the literature on sexuality overlaps with that on gender (Herdt 1982, 1984), as we shall see. Most feminist writers are women, but obviously gender cannot purely be about women, as there could never be a single gender without erasing the concept altogether. Gender is thus a relational concept, deriving from the creation and maintenance of difference. It has taken some time for a relational model to become a starting point for discussions on gender. Wylie (1991) has pointed out that explorations of gender in archaeology have gone through three main phases: a critique of androcentrism; a search for women in the past and (now) a fundamental rethinking of issues of difference and relatedness. Similar processes of thought have gone on in anthropology (see Moore 1988), but at a slightly earlier date, although anthropology does not have the same problem in recognising gendered individuals and has made more progress in reconceptualising the field of gender relations.

Feminism has an explicit political agenda which aims to expose and over-throw women's oppression in all areas of life and in any society in the world. But to develop such an agenda is not a purely practical matter: it also necessitates considerable theoretical work on how gendered relations are constructed in various parts of the world and in different areas of life. Such a programme raises questions of power and motive on the part of the analyst. Particularly difficult questions revolve around how far anthropology and archaeology as western constructs in origin and conception impose their own views of the world on the rest. It might be held that women face the same problems of subordination and male bias the world over, and this allows some sort of general approach to be developed to global problems. On the other hand, it can be argued that feminism and much of the thinking on gender connected with it, arose in the First World and has been imposed on the rest. If women and men are not universal categories, but are created through culturally and historically specific sets of relations (Moore 1988: 7), then the study of gender as a generality can never take place, but should only be carried out with modes of thought sensitive to particular cultural contexts. In particular, westerners should be wary of seeing any form of inequality between men and women as being the same as western inequalities.

For these reasons, part of any approach to gendered relations must involve a critique and unlearning of western assumptions and should eschew any temptation to universalise the nature of relations between men, women and children (of course, the same could be said for any area of anthropological or archaeological study). I will tackle these tricky issues with primary reference to one particular work: Marilyn Strathern's (1988) *The Gender of the Gift*. This difficult book is important not only because it contains her first statement of a relational approach to people and social groups, but also because Strathern attempts to uncover the assumptions in western liberal thought which shape our thinking about gender.

Let us start with what Strathern calls an 'ethnography of western knowledge practices' (1988: xi) and the concomitant 'claims to comprehension that anthropology can and cannot make' (1988: xii). She provides not so much an account of what Melanesian forms of representation and thought are, but what they look like when viewed through a lens ground out by western preoccupations.

For Strathern a central feature of liberal thought is the distinction between the individual and society. Society, which is in fact a category generated by analysis, is often seen as a real object and is made up of combinations of individuals. Society is a series of connections between people that holds them in some form of unity and the Radcliffe-Brown image of kinship structures in the forms of trees is one which resonates broadly in the western mind. Individuals are the building blocks of society and each of us is seen as a sovereign entity, the author of our own acts and therefore responsible for them. We are separate bounded entities by virtue of our bodies, which create boundaries between self and other. Each bounded self is an agent in the social world, affecting others through their acts and dividing up the material world through ownership: each individual owns objects as their property and can dispose of this property in particular ways so that objects become extensions of a person's agency. Not all people are equal or the same and are divided up into groups on the basis of class, age and gender and these divisions act as fracture lines within society dividing people in all contexts of action. Men and women are essentialised so that their respective actions are seen to be different in all situations they confront each other, even though those responses may be modified in some ways by context. Men are seen to control the public life of any group, and women, as far as they have power, exercise this in the domestic sphere where children are born and nurtured and spouses supported.

Contrast these bourgeois views of social life, as outlined by Strathern, with her evocation of a Melanesian world which is one without any fixed concept of the person or society. People are not individuals, but 'dividuals' (a term she takes from Marriott's (1976) views on India). People are plural and are best seen as shifting nodes in sets of social relations, composed of all the different relationships in which they are enmeshed. Individuals have no fixed set of characteristics, but are like colours which change depending upon the mix of hues pertaining in one social encounter. Because people are composite, the bringing together of many like people is analogous to the bringing together of one, so that the plural and singular are homologues of each other (Strathern 1988: 13). But not all groups of individuals or collectivities are internally identical and dyadic relations are both the source and outcome of action. There are two forms of plurality: the composite and the dual. One of the chief forms of duality is that between men and women. But this dual state is not one that exists irrespective of context, but is evoked under certain circumstances. Gender is not a pre-existing condition of social action, but the precipitate of social action, so that men and women are differentiated only under some conditions. It is not the case that boys will be boys in any pre-ordained fashion, but rather that maleness will be emphasised in some social arenas and not in others. As composites, both men and women have combined male and female characteristics, to be emphasised or forgotten as the situation allows. This also runs counter to the view of gender as constructed through socialisation, whereby people who are initially ungendered are given a gender identity through socialization into general norms. It is as if different genders recruited members to their group from those seen already to possess the qualifying attributes for membership (Strathern 1988: 64).

At the broadest level of generalisation, Strathern makes the point that any construction of identity and gender needs to be tied into a general social scheme of thought and representation which outlines the aesthetics of human action and the material culture which is an integral part of this action. A crucial question about Melanesian forms of representation, or rather western depictions of these forms, is how to specify the varying relationships which exist between public cult activity, ceremonial exchange and warfare on the one hand (glossed as the public sphere by the west) and gardening and domestic nurture on the other (the private/domestic arena for western thought)? The consensus view of Melanesia amongst anthropologists is that men have dominated in the public sphere and expropriated women's labour in the domestic sphere in order to fund exchanges, cults and war, all pursued for reasons of personal prestige. Men's prestige and dominance is produced through both the exclusion of women and by siphoning off domestic products. This, says Strathern, is too simple a view, resting on a dichotomy between women and men which is seen to pre-exist social life, rather than differences being produced differently by various areas of social life.

In the area around Mount Hagen in the Western Highlands men have to be effective in discharging their domestic obligations. This is not a matter of temporary male involvement in the primarily female domestic sphere, but rather a mutuality of women and men in undertaking tasks of gardening, house maintenance and child rearing. Children do not grow to be sovereign individuals in the home, but mature into a set of social relations which have male and female aspects, both of which are derived from each of the parents (Strathern 1988: 89–92). Men and women can be seen to have different, but overlapping, spheres of efficacy, each of which is dependent on all the others.

Unlike in the west where men and women are seen to be in a continual relationship of difference, gender is created and transacted in Melanesia. In his analysis of Abelam art Forge (1973) noted that objects did not represent things which existed in the world, but were rather about sets of relationships between things. These relationships can appear quite confusing from a European point of view. The fronts of men's houses are decorated with a whole series of figures, which have varied pendulant appendages. Although these appear to the outsider to be similar, some of these appendages are seen by the Abelam to be breasts and others to be penises, so it is as though men and women were variants of each other. Can we see the phallus as a male breast or the breast a woman's penis? Such questions might only have local Abelam interest if it were not for the fact that such ambiguity is found in many places in Melanesia. Flutes, common in male initiation rites in the Eastern Highlands, are seen as female, but as a female penis. A men's house may be seen as a womb and the blood drawn from a penis during an initiation rite may be seen as menstrual.

Some have seen the male initiation cults as a reflection of male anxiety about their inability to reproduce and as a consequent attempt to appropriate female powers. But to follow this interpretation, Strathern (1988: 126) says, is to see that women and men are always conceived of as being different. She also feels that to see breasts as always female and penises male is to start with a notion of possession which fits in well with European conceptions of property, but makes it much harder to grasp the aesthetic schemes in use in Melanesia. Perhaps a transactional scheme would be more resonant with Melanesian thought. Many of the rituals create male and female attributes at special stages of the process and these are moments in an overall pattern of action. Genders are not pre-set but arise out of transactions between men and women and bodies are the outcome of actions: a penis can become a womb in a particular context, being enclosing rather than penetrative. Context is all and the major enframing context is that created by exchanges between men and women, who are themselves created out of the exchanges. Thus men do not control or overcome women, but each needs the other as a perpetual set of spurs to actions which precipitate special relationships with their own gendered qualities (Strathern 1988: 131). The continuous creation of gender reinforces Strathern's major point, that all people are composite and created through sets of relations to others. Maleness and femaleness are especially important outcomes of such relations, but are parts of people rather than their essence. Such a point of view leads to the question of what aspects of social action lead male or female qualities to be emphasised.

An important aspect of the scheme of representations through which gender is produced is that which westerners would call political economy. Here the distinction between gift and commodity is vital and this goes back to Malinowski's work on the difference between western and non-western economies and the use that was made of it by Mauss and others. Strathern uses Gregory's (1982) formulation of the problem. Since Mauss (1969) gifts have been seen as a means of setting up obligations: if a gift is not reciprocated within a period felt to be reasonable by both parties, then the receiver is under obligation to the giver. Giving is ordered so that the maximum number of relationships can be created and maintained. But Gregory draws on Marx to show deeper schemes of representation underlying different forms of giving. Under capitalism people desire particular goods and are less interested in social relations with the people who made and sold the goods: social relations are subordinated to material relations. In a gift economy people use things to expand their social relations. This stress on people has two consequences: gifts may assume the social form of persons and gifts maintain an attachment to people who made or previously owned them (this latter is often glossed as the problem of 'alienation' (see *Man* 17: 340–5; 18: 604–5, for a discussion of the problematic notion of alienation). The continuing connection between things and people means that a dense social world is set up and people work their way through a network of connections which ramify off in all directions.

In all Melanesian societies gifts are the dominant form of exchange, but in some, especially the Western Highlands, there is enormous emphasis on ceremonial exchange in which men can be seen to dominate. A whole range of items are exchanged in such systems, including marine shells, Bird of Paradise

plumes, oil, salt and now money and Toyota Landcruisers, but one crucial element is the pig. Pigs, in turn, represent the point of articulation between the
public sphere of ceremonial exchange and the domestic realm of subsistence
production. In the home things like pigs are 'multiply authored' (Strathern
1988: 159) by men, women and children and this joint effort and responsibility is recognised by all parties. However, through ceremonial exchange this is
transformed into a singular relationship between men and wealth objects
which are used to bind them to other men. A male multiple identity in the
home is transformed into a unitary identity in exchange and this is carried out
partly at the expense of other aspects of male identity, so that men succeed in
ceremonial exchange by paring down other elements of their characters.
Strathern argues, in contrast to Josephides (1985) for instance, that this is not
a straightforward matter of men exploiting and appropriating women's labour,
as the sole male use of items made by women would be in a capitalist regime.
Rather, women's role in the production of gifts is always acknowledged by
men and this embeds part of their identity more deeply in the family sphere.
Also, what men gain in public prestige they lose in terms of the general multiplicity of their identity which channels much of their efficacy down the path-
ways of ceremonial exchange at the expense of broader forms of social
agency.

Strathern also argues that similar things occur in the Eastern Highlands
where initiation and cult activity dominates. Here there are a plethora of
forms of initiation of boys by older men, which involve complex forms of
symbolism surrounding flutes and, often, sex. There has been long debate
about the nature and social embeddedness of these rituals with some saying
they emphasise male power, but others feeling that all this activity betrays a
deep anxiety about maleness and especially men's inability to reproduce
(Herdt 1982, 1984). Strathern makes a parallel between the initiation rites and
ceremonial exchange in that both of them are transformations of things into
wealth, or in the nature of items such as flutes in cult ritual which in turn
transforms the people involved. Through these forms of public activity men
work on and change their relationships and identities (which are the same
things by different names in Strathern's view). Domination in gift economies
is by those who determine the connections made by objects and the sets of
symbolic conventions connecting people and things. A major element of these
distinctions is that of gender which both produces particular forms of relations between people and things and is produced by them.

Strathern's ideas are stimulating but difficult. An excellent concrete example
of some of her ideas in action is provided by the work of Maureen
MacKenzie looking at looped string bags in Papua New Guinea (known as the
bilum in Tok Pisin) and focusing especially on the Telefolmin area (MacKenzie
1991). String bags are integral to life in most areas of Papua New Guinea and
MacKenzie (1991: 21) feels there has been little attention paid to them as they
are women's work. While MacKenzie wants to redress this androcentric bias,
she feels that the reverse strategy of taking a women-centred approach, as

advocated by Weiner (1977, 1980), misses the chance of looking at the ways in which women and men shape each others' personalities, cosmologies and spheres of action.

The area that she is looking at is that of the Mountain Ok, a group of about 30,000 people who live in central New Guinea mostly in Papua New Guinea, but also over the border in Irian Jaya (Figure 6.1). Most of the Mountain Ok have a self-conceived unity as descendants of Afek, a female creator spirit who travelled across the area stopping last at Telefolmin where she left her mythical relics in the cult house in Telefol village.

The *bilum* is produced by women through a looping technique which is flexible enough to produce a range of different bags, with varying forms of decoration and purposes. In all, the Telefolmin distinguish between twenty-seven named types of *bilum*, used by both women and men. Their different uses reflect gender-specific tasks within Telefolmin society. Women use the *bilum* for carrying garden produce, household items and their babies. Women live in family houses, while the men sleep in men's houses. This separation is also reflected in their respective tasks, whereby men hunt and fish and do the heavier labour involved in setting up gardens, whilst women gather plant foods and do the day-to-day work of gardening. The divisions between the genders are reinforced by food taboos, such that only women can eat marsupials and only initiated men can eat pork. However, this separation of the sexes is more apparent than real and does not lead, in MacKenzie's view, to the domination of women by men. To see why this is so, it is necessary to look at the nature of work in the light of Strathern's concept of multiple authorship.

Like Strathern, MacKenzie stresses the multiple authorship of the *bilum*. In the west there is a notion of a unitary relationship of the producer and her or his product and this view of people being the authors of their works is basic to our view of agency. In Melanesia work is more socially effective when it is carried out for others. In the Telefolmin case the *bilum* is made by a woman but decorated with feathers by a man in the course of his initiation rites: 'Men elaborate only the outward facing side of the bilum. When they carry their bird feather bilums the actual meshwork, looped by a known and loved female relative, remains in contact with their skin' (MacKenzie 1991: 160). MacKenzie does not take a static view of the *bilum* as an item of material culture, but instead looks at its biography as it passes through different stages of production and use (a point we will return to in the next chapter). The crucial element to the biography of the object is the set of relationships through which it passes.

As an embodiment of labour the bird feather bilum stands neither for female or male, and is not reducible to the interests of either. As Strathern points out, the labour cannot be measured separately from relationships, for the transfer of labour is embedded within a *particular* relationship. The woman's looping work is the mark of value she holds for her father/husband/son, while the work that both a mother and a father

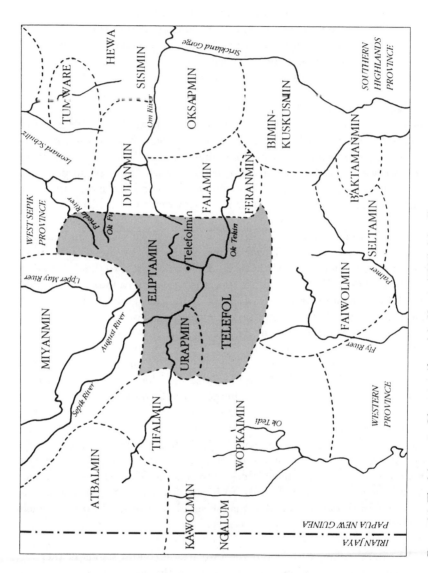

Figure 6.1 The Mountain Ok region (from MacKenzie (1991): Map 3)

do in making their son's *dagasaal men* [first initiation *bilum*] is a mark of their commitment to their son. The elaborated bilum cannot be exclusively identified with either producer or recipient, woman or man. A metonym of the *relation* between women and men, it is recognised as the product of multiple authorship.

(MacKenzie 1991: 160)

Men decorate and use their *bilums* in the confines of the men's house, in ritual situations from which women are excluded, and this may seem to contradict the argument that women are not dominated by men. However, a closer look reveals a more complex situation. To simplify drastically it is possible to say that cult activity is carried out in two main areas: the use of ancestral bones to create fertility in gardening and effectiveness of hunting; the initiation of young boys into manhood. I shall look at initiation first. Initiation is a staged process, with boys being progressively trained in knowledge, such that it is only the older men who have seen the whole cycle of ritual who can appreciate the rites as an interlocking and coherent whole. There are three main grades of initiation (although they are not conceived in quite such formal terms) found throughout the Mountain Ok region. Each is associated with a different bird: the megapode, the hornbill and the cassowary. MacKenzie feels that one unacknowledged aspect of the association with these birds (here she is criticising Barth's [1987] view of Ok ritual) is that all nurture their young and may be seen as 'male mothers'. An emphasis on male nurture has resonances with the use of the *bilum*, which itself is a provocative symbol of female fertility and motherhood. Early elements of the ritual revolve around the initiates giving birth aided by a Mother and a Father (both biologically male). Menstrual blood is also mixed with initiates' body paint in order to give strength, which contrasts starkly with daily life where all aspects of menstruation and birth are seen to be polluting to men.

Women control the cosmological processes on which male cult is founded and the main message of the cults, as perceived by MacKenzie, is that antithetical opposites must be synthesised to allow creativity. Focusing on the *bilum* allows the full complexity of human relationships and their attached symbolism to be drawn out (not that I have been able to do justice to them here and the reader is recommended to read MacKenzie's work for themselves). In MacKenzie's own words:

> my biographical focus on a single artefact, the bilum, as a complete object made by women and men, will give me a technological and sociological understanding of its combinatory symbolism, and reveal spheres of activity that an analysis of either female work or male cult activity would miss.
>
> (1991: 28)

Strathern's work moves us a long way from the study of women or of men as separable entities and is a perfect demonstration of the general point that the emphasis of study should be on gender as the outcome of a set of relationships. These emphases fit in well with what is known as Third Wave Feminism (see Meskell 1998a). The writings of Butler (1990, 1993), especially have been influential in moving consideration away from gender in isolation to looking at aspects of identity together. Gender means little if not modulated through a consideration of age, class, ethnicity or sexual orientation. Categories are certainly not binary, with men opposed to women, but multiple and multiplying, with more dimensions to life than can ever can be accommodated within analysis.

An equal strength of Butler and Strathern's work is that they destablised many of the basic categories of anthropological and archaeological analysis. If we take Strathern's view of dividuals seriously then the individual and society both disappear as simple categories, as do many notions of agency. The idea that individuals have free will which is not overwhelmed by social forces is a crucial starting point for western social science (Giddens 1984). The startling image of the fractal person (Wagner 1994) provides a very different starting point for social analysis. Just as fractals are composed of a series of identical forms at different scales, then the fractal person is made up of a set of relations of the same structure as themselves, but at a smaller scale, just as they represent the same patterns as society but in miniature. The movement from individual to society is not a shift from one form of reality to another, but simply a change of scale with the pattern remaining the same.

Ideas of practice and of transformation could be usefully combined, with the ritual theory of Bell providing something of a bridge between the two. Bell is starting to explore how the formalisation of action in some arenas of life can affect action in another and in doing so is approaching a relational theory, but still keeping an emphasis on embodied action and the material settings of life. If such ideas are useful in anthropology, they should be even more so in archaeology where material culture and the physical locales of action are a major form of evidence. I shall consider how far such notions have informed the archaeology of gender, before looking at the way in which such arguments could be usefully developed.

Gender in archaeology

In the study of gender, archaeology has taken much from anthropology, but is now also starting to develop a set of traditions and conversations of its own. Although the literature on gender in archaeology is growing at a considerable rate, the subject can still be traced to discrete origins which are always recounted in the same way. In the beginning was the article by Conkey and Spector (1984) addressing problems of male bias and highlighting the need for a more balanced archaeology in terms of implicit or explicit considerations of gender. Then have come a series of edited volumes with differing theoretical and empirical concerns (Claassen and Joyce 1997, duCros and Smith 1993, Gero and Conkey 1991, Hager 1997a, Marshall 1998a, Moore and Scott 1997,

Wright 1996, plus a growing number of articles: Engelstadt 1991, Øvrevik 1991) so that there is no doubt that gender is an issue for all areas of archaeology. However, gender studies is by no means a unified field and there are considerable differences in how gender is studied. Alongside work which counterbalances androcentric views in which women or gender relations were ignored, archaeologists are beginning to argue that gender cannot be studied on its own but has to be situated within broader sets of age, hierarchy, sexual orientation and so on (Butler 1993) in line with the so-called Third Wave Feminism. I shall concentrate on these recent arguments, as some of the most vital within the broader arena of discussions of practice, performance and transformation. Partly because archaeological discussions of gender are still relatively recent, much of the presentation of argument and data has been in the form of articles. I would like to start by looking at a single-authored study, Gilchrist's *Gender and Material Culture* (1994), which demonstrates how issues of gender can be discussed in an in-depth manner when considering a particular body of archaeological evidence, in this case nunneries from late medieval Britain. This study is also useful as it draws upon the notion of habitus and can easily link into Bell's arguments on ritualisation.

In order to become a nun, postulants went through a ceremony in which they put on bridal garments and the nun's finger ring, which resulted in a lay woman being transformed into a bride of Christ and committing her virginity to Christ. The nun's hair, a symbol of sensuality, was then cut and she was given the uniform of her order. Individuality was further stripped away by renouncing all personal property and observing the strict timetable of the nunnery which left little latitude for personal activity (Gilchrist 1994: 18–19). This might seem a straightforward case of women committing themselves to a male god, in a patriarchal society, in a manner that left no latitude for the expression of individuality or femininity. But, as usual, life was a lot more complicated and interesting than that, as Gilchrist shows. Christ was not a straightforwardly gendered figure and in his image as the suffering Lamb of God, the feminine elements of his personality were also emphasised. Nor was Christ the only pole of attraction within the church, with the Virgin Mary and Mary Magdalene both providing different archetypal figures for women entering the institution. And although elements of individuality were given away, new areas of personal exploration were opened up. Celibacy made the nun's body a private space and her sensuality, although allowed little material expression, made itself felt through the tradition of female mystics, such as Julian of Norwich or Hildegard of Bingen.

Gilchrist uses archaeological evidence, with assistance from the textual material, to trace some of the complexities of this world. In part because of the nature of the archaeological evidence available, she concentrates on space. As was discussed above, Bell concentrates on ritualisation and the locales in which action is given a formal ritual quality. This is very much the approach that Gilchrist takes, looking at the interaction between space and religious personality (although not using Bell's work directly). It is possible to look at the manner in which activities would have been channelled by architecture and the process of interpretation of the spaces within which nuns lived. The lived spaces of the nunneries represented the finest spatial scale at which women acted and Gilchrist also considers the relationship of nunneries to their land-scape, the set of social relations within which they were embedded in late medieval Britain and the comparisons and contrasts with monasteries.

Drawing on Bourdieu, Gilchrist (1994: 192) looks at religious institutions in terms of the forms of habitus created within them. In the late medieval period there were around 150 nunneries, as compared to roughly 900 monasteries. Nunneries started up through being affiliated to existing monasteries and had close links to the local gentry and hence local village and manorial communities. Nunneries did not generally attempt to be self-sufficient, so that there was little farming or industry carried out and the nuns lived a much more symbi-otic life with local communities. There was not the same separation between nunneries and the surrounding world as there was with monasteries and this was reflected in the plans of the nunneries, which were partly structured around an internal separation between the nuns themselves and members of the local community who came to worship. In spatial lay-out nunneries had influences from both monasteries and manor houses.

Many nunneries were poor in comparison with monasteries and a prevail-ing explanation has been that female piety was less valued by the community than its male counterpart. But studies of wills and benefactions shows this not to be true and that the community retained faith with nuns, long after scepti-cism had set in about the holiness of monks (Gilchrist 1994: 190–1). Rather than being a slighter version of male piety, women's religious avocations were constructed differently. Here it is important to situate nuns not just in rela-tionship to monks, but also in regard to lay religious women. Material culture from nunneries, plus the textual evidence, suggests that nuns dedicated them-selves to Christ through the Virgin Mary in a spirit of purity resonating with that of the Mother of God. Nunnery seals have a range of imagery on them, but depictions of Mary predominate (Gilchrist 1994: 143–8). Outside the nunnery a range of religious lay women lived and worked. These included *beguines*, sisters in hospitals, anchoresses and female hermits, many of whom lived in towns and were active in the outside world, unlike the more contem-plative life of the nunnery. These alternative avocations were themselves vari-ous, but held a theme of penitence and the expiation of sin in common. The iconography and piety of the nunnery was constructed not just through influence from, and contrasts with, the monastery, but also existed in a broader spectrum of female religious observance, which helped shape and give it context.

The life of a nun was constructed through forms of material culture, which was not deployed in a vacuum but according to special spatial forms. The con-struction of church and cloister followed the monastic pattern, although the plans of the buildings were less elaborate in nunneries and the building mate-rials less costly. On occasions features such as moats were added, which owed more to manorial ground plans than religious architecture. Although simple, the churches often had internal divisions (Figure 6.2), to separate the nuns' from members of the parish, indicating the nuns' ambiguous position as part of, and apart from, the local community. Considerable elaboration was reserved for the north cloister. In Christian cosmology the north was associated with night and cold, as opposed to the warmer, brighter south, with the moon, the Old Testament and female aspects of life also connected with the north (Gilchrist 1994: 133–4). Further manifestations of this division are found in the prevalence of female burial to the north of churches in many parts of the Christian world and the association between female saints and the north wall. Importantly, there is also an association between the Virgin Mary and the right hand side of Christ, which is translated through the analogy between the church and the body of Christ into a position on the northern side. Other historical associations were also at work in the iconography of the church. Refectories tended to be two-storied, by reference to the house of Mary in Jerusalem in which women met in the upper storey in the early days of the church. The nature of decoration in the nunneries also indicates patterns of movement and exclusion. The sacristy is the room where the priest's robes and sacred vessels for the Mass were stored. It was here that male representations were most common, whereas female representations were most frequent in the interior private spaces of the nunnery (Figure 6.3). In the monastery the sacristy was in the heart of the building, whereas the most secluded space in the nunnery was the dormitory of the nuns.

Gilchrist's study locates the lives of nuns within a broader spectrum of religious practice, both male and female, and plays with some of the different dimensions of medieval life, rather than seeing gender as a single construction. More recent work has stressed multiple dimensions even more strongly. This is partly in terms of a discussion of the relationship of the individual to society as a whole. Many views of this relationship have implicitly seen individuals as atoms (especially in so-called small-scale societies) which come together to make the whole, in the same way that atoms form a molecular structure. We have already seen how Strathern's notion of the dividual challenges such a view and archaeological work is now starting to explore the multiple influences on the individual, which may mean that no two individuals are ever identical, with each having their own set of relationships to the collectivity. One example of the analysis of different influences on identity is Meskell's study of tombs from the New Kingdom site of Deir el Medina (c. 1500–1100 BC) during the Eighteenth Dynasty (Meskell 1998b). She concentrates partly on two individuals, Kha and Merit, who were man and wife. They were both buried in a tomb together, each with their own grave goods, the possession of which can be determined from the fact that their names were written on them, which derives from the Egyptians' long preparation for death (Meskell 1998b: Table 1). Kha was the pharaoh's chief architect and his tomb mirrored the fashions of the pharaohs' and also contained personal gifts from them. Differentials in wealth between man and wife even extended to the treatment

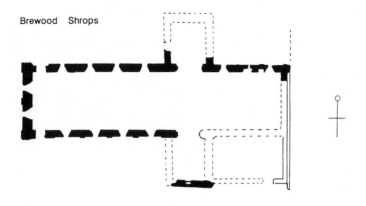

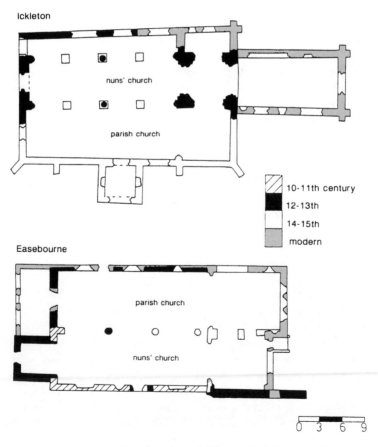

Figure 6.2 Plans of nunnery churches (from Gilchrist (1994): Figure 4.1)

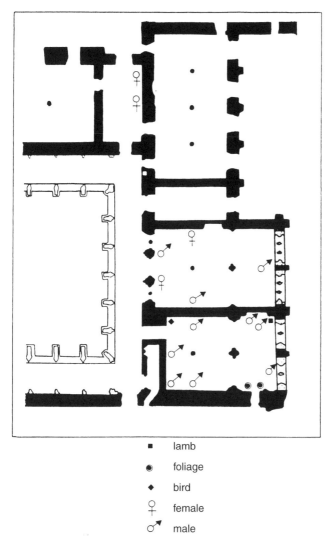

■ lamb

◉ foliage

◆ bird

♀ female

♂ male

Figure 6.3 Symbolic architecture and iconography: the distribution of carved pil-
lar bases at Lacock, Wilts. (Exclusively male representations were used
in the sacristy, and some were present in the chapter house, but only
female representations figured on carved corbels in the more private
spaces of the nunnery.) (From Gilchrist (1994): Figure 64)

of the body, with Kha's being much better prepared (and thus preserved) than
Merit's. The naming of Kha and Merit's goods allows a detailed analysis of
their connections in life and the ways they constructed their lives, but overall
the discrepancies in wealth indicate a fairly predictable picture of male advantage. However, Meskell shows that a broader view modulates this picture.

Kha and Merit were buried in the Western Necropolis at Deir el Medina, which shows general inequalities between the wealth of men and women. However, these discrepancies are not invariant, but seem to increase as overall wealth and status rise, so that poorer couples were more equal in death (and presumably life). However, in the Eastern Necropolis at Deir el Medina status was differently constituted, with age and possibly marital status being the main differentiations. Meskell (1998b: 376) makes a distinction between emotional relations between individuals as lovers or parents and children and the general cultural practices of the time, so that each individual constructs life through a combination of their own personal circumstances, made up of accident and design and the broader social forces shaping everyone's lives. A stress on intimate relations can provide an antidote to the more usual perspective found within archaeology: that of society as a whole, which concentrates on more global relations of hierarchy and power (Marshall 1998b).

The Egyptian example is a good one, as Egyptian society is supposed to be rigidly structured by class, status and gender, as indeed it was in many ways. But these categories were not simple pigeon holes, but a strict set of rules with which people could work and manoeuvre to create an advantageous position for themselves. The importance of a multi-dimensional view is even more necessary when looking at cultural forms which emphasise ambiguity, such as those of the Northwest coast of North America. Marshall (1998b) discusses some of the imagery embodied in prehistoric forms from this area and the manner in which meaning derives from relationships expressed and not the figures depicted. A striking instance of relationships and ambiguities is the Sechelt Image (Figure 6.4) as discussed by Duff (1975) who put on an exhibition of Northwest Coast art in the 1970s.

> The Sechelt image has just such an ultimate ambiguity: its mighty phallus is at the same time its partner, and they clasp each other in the same embrace. The human head on the club: is it a fetus or an old man? . . . And what of the little punned phallus man, the part that is also a whole?
>
> (Duff 1975: 18, quoted in Marshall 1998: 312)

Here was a cultural aesthetic where play and shape-shifting were paramount. It is impossible not to be reminded of Strathern's arguments against essentialism and how relationships constitute entities, the entities themselves changing depending on what one takes to be part and what the whole. But the Sechelt image also reminds us that there is a set of dimensions linked to sex that we have not explored as yet and these are to do with sex and sexuality.

Sex and sexuality

A lurking presence in all discussions of gender is that of sex. It is worth making a distinction at the start of this discussion between sex, as biological difference, and sexuality as denoting images, actions and relationships connected

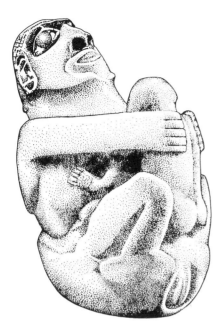

Figure 6.4 The Sechelt image (from Duff (1975): Figure 29)

to varying sexual orientations. Sex is conventionally seen in feminist thought as a biological difference which was culturally elaborated in the form of gender. However, such a view assumes that sex is determined by the facts of biology as we conceive of them now: as a set of differences in genitalia and other aspects of the body. But it has recently been realised and documented historically that our binary view of sex is itself a cultural representation of physical differences and not the invariant foundation for gender differences. Such a change of view complicates things in that the relationship between sex and gender is now the set of linkages between two schemes of representations: the body on the one hand and the roles and experience of gender on the other. Whilst by no means the same these two schemes of representation are linked, as conceptions of the body inform views of gendered action, and culturally influenced patterns of action form part of the context within which concepts of the body are formulated.

Laqueur (1992) has documented how within European thought views of sex have changed, so that the scheme of representation inherited from the Greeks broke down in the eighteenth century. This was a change from seeing women as pale reflections of men (what Laqueur calls the one-sex model), to viewing the two sexes as unbridgeably different. 'Organs that had been seen as interior versions of what the male had on the outside – the vagina as penis, the uterus as scrotum – were by the eighteenth century construed as of an entirely different nature' (Laqueur 1992: viii). Our present view he terms a two-sex model, which holds a whole set of heterosexual prescriptions within it. At the end of the book he concludes:

> The ways in which sexual difference have been imagined in the past are largely unconstrained by what was actually known about this or that bit of anatomy, this or that physiological process and derive instead from the rhetorical exigencies of the moment.
>
> (Laqueur 1992: 243)

The replacement of one scheme by another was not the result of advances in medical science, but rather of subtle shifts in conceptions of men and women, their bodies, their sexual activities and views about what the proper state of all these elements should be.

Sex, as biological difference, which once seemed a solid fact is now best viewed as a cultural construct. If this is so, it can no longer act as the foundation for gender differences, but becomes part of a field of actions and practices which are mutually influencing. In many parts of the world children achieve a biological sex through the same set of processes through which they come to a gender. Bell (1990) looking at the Creek Indians of northeastern Oklahoma says that until a child can talk it is carried by its mother as 'it has no bones' and in this state all children are female and still connected to the mother. Once a child can speak, it also has to walk by itself and can start to enter into gender-specific tasks through which it is socialised. Biological sex and gender are recognised and made socially salient at the same time, one informing the other. Now many realise that the relationship between sex and gender is very under-theorised (Moore 1994: 12) and that categories of gender have been 'constructed by sex, sexuality, stages in the lifecycle, physical deportment and social status or occupation' (Gilchrist 1996: 122).

Biological sex constitutes an area of especially sharp debate in the area of skeletal analyses. The older the skeletons, the sharper the debate, so that one of the oldest skeletons of all, 'Lucy' found in Hadar in Ethiopia was immediately thought by its discoverers (Johanson and colleagues) to be female on the basis of small size and pelvis structure. However, as Hager (1997b: 10–11) points out, there is no guarantee that the pelvic morphology of *Australopithecus Afarensis* is analogous to our own, as means of walking and birth might have been quite different. The identification as female was reinforced by the skeleton's supposed small size, even though sexual dimorphism is poorly understood for *Australopithecus Afarensis* due to small sample sizes. Even if the skeletal criteria were clear, it is not certain what being female means in the context of this species, so after all the discussion expended on biological characteristics no one knows how these might translate into action. The need for a multi-dimensional approach both to biology and its correlates in action is marked: 'we need to be able to account for all levels of variation before we can assign a fossil to a taxonomic category and before we can understand its evolutionary history' (Hager 1997b: 11).

The study of sexuality, past and present, is a growing field within both archaeology and anthropology, partly through the links between sexuality, gender and performance (Morris 1995). But this is not just an exploration of new ground, but a return to old areas of interest with newer theoretical apparatus. Malinowski (1929) produced a full length study of sexuality in the Trobriand islands and the publication of his diary has raised a host of questions, many of a prurient nature, about sex and the fieldworker. This is a theme taken up in a recent volume of essays, where many of the contributors see the denial of a personal interest in sex during fieldwork as part of the limited nature of anthropology, which has denied the emotive and experiential background to work in exotic places (Kulick and Wilson 1995). This is all part of anthropology's reassessment of fieldwork, the relationships brought about through the process of fieldwork and the sorts of knowledge created through these relationships. Margaret Mead (1939) concentrated on sexual relations in the process of growing up in places like Samoa and New Guinea and evoked great public interest through her comparisons with adolescence in the US, whereby her home culture was seen as unhealthily repressive (see Freeman (1984) for a controversial and critical review of Mead's work).

Much of the recent work on sexuality has been influenced, either positively or negatively, by Foucault's *History of Sexuality* (1981) and many authors find the need to distance themselves from Foucault's scheme, which emphasises the links between sexuality and power and the creation of sexuality as a subject of discussion and study (rather than as an arena of pleasure and procreation) in the last two centuries (see Giddens 1992 and Laqueur 1992 for two authors who maintain a decent distance from Foucault). By contrast there have been few attempts to trace the prehistory of sexuality and the best known is that by Taylor (1996). This work combines the salacious and the scholarly and is ultimately disappointing as it leaves untouched any of our western preconceptions about the links between sexual pleasure, biological differences and gender. Taylor employs a two-sex model throughout and takes at face value much of the biological work on sexual dimorphism in human evolution and more recent prehistory. At the other end of the scale is Yates' (1990) attempt to locate both sex and gender in Bronze Age Scandinavian rock art in such a way as to shake our preconceptions of both. However, while containing occasional insights, this was an essay marred by incomprehensibility and has had much less influence than it might as a consequence.

Again, human evolution is one of the most intractable and thus interesting areas of the study of human sexuality. Following the dominance of Darwinian theory in most discussions of the early human past, sexuality is often linked with reproduction, so that it is assumed that most human sexual relations will be between men and women for the purposes of reproduction, reflecting longstanding Protestant views on sex and pleasure. Recent studies in primates have shown that same-sex relations are actually quite common and cannot be explained away as relations which are set up only when partners of the opposite sex are not available. Vasey (1998) in a study of Japanese macaques shows how frequently females have sex with each other and the effects that this can have on males who are excluded. Female homosexual relations can have a crucial influence on group dynamics and can be understood through ideas on sexual pleasure, rather than within sexual selection theory. Vasey extends his argument to look at the notion of sexual pleasure in prehistory, especially the Palaeolithic. Vasey makes the important point that sexual pleasure is not simply a biological matter, to do with the messages passed from the skin receptors in the erogenous zones to the brain. Rather the brain learns to interpret these signals in different ways:

> This interpretative process is a subjective one and depends, in large part, on personal experience and cultural context. Hence, one individual might interpret certain sensory signals emanating from erogenous zones as sexual nirvana, while another may very well react to the same stimuli with indifference and even nausea.
>
> (Vasey 1998: 418–19)

Such a view returns us to Bourdieu and habitus. In a strictly biological view of culture the needs and capabilities of the body constrain and channel human responses and the cultural forms built upon these responses. Bourdieu tends to reverse the arrow of cause and effect, saying that the body and its responses are shaped by cultural forces. 'Hexis' is the name Bourdieu gives to the embodiment of culture, so that differences of gender and class are written into the body and displayed through forms of comportment and body language. 'What is learned in the body is not something one has, but something one is' (Bourdieu 1990: 73). Vasey adds an extra dimension to the discussion, showing that it is the interaction between social learning and physiological processes that is at the basis of human experience. We learn what sexual pleasure is within a cultural context, but on the other hand there are certain physiological processes connected with sexual experience which may give some commonality to sex the world over. However, the fact that culture channels our physiological responses is vital, showing that culture creates different worlds to live in and it is not just material culture and landscapes that vary round the world, but human responses to material things are structured differently.

Similar points have been made within the anthropology of art and aesthetics. For Coote (1992) perception is a cultural phenomenon, in which certain skills of perception are developed so that each culture has its own repertoire of skills in perceiving the world. But the world is not simply sensed, it is also valued. Perceptions are disturbing, enlightening, unusual or comforting: they cannot be simply neutral. 'All human activity has an aesthetic aspect. We are always, though at varying levels of awareness, concerned with the aesthetic qualities of our aural, haptic, kinetic and visual sensations' (Coote 1992: 246). This raises the possibility that it is not just that cattle-keeping peoples of the Sudan, such as the Nuer, find their cows beautiful, but that the beauty is manifest to them in ways initially denied to those not trained to see in local ways. It is not that beauty is just in the eye of the beholder, but in all our senses, and it is not just beauty, but all the complex valuations of our lives which we create through our perceptions. If to sense is to evaluate, then the body itself is a crucial nexus of many values. Gender, sex and sexuality are three names we have for some of the more important dimensions of these values. We must not mistake these names for solid properties, but they are part of the way we divide up and give value to experience.

A stress on aesthetics helps bind the two different approaches I have highlighted here. An emphasis on practice shows how cultural skills and norms are embodied, given substance and continuity. Thoughts about transformation show that what is learned is not all of a piece, but can be re-ordered between one context of life and another, as well as over time. Gender, sexuality and so on are learned embodied practices, taking on local colour and nuance. But they are never invariant entities, connecting up with all the other aspects of life which change through context. Aesthetics, as culturally channelled physiological responses which are basically about value, are created through practice but also influences transformation. If cultures are made up of many locales in which transformations take place, where femaleness is emphasised, for instance, along with notions of dominance and submission, then these transformations will also be in accord with local aesthetic schemes, which sketch out what is possible and desirable. Aesthetics, of course, is not just about valuations placed on the body, but the body in the context of landscapes and sets of material culture. It is to these we turn in the next chapter, looking both at local practice and how far transformations can be understood through schemes of history.

7 Material anthropology
Landscape, material culture and history

This chapter explores the material dimension of life, which is obviously the area where archaeology and anthropology meet most closely. A consideration of topics such as landscape and material culture crosses the boundary between the two disciplines so regularly as to blur any real distinction them and the will to break down boundaries is now quite pronounced, especially in Britain.

Any notion of material anthropology needs a solid consideration of the material itself. For purely heuristic purposes we can divide the material world into two: landscape and artefacts. Without wanting to overplay this difference, such a contrast is useful to highlight different centres of gravity in social life: the long-term, stable nature of landscape is far more likely to change slowly than mobile material culture which moves across the landscape, linking or dividing social groups. However, when considering the built environment composed of structures ranging in permanence from an overnight camp to the pyramids, it is harder to assign long-term change to the landscape and more ephemeral aspects of life to artefacts.

History runs through all considerations of materiality and as nothing social or material lasts for ever, change must be a constant topic. Anthropology has embraced history in a major way over the last twenty years, although not all anthropological history is material. The consideration of history represents a slight digression, in that we shall consider some attempts to join anthropology and history, such as that of Sahlins, which emphasise the symbolic not the material. However, I shall argue that a proper consideration of history is impossible without some attempt to ground it in the material conditions of people's lives, not least because in many parts of the world oral or written histories only cover the recent period and longer sequences of change involve the conjunction of archaeology and anthropology around the material evidence.

Finally, living in the material world always involves aspects of style and aesthetics. Aesthetic considerations do not just have to do with art, but with life in general. Aesthetics is commonly conceived of through cosmologies, which describe sets of physical relations within the universe, and the origins and the place of human beings within these relations in terms of moral correctness. The combination of the physical and the moral in a cosmology mean that they embrace all aspects of life, laying down the most sensible patterns of work in terms of the physical properties of materials, but also the moral consequences of relationships within the physical and the social worlds. Aesthetics and cosmologies allow us to consider particular styles of life and how people create these over time. Creating an aesthetic of mundane and ritualised performance is the equivalent of creating a world to live in, a world both of work and of meaning. It is to this end that material anthropologies can eventually aspire: to uncover how people create worlds for themselves and how these change over time, either through their own internal dynamics or through encountering other people's worlds with a different cosmological and aesthetic basis.

Landscape

The study of landscape is appealing partly because it crosses the boundaries between geography, art history, anthropology, archaeology and other disciplines. The transgressive nature of the topic allows a variety of approaches and subject matters to be considered under the topic of landscape, which make it both a rich and an indefinable field. Common ground can be found, however, and at the most basic level this is seen in a shift in perspectives about landscape from abstract and objective spaces to the lived experience of place. The word 'landscape' comes from the Dutch term *Landschap* (originally rendered in English as 'landskip') and was borrowed in the sixteenth century by painters (Thomas 1984). Scenes of landscape were constructed using perspective, allowing an appreciation of depth and distance, as well as creating a view from a particular vantage point. Painted representations of landscape have come to dominate our appreciation of the real thing, so that we may say something looks 'picturesque' highlighting its resemblance to a picture. For westerners landscape became something out there, to be appreciated in visual terms and constructed through the rational principles of perspective. Distanced geometrical images of landscape were reinforced by cartography, within which land and sea were rendered in two dimensions, to a particular scale and with a grid laid over it. Landscape was not lived, but looked at, being seen as something external to people; nature versus their culture.

Both views of landscape, as picture and as map, have had a vast influence on everyday lived experience and on academic views of the world. They form known subject matter for our repertoire of visual skills, as discussed in the last chapter, and the linguistic emphasis on view and viewpoint reflects the dominance of this one sense. Bernard Smith (1985) saw that there were different visual modes of representing Pacific landscapes by early European explorers. On the one hand were images of Arcadia and Eden, counterpoised by visions of primitivism and savagery so that the peoples of the Pacific were constructed through predefined conventions which structured observations, clustering them round either positive or negative associations. In addition, there was the objectified drawing of plants and animals for the purposes of scientific naming and classification in which people, as an element of the fauna, were often included. Landscape and representation have been linked ever since the words came into the English language and part of the recent interest in the former has come from exploration of visual representations other than the rational and perspectival. Pinney (1995) has explored the politics of representation in Nagda, an industrial town in India, where oleographs combine the depiction of Hindu deities and real individuals (like Gandhi) against a variety of backgrounds in a manner that works through some of the problems of traditionalism, modernity and nationhood in contemporary India.

The analysis of Cartesian space in the form of maps entered the New Geography and Archaeology in the 1960s in the form of spatial analysis. It was thought that much could be understood about the social process from the analysis of the spatial arrangements of settlements or the distribution of artefacts (Chorley and Haggett 1967, Clarke 1977, Hodder and Orton 1976). This analytical movement took little hold on anthropology, perhaps because the concentration on the details of lived experience made such abstracted views less appealing (although see Smith 1976). Recent approaches to landscape have represented a movement against spatial analysis, which reduces human action to a series of numerical variables suitable for understanding the relationship between the friction of distance and economic and social behaviour. Indeed, much recent literature on landscape has made a point of anatomising the sorts of logics lying behind the use of maps and forms of abstract space (e.g. Thomas 1993). There has also been a big reaction against anything that smacks of environmental determinism, with the stress instead on the mutual creation of people and landscape. Here Bourdieu is influential, with landscapes and habitus being seen as mutually creative. The notion of the cultural (or social) landscape is one that goes back to Sauer (1963). Such practice-based approaches blend into those influenced by Heidegger and phenomenology, looking at the lived experience of landscapes (Gosden 1994, Ingold 1993b, Tilley 1994). There is also considerable mutual influence between recent geography and anthropology, both partaking of the same underlying influences of the practice theorists and phenomenologists (Harvey 1989, Soja 1989, 1996).

One excellent example of the mutual creation of social and spatial arrangements is Moore's (1996a) *Space, Text and Gender*, as this brings together some of the theoretical literature with a compelling anthropological example of space and gender relations. Moore looks at the Marakwet, a sub-group of the Endo, who live in the Cherangani Hills of western Kenya (Figure 7.1). This is a highly structured spatial world, partly due to the position of Marakwet villages on the edge of a steep escarpment, whereby people are moving up and down hill all day (Figure 7.2). It is also partly structured by a binary division between women and men, suspiciously reminiscent of structuralism. Marakwet villages are made up of a series of households, each with its own compound. The spatial organisation of the compound is along lines of gender, reflecting the division of labour between women and men. Both are seen to contribute to the household: the

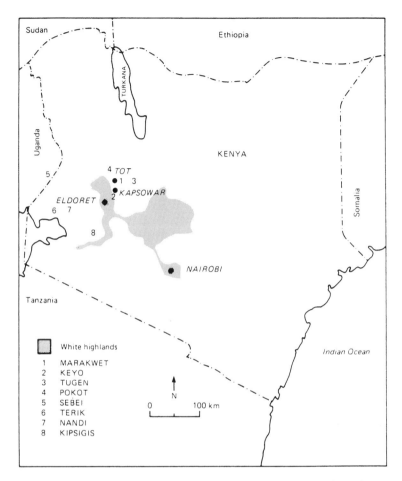

Figure 7.1 The location of Marakwet and the Kalenjin peoples (after Moore (1996): Figure 1)

man provides land and livestock and looks after the animals; the woman provides agricultural and domestic labour and gives birth to children. Moore
points out that as there are no public buildings or communal spaces in the
Marakwet world, social and spatial relations are concentrated in the compound. Following the view put forward by Giddens (1984) and others that space
is both produced by and producing of social action, Moore looks at how gender structures the spaces of the Marakwet compound and how these, in turn,
reinforce and alter relations between women and men.

The Cherangani escarpment runs north–south and compounds are built on
levelled platforms with stone revetments cut into the slope. Houses are not
allowed to face out over the valley and therefore all have the doors facing either

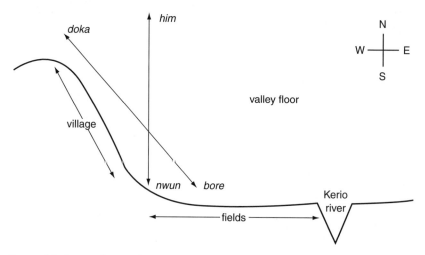

Figure 7.2 Axes of spatial orientation among the Marakwet (after Moore (1996a): Figure 17)

north or south. Houses are roughly circular and the internal layout is invariant, with beds, food preparation and storage facilities always in the same places. This is because the bed is always put behind the door, as the most private spot in the house, and everything else is arranged with respect to the bed. In earlier times most compounds would have had two houses, one for a man and the other for his wife (Figure 7.3); these days the two dwellings are seen as a sleeping or enter-taining house and a cooking house respectively, although they still have strong associations of gender, as the woman does most of the cooking. The exact num-ber of houses in the compound will depend on the stage in the life-cycle of the family living there: an older man may well have more than one wife, as well as children and large herds, all of which necessitate a larger compound or extra house spaces nearby (Moore 1996a: 99–109). However, the elaboration of the household follows the same sets of principles as the simpler types.

Of considerable interest to archaeologists (Moore's study was partially con-ceived of as an ethnoarchaeological project) is the pattern of rubbish disposal around the compound which is strongly structured by relations of gender. The Marakwet distinguish three kinds of rubbish, which are deposited in different areas: ash, animal dung and chaff from finger millet or sorghum. All rubbish is thrown down the slope below the compound. Ash is thrown behind the house from which it comes and ash from different houses should not mix; chaff accumulates on the edge of the compound where a woman has done her winnowing; dung is swept over the edge of the compound below the animals' quarters. The main reason for separating these materials is that women will be buried near their chaff and men with the animal dung and, when buried, peo-ple are placed so that their head faces the compound with their feet towards

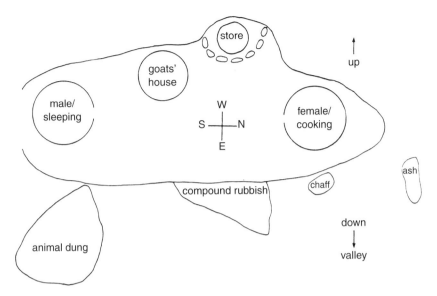

Figure 7.3 A typical Endo compound (after Moore (1996a): Figure 24)

the valley. The exact position of the different types of rubbish will vary because they are all placed relative to the house and the position of the house within the compound is not invariant. However, ash and dung must never be mixed because this can result in the goat herd dying. Women are seen to control the domestic space of the houses and only a woman can remove the ash from her own hearth. Ash is an ambiguous substance, because it represents domestic nurture and continuity, but also consumption and destruction. Ash is further associated with the potentially destructive nature of female sexuality and power. Dung represents a more male form of fecundity deriving from their herds. Marakwet ritual is aimed at maintaining a balance in the world through respecting the traditions of the group. It is only through showing respect that the health of the goat herd can be maintained, on which the prestige of individual men and the clan as a whole depends.

The relationship between ash and dung, two substances which seem to westerners to be trivial and unexciting, is a microcosm of much of the relationship between men and women. Women control the household, through food and its waste; the male realm is that of the herd and public life through which politics and ritual are conducted. The spatial separation of ash and dung derives from a broader scheme of cultural representation enjoining right action between men and women and between people and cosmological forces. But also the manipulation of these two substances allows for creative play within which the tension in the roles between women and men can be worked out and rethought. The spatial separation of dung and ash is created by broader cultural schemes, but also allows play with these cultural schemes through which changed relationships can emerge.

Moore's approach concentrates on action in the landscape and the lived experience of these activities. Thus it is not the objective qualities of any landscape that are important but the cultural logic and structure of action by which landscapes are perceived and used. Different cultures render the same landscape in very different ways. As Strang (1997: 4) says in her exploration of Aboriginal and white pastoralist communities in northern Australia:

> Emu Lagoon is only one place, but it is also many places – all the different places that people make of it. Though they move through the same world, people see, understand, experience and value quite different things. They can walk around the same water, scuff the same dust and sit under the same trees, but they are not in the same place.

In such discussion the notion of values is crucial, as is how such values are attached to space and place through the things people do and where they do them. Discussion of values will take us back to the notion of an aesthetic.

To use one, very influential, example of the creation of value through action I shall turn to Nancy Munn's work on Gawa, an island in the Milne Bay Province of Papua New Guinea, whose inhabitants play an important role in *kula* transactions. Munn (1977, 1983, 1986, 1990) pursues a particular set of issues within symbolical anthropology and concentrates explicitly on the nature of experience and its historical basis. This leads to a stress on 'the practices by means of which actors construct their social world, and simultaneously their own selves and modes of being in the world, are thought to be symbolically constituted and themselves symbolic processes' (Munn 1986: 7).

In the process of transforming personal and material values Munn places great stress on the production of time and space, which are both relevant to landscape and the values attached to it. Gawa is a relatively small island towards the northern end of the *kula* ring, which has a series of links with the Trobriands, Muyuw and islands to the south (see Figure 4.4). These spatial connections are built on and reinforced by ongoing practices which have their own rhythms and times. The practice of exchange and the dynamics of travelling and giving connects Gawa to distant people and places, creating social concepts of space and time. Space and time are intimately connected to social standing and for Munn they are not a passive, abstract medium in which action occurs but are themselves created through social acts. The regional world is not given but lived, and history is the temporal aspect of regionality.

Munn (1990) looks at how regionality is created in experience. Drawing on the work of Husserl she points out that regionality is a temporal as well as a spatial construct, and it provides an event history, patterning happenings on both a local and regional scale. The particulars she focuses on are a series of illnesses and deaths which result from witchcraft deriving from disputes on Gawa itself about *kula* transactions. In 1974, Silas, an important Gawan participant in the *kula*, fell ill. A public curing meeting was held to stop local Gawan witches killing him. In the minds of many at the meeting Silas's illness was related to his transaction of Manutasopi, a famous named *kula* shell. This had come from Boagis Island, by-passed Gawa and other islands through which it should have passed on its path and landed in Kitava. Silas was implicated in the transaction and the fact that the shell had missed Gawa. His illness was linked to unrest on Gawa among those who might have received the shell but did not. As Munn tells the story, the event of his illness was set in a regional sphere and influenced by two of the most powerful cultural forces in that region: *kula* and witchcraft. These forces operate in opposite directions: *kula* acting to join people together, witchcraft acting as a negative pole causing ruptures in the social fabric.

Silas recovered from his 1974 illness, but fell sick again in 1979. Thomas, another phratry leader and important force in the *kula*, felt that he had been accused of causing this second illness by another bigman, Daniel. Thomas was one of those who may have felt aggrieved at missing out on the Manutasopi transaction in 1974. The events started by the Manutasopi case penetrated ever more deeply into the life of the community, changing people's sense of the original events and altering future actions. One new project affected by the transaction and the illnesses was the *uvelaku* competition, a cycle of *kula* transactions moving around the islands. The winner of the opening *uvelaku* must sponsor the next with valuables which come from the opposite *kula* direction. An opening competition involving necklaces on the northern island of Kitava sets up the expectation of an eventual closing transaction of armshells on a southern island such as Muyum or Yegum. Time and space are again linked in particular patterns through the medium of the *uvelaku* exchanges.

In 1979 a competitive necklace exchange on Kitava was co-sponsored by Silas and won by Thomas. Thomas and Daniel were supposed to co-sponsor the next competition but this co-operation was hampered by the bad blood between them over Silas's illness. Daniel then died. Peace was restored between Silas and Thomas through joint planning for a future *kula* transaction. *Kula* could be seen to put together what witchcraft (and *kula* competition) had previously rent asunder. In telling this story Munn is attempting to probe the cultural structure of history-making and the creation of space, which involves the specific ways in which past and future are implicated in events. She is asking the question 'what frameworks can we develop to conceptualise the on-going constitution of a lived world?' (Munn 1990: 14). The general cultural framework relevant to this Gawan case is the dialectical play between the negativity of witchcraft and the positive effects of *kula*. Munn's work is useful in that she stresses that regions are created as lived spaces given sets of values through action and material culture, in this case connected with *kula*. Regions can be seen as aesthetic constructions, but in quite a different sense to landscape painting. The lived landscape has areas of positive attraction and areas of danger and avoidance: nowhere is neutral. Integral to this construction of landscape is the use and movement of material culture.

Material culture

Strong claims have recently been made for the study of material culture: that it can form a new cross-disciplinary area in its own right, as all human life is there (Miller 1987). Certainly if we consider material culture in its different moments of production, exchange and consumption then little is left out, especially once each of these is set within its social contexts and consequences. Production, exchange and consumption are sometimes considered in a linear sequence, one happening after the other. However, it makes more sense to see them as a circle, because all production consumes material and all consumption has some productive effect. It has been claimed that both production and consumption have been relatively ignored within anthropology and there is some truth to this, although no one could ever say the same for exchange. For this reason, and because I have considered questions of exchange extensively in many of the previous chapters, I shall concentrate on production and consumption here, starting with the former.

Productive practice links the body and technology, so that the history of the body and techniques are interlinked as the one has always shaped the other. As we saw in chapter 5 Leslie White defined technology as an extrasomatic means of adaptation, so that tools were a physical extension of human muscles and technology became a purely utilitarian means of extending human physical powers allowing us to extract more energy from the environment by expending less effort ourselves. For White technology was about economy and energetics.

Maybe it is such dry and abstracted views of technology that have led to there being so little interest in the subject over the last thirty years. As Pfaffenberger (1988: 236) points out, there is a mystery as to why technology should have received so little academic attention, as it lies at the heart of the west's self-image, as modern, progressive and at the vanguard of history. Technology is at the heart of how we see ourselves and its study is connected to two contradictory attitudes. The first is that technology is developed by technicians and then put into use: it is morally and ethically neutral and does not really connect to the social process as a whole. The second is that of economic determinism, where society is shaped by technology and technological development, but that these are external forces, which then have an impact on the workings of society. Neither attitude makes it possible to examine the interlinking of the social and technological forces, seeing each as heavily implicated in the other. This is partly due to the influence of class, as the middle classes who form the bulk of academics are exempt from manual labour and, although they may not be disdainful of it, much of the work of the world is hidden from them (Sigaut 1994: 420).

Problems in understanding practical action also arise from the general nature of the terms we use: to look for the relations between technology, language and intelligence, for instance, presupposes that these generalised terms are helpful. As Ingold (1993b: 436) points out it is only with writing that notions of correct spelling and grammar come about, which lead us to the view that language is an objective system which can be understood by linguists divorced from its contexts of use, and privileges the written form of complete and grammatical sentences over the partial, messy, incomplete utterances of speech. Similarly there is no such thing as technology in the real world, existing as a neatly bounded set of mechanical contrivances and techniques, but rather a series of things that people do, which are messy, contradictory and partial, but nevertheless effective in shaping the social and physical world.

Ingold (1993b: 439) feels that this view of technology comes partly from changes in technology itself, due to the Industrial Revolution. The western view of technological history is one of complexification of individual steps and linkages, leading to a greater range of products and increased efficiency in production. Echoing Marx's view of the alienating consequences of factory production, Ingold sees technology as having undergone objectification and a move from the subject-centred knowledge and skills of the traditional artisan to a rational understanding of the principles of mechanics which lie behind machine production. Sigaut, in partial support of the old view of complexification, talks of lineages of techniques, so that certain developments must be predicated on what went before: all the various developments in car design depend on the existence of the internal combustion engine and without it would make no sense. Technologies develop along paths defined by past inventions and there is considerable happenstance in the matching of invention to social needs. It is only inventions which are socially necessary, as well as practically effective which will be taken up and worked with further. Such a matching of social need and technical efficacy leads to lineages of a very different type from Pitt Rivers' progressive complexification of artefacts, seen as ever more suitable ways of meeting human needs.

In contrast to these views Pfaffenberger puts forward the idea of technology as a total social fact (in the sense that Mauss used the term) involving political, symbolic, social and legal dimensions and with a history linking it to the history of society. Pfaffenberger sees technology as humanised nature and as world-making. Following Marx, technology is the means to shape the world, which also then shapes people. As Engels said, the hand is as much the product of tools, as tools are the product of the hand. Technology reaches far beyond the physical into the psychological and existential. To reformulate Foucault's phrase, people are formed as subjects by the technology they use. An often used example is that of the car, where design concerning aerodynamics and the efficiency of fuel use blends with social aspirations and erotic fantasy. Nations such as the United States or Australia, where there are vast distances to be covered, have been basically shaped by the internal combustion engine and the older nations of Europe and Asia have seen their cities remodelled and countryside reshaped to accommodate the needs of millions of cars. The impact of the car on film, music and literature has been enormous and our notions of time and space have been changed by the ability to travel at speed. The car is a technology that reaches deep into the lives of many in the world today and we as social beings have been fundamentally affected by its existence.

Technology is never simply that; it is always more than a set of procedures for altering the physical shape of the world. However, we should not neglect the physical reshaping of the world that has come about through technology. The Industrial Revolution has obviously massively reshaped the world, but this is not the only time large-scale change has occurred. Sigaut (1994: 450) argues that the ancient world, conventionally seen as technologically static and making up for this deficiency through the use of slaves, in fact produced a mass of technological innovation. The Greek-speaking world of antiquity developed the first widespread use of iron tools for wood-working and agriculture, but also the first rotary machines (olive crushers, mills, water-lifting devices, etc.). New developments were also made in the areas of architecture, agriculture, ship-building and horse-drawn vehicles, many of which are still used today. If we extend technology beyond mechanical devices, which Sigaut does not, to include plants shaped by people then the development and impact of olive growing and viti-culture need to be included.

Descola's (1996) discussion of the technology of hunting, gathering and gardening among the Achuar Indians of the Upper Amazon is exemplary in fitting together the technical and the social elements of all these processes and blending considerations of landscape into an overall view of the social process. Hunting and gathering take place in the rainforest to a large degree and these activities help shape the perception of the rainforest as a realm of seclusion and danger:

> relations with the animals of the forest demand the entire range of conciliatory and bellicose capacities in the human repertory. Together with lovemaking and warfare, hunting is the third pole of those conjunctive relations set in the forest. It resembles the first two in both the pleasures it affords and the technical and magical skills it requires.
>
> (Descola 1996: 222)

Hunting is not simply a matter of being able to make and use blow guns (male activities) or train a good hunting dog (female activities), although it involves both these things, but also requires knowledge and skill and the ability to set up proper relations with the spirits of the animals to be killed. In both hunting and warfare the animals killed or the human enemy are seen as affines (kin), but whereas killing a human affine severs alliances, the killing of an animal maintains a link with its guardian spirits as long as the correct magic and charms have been used. Hunting is not quite a total social fact, but brings in many aspects of life beyond the production and skilled use of the technical means and these techniques can only really be understood in terms of their relationship to a cosmology, relating people to the non-human world.

Technology is often linked with production, but this is only generally socially effective once things are consumed and it is to studies of consumption that we now turn.

Creative consumption

Consumption is hard to define in its anthropological usage, the more so because the use of the term has drifted away from its common-sense connotations. Consumption sounds rather final, as if things are used and used up at the same time, as food is in the act of eating or fuel in a car. Using up material things in social acts is part of what people mean by consumption, but it can also refer to acquisition through gift exchange or commercial activity, or to acts with long-lasting consequences, like furnishing a house. Consumption does not mean the end of objects, but is part of their overall biographies, so that things may be consumed many different times in different settings. As we shall see, the historical aspects of consumption of objects which have long histories is one of the most interesting aspects of the topic.

A number of studies of consumption within anthropology have been critiques of economics and rational choice theory. Douglas and Isherwood (1979) showed that people used material items to create cultural order, so that things were bought and used which reflected and extended cultural categories. They defined poverty as an inability to participate fully in a cultural sense, making it a relative term, rather than some absolute shortage of money or resources. People are not rational consumers in the sense proposed by the economists, always buying cheap and selling dear, but instead respond to their own cultural logics which make sense of the consumption and use of goods. For Douglas and Isherwood material culture is about relaying messages and the more expensive the production of goods in terms of labour time or skill, the greater the imperative to get the message across. They use studies of ranked exchange spheres to look at how society is structured around restriction of goods in order to maintain their value and thus the rank of the people who have control of them. The Tiv of west Africa are generally regarded as the classic case of ranked exchange, as discussed initially by the Bohannons (Bohannon and Bohannon 1968). The top rank of exchanges is about the control of marriage alliances and only people (generally men) who have the right combination of rank and wealth can operate in this sphere. The second sphere is formed of prestige goods, such as guns, metal or cloth, while the third, in which everyone can participate is concerned with everyday objects. Those who controlled the upper two levels could regulate the economy as a whole and this was partly due to the management of exchange values, but also due to access to greater information that went along with management (Douglas and Isherwood 1979: 137–9). Such a model seems simplistic and suspect today, with its talk of the control of women in marriage and stress on information, not the objects themselves. However, it was very influential at the time, especially when it came to discussing poverty and wealth in terms of differential access to the core areas of society in a manner which broke down any distinctions between western societies and all other cultural forms.

Bourdieu (1984) sets up his study of consumption in contemporary France as a critique of aesthetics, rather than economics. In his view there is no such thing as pure aesthetics; beauty does not adhere to the object itself but rather derives from standards generated within its context of use. No society has an overall aesthetic standard, but a series of different forms of appreciation and taste based on overall patterns of life and in western societies the major fracture lines creating different standards of taste are class divisions. Comparing working-class and middle-class taste in France as manifest in home furnishing, patterns of sociability and so on, Bourdieu argues that each class has its own standards of human decency that others fail to meet. Working-class social life is open and communal, taking place in bars, clubs and restaurants, whereas the middle classes are more likely to socialise at home in surroundings which, to working-class eyes, privilege empty form over substance. Bourdieu shows that these differences are not just due to money and discusses a series of different forms of capital, crucial amongst which is cultural capital accumulated through formal and personal education which provides a command of elite French culture so vital to middle- and upper-class taste.

He illustrates his arguments with a series of charts and diagrams which counterpoise such factors as income and cultural capital as determinants of what sorts of films, music or newspapers people prefer. One of his more immediate presentations shows preferences for types of homes favoured by members of different classes, on the basis of interviews conducted. His major point is that an emphasis on the aesthetic properties of a house grows as one moves up the social hierarchy, just as the desire for a functional environment (clean, practical, easy to maintain) declines (Bourdieu 1984: 247). Bourdieu's argument that patterns of consumption are based on tastes derived from class could be applied to many a western society. His argument here also links in with that in *Homo Academicus* (1988), perhaps his most accessible book, which looks at the construction of cultural capital through education and the links between class, institutions and patterns of culture. Taste is something which is difficult to define, but easy to recognise in practice, forming a vital part of social life and the discriminations we make between things and people.

An important area of taste is food, where the figurative and literal meanings of the word meet. Food is a constant need, something that people consume every day and around which there is often considerable cultural elaboration. Both Lévi-Strauss (1969b) and Goody (1982) have looked at food in terms of either classification or the role it has played in creating and reifying class differences. Appadurai (1981, 1988) has pointed out that food is a powerful element in the battle for various cultural resources and coined the term 'gastro-politics' when looking at the Hindu case, where he shows that the sensory nature of food acts as a powerful evocation of memory, bringing situations far distant from the present into reach, making it a potent element in battles for power within the family and beyond. Archaeologists and anthropologists are realising that innovation in growing plants and keeping animals often occurred in those species that might be considered to be luxuries and not staples. The consumption of plants involves not just nutritional considerations, but also mind-altering substances (Goodman *et al.* 1995). These can only be understood through situating food and drugs within patterns of consumption as a whole. One of the benefits of emphasising consumption is to tie food into material culture, so that the pots to prepare or eat food are indicative of where and how consumption took place, plus the sets of cultural categories lying behind different forms of food and drink. Food, and its consumption, leads into discussions of material culture more generally. Mintz (1985), also taking an historical perspective, has looked at the history of sugar in Europe. In a period of rapid industrialisation in Europe it provided a major source of energy, but in the Caribbean and elsewhere it led to the setting up of plantations, often worked by slaves, and had a series of far-reaching and widespread effects. Sugar, like tobacco, tea and coffee (Goodman 1993), has had the effect of making Third World economies dependent on First World fashion and taste.

Much recent work on consumption has concentrated on mass consumption and here the work of Miller (1987, 1995) is key. Following in the tradition of Douglas and Isherwood (1979) and also strands of thought going back to Veblen (1924), Miller attempts to reform economics and re-orient anthropology. Miller is sceptical about the existence of the rational consumer on which so much of demand theory in economics is based. Economics is a dismal science insofar as it cuts choice off from the social milieu in which it exists. For Miller consumption is about 'objectification' (a term drawn from Hegel), in which people create a world of their desire in physical form through buying things and making use of them. Shopping has been academically ignored, as a mundane, trivial activity which is manipulated by the power of advertising and transnational companies trying to create desires that never existed before for purposes of profit. All these assumptions are challenged by Miller, who, in polemical vein, argues that we are in a new phase of consumer-led capitalism which has profound implications for the workings of western democracies and the division of labour between the First and Third Worlds (Miller 1995). The western household is neither the locus of cold, rational decision-making as the economist would have it, nor the point of creation of a shallow, value-less global culture as assumed by sociologists and anthropologists. It is, Miller argues, the place in which a moral, cosmological and ideological universe is created, so that the weekly shopping represents love and care for the family (mainly by women) and the constant creation of class-based values in a manner demonstrated by Bourdieu for France.

Such conclusions derive from an earlier study (Miller 1988) of kitchens on a north London council estate. The estate was built in the early 1970s and consists of flats in low-rise blocks. The people living there were predominantly West Indian, Irish or of local origin. The crucial thing from Miller's point of view was that all flats started out with identical kitchens, so that he could look at the modifications brought about by the inhabitants and how these changes reflected patterns of sociability and ethnic background. He interviewed forty tenants (about 13 per cent of the total) and photographed thirty-four kitchens as they were at the time. The degree of alteration of the kitchen varied from being virtually unchanged to having had all the original fittings thrown out and new, commercial fitted kitchens installed (Miller 1988: 356). The degree of alteration was tied into patterns of sociability. Single white males were often the most socially isolated and had done little or nothing to their kitchens; whereas single black men had changed their kitchens quite considerably, showing an interest in cooking and socialising. The most sociable had made the greatest changes, which involved both changing the fittings of the kitchen, but also adding personal decorations and ornaments. Overall, financial constraints emerged as much less important in the changes brought about to kitchen than ethnicity, gender and sociability, so that the kitchens represented an exercise in self-creation, as people tried to overcome their feelings of being tenants and to create a style of life that generated and reinforced their self-image.

The kitchen is the centre of consumption in many homes, reflecting current tastes and their changes over the years. The ability of modern retailers to keep electronic records of what they sell and to analyse these constantly means that they can keep up with the changes in consumer demand, so that organic food or copies of the latest designer clothing can be on the shelf rapidly. Miller (1995) sees consumers as setting their own agendas, rather than being pawns of marketing, with political parties rising and falling on their ability to combine low taxes and low prices, the ultimate bedrock of any popularity. Miller claims that if power is dispersed throughout society in the way that Foucault described, the main loci are consumers, often the housewife, whose sturdy independence and practice of thrift makes her a power for world domination. Those dominated are, of course, the Third World producers so that if northern hemisphere fashions change then producing nations can be driven to the wall. Swallow (1982) shows the impact of a fluctuating demand for cheesecloth in the west on Indian producers and this example could be multiplied endlessly. Although effects on producers are real enough, many have denied that mass consumption is breaking down a previously authentic culture, swamping it with Americanised tastes and tat, an argument we shall revisit in chapter 8. Miller also sees some puritanism on the part of anthropologists who want to marginalise the role of western goods, and if these are emphasised then it is in a context of resistance to consumerism, such as through cargo cults (Worsley 1957).

Not only is local culture not being swamped by global forces, but there is increasing interest in how pre-colonial regimes of value and use of material things have shaped people's encounters with capitalism. Thomas (1991) has argued that the different forms of exchange throughout the Pacific were a major factor influencing the reciprocal relations between incoming westerners and islanders. Consequently the varying forms of state society which have grown up over the last 200 years are as much the product of pre-colonial forces as they are of the incoming capitalist structures. In a provocative piece, Gell has argued that gift exchange, one of the quintessential elements of non-capitalist societies, may actually have been an outcome of colonialism in Papua New Guinea, replacing older forms of inter-group movement of objects which looked more like commodity exchange (Gell 1992a). If this is true, even partially, then it will necessitate a rethink of the histories of Melanesian societies and their crucial forms of exchange. To explore a proposition like this necessitates a combination of archaeology and anthropology, to document the nature of exchange in the present and its changes over the last century, or more thorough historical documentation and an analysis of the types of movements of objects in the prehistoric period, where this is possible. A precondition of such studies is a theoretical structure which will enable us to look at long-term and shorter spans of history. It is to problems of history that we now turn.

History

As we have seen before, anthropology has had a complex and fluctuating relationship with history. For much of this century, in Britain at least, any close relationship was made difficult through the stress on the synchronic within structural-functionalism. A major change was heralded by Evans-Pritchard's (1950) break with Radcliffe-Brown, although this article led to no flood of publications on historical change and it is not until the last twenty years that the fiction of the 'ethnographic present' has been finally been dispensed with, leading to the complementary realisation that all societies have histories and no cultural or social study is possible that does not give some recognition to this. In recent years there has been an outpouring of historical writing within anthropology (Biersack 1991, Borofsky 1987, Comaroff 1985, Foster 1995, Rosaldo 1980, Wolf 1982) and also increased consideration of the effect of excluding time from anthropological analysis (Fabian 1983, Thomas 1989). There is a related, although rather differently oriented, literature on local conceptions of time and change (Gell 1992c, Munn 1992). However, I shall consider one main example of work on history and time, with the major justification that the work is probably the most influential of recent years: that of Marshall Sahlins.

Anthropology has throughout its history attempted to reconcile the problem of order (what holds societies together as coherent if conflictual entities?) with the problem of change (how can alteration occur without causing social disintegration?). The power of Sahlins' recent work (1981, 1985, 1995) is that he attempts to overcome the perceived opposition between order and change. Sahlins' attempt to combine an understanding of order with an appreciation of change is through the juxtaposition of structure and events. Structures are primarily to do with signification: they are a set of relations between cultural categories, symbolic orders through which the world itself, people's place in the world and patterns of action are made meaningful and evaluated. Structure is both the medium and outcome of practice; 'cultural schemes are historically ordered, since to a greater or lesser extent the meanings are revalued as they are practically enacted' (Sahlins 1985: vii). In areas of the world like Polynesia the set of cultural categories and their relations are concerned with cosmology. The ordering of the universe rests ultimately on the relations between gods and nature. People's roles are defined in terms of their relations to these transcendent categories, so that chiefs mediate between gods and commoners and in so doing help control the fertility of the human and natural world. These roles and relations are not automatically reproduced but challenged and put at risk by events, which are always contingent on a host of factors. Events are never straightforwardly meaningful, but always interpreted, interpretation deriving from the cultural schemes they put at risk. There is a continual dialectic between structure and event whereby each derives from, but yet challenges, the other. As is well known, Sahlins is especially interested in sets of events that bring about challenge and change. These he terms structures of conjuncture.

The meeting of different social logics, through the process of European exploration and colonialism, provides Sahlins with his prime case of a structure of the conjuncture and the best example of such a case is the death of Cook in Hawaii. Sahlins' idea that Hawaiians took Cook to be Lono, one of their major categories of the divine, in order to assimilate him into their own views of the world and to create meaningful patterns of action towards him has been criticised by Obeyesekere (1991). Obeyesekere's attack on Sahlins was based on the sound point that Europeans may be rather too prone to see themselves as gods, but runs up against the evidence that many Hawaiians did, in fact, take Cook to be Lono. According to Sahlins, Cook and his crew sailed around the big island of Hawaii in the same direction and at the right time for the Makahiki festival. This was an annual festival, four months in length, during which processions took place in a clockwise direction around each of the Hawaiian islands with the god Lono at their head. Lono was the priests' and people's god and the Makahiki represented a period during which the normal social order to was overturned. During this time the chiefs went into hiding and their god Ku with them. At the end of each Makahiki there was a ritual confrontation between Lono and Ku through which Lono was driven off, not to return again for another eight months until the start of the next Makahiki. This confrontation restored the rule of the chiefs.

Cook came ashore at Kealakekua Bay on 17 January 1779 to the most rapturous reception he had received anywhere in the Pacific, with an estimated 10,000 people there to greet him. He left on 4 February, which was just a little later than the Makahiki calendar allowed and all would have been well had he not been forced to return when the foremast of the *Resolution* was sprung. Coming back to Kealakekua Bay to get a replacement mast, Cook and his crews were met with a totally different reception, which Sahlins sees as being due to the chiefs' dismay that Lono had returned to confront them, threatening an overturn of the whole social order. Thefts and confrontations escalated over the next three days, eventually leading to Cook being stabbed in the back with an iron dagger, made in Birmingham and traded by his crew to the Hawaiian nobles.

For Sahlins the death of Cook represents the classic clash of different social logics. Each side interpreted the events leading to Cook's death in a manner which made sense to them. Had each had some insight into the thoughts of the other, then events would have turned out differently. The death of Cook is a microcosm for the encounters of colonialism, showing how unprecedented encounters could only be worked through existing logics of thought and action. It is unusual in bringing about European, rather than a local, death. In order to understand this set of events from the Hawaiian point of view we need to look a little more at the schemes of culture and history that structured these events.

Hawaiian history and philosophy of the pre-contact period is known today from sources written down in the early and middle nineteenth century. Many of these are internally consistent and coherent, but may have some missionary influences which have provided consistent bias, for instance in imposing European views of the role of women in the ritual system (Linnekin 1990).

Hawaiian history is constructed within a framework which links philosophy and action so that general precepts can be translated into guides for living well. Much of this history is contained within genealogies which go back to two ancestral figures, Wakea and Papa, whose story helps lay out the basics of the system of religion and *tapu*, together with crucial principles of relatedness. Wakea (sky-father) and Papa (earth-mother) are parents of the islands of Hawaii and human offspring (Kame'eleihiwa 1992: 23–4). Their first-born human child was a daughter, Ho'ohokukalani, whom Wakea desired to sleep with. In order to have an excuse to be apart from Papa he caused, through the medium of a *Kahuna* (priest), the *Aikapu* system to be created, where women are seen as defiling in contrast to the sacredness of men. The two genders must not eat together, and women are forbidden to eat certain foods, such as pig, coconut and bananas which have male symbolic connotations. The separations brought about by the *Aikapu* system enabled Wakea to have sex with his daughter. Their first offspring was born partly formed, so was buried and grew into the first taro plant, Haloa. Their second child was a human male, given the same name as his elder sibling, emphasising the close relationship between people and taro.

In this story is contained a whole series of prescriptions for everyday life, plus the most prestigious forms of relatedness for the aristocracy. As we shall see below, the spatial arrangements of settlements are based around the *Aikapu* system and lying behind this, in turn, is the organisation of both domestic labour and work on the land. The philosophical precepts of the religious system had a massive impact on everyday life, but also arose out of those patterns such that actions, constantly repeated, provided a source for the philosophy. Also, the *Aikapu* system which divided men and women provided the basis for even more divisions, such as those between chiefs and commoners. And the emphasis on incest within chiefly families was the ultimate expression of exclusion which again ran through the landscape and settlements ensuring that commoners (*maka'ainana*) and chiefs (*ali'i*) maintained a proper distance between each other. The basis of this distance was cosmological: the chiefs were closer to the gods than were the commoners and more able to influence divine powers.

The divine was divided into four main categories of generalised gods – Ku, Lono, Kane and Kanaloa. Each of these categories has a multitude of particularised forms which together encompass the whole of reality and human action within the world. There is an ambivalent relationship in which people are generally dependent on the actions of the gods, but can influence these actions through anthropomorphic images of particularised divine forms and through sacrifice.

There are also a whole series of temporal implications deriving from Ku, in his general and particular forms. As we have seen with the death of Cook, the ritual calendar of Hawaii divided into two parts: a roughly eight-month period in which Ku was dominant and with him the power of the chiefs, which was counterposed by four months in which Lono ruled through the ceremony of the *makahiki*, in which the commoners and their priests had more influence. But also individuals were more connected to some gods and the categories of action they represent at some periods of their lives rather than at others.

Kamehameha, the chief who unified the Hawaiian islands into one political structure at the beginning of the nineteenth century, had a changing relationship with Ku throughout his lifetime. Valeri (1991) makes a link between the shift that happened every year from Ku as wild destructive power domesticated in the temple through sacrifice, who then gives way to Lono, a fertilising power for both land and people, and that which occurred within Kamehameha's lifetime in a shift from a warlike conquering phase to peaceful statesman.

Contained within this mixture of power and cosmology are a whole series of timescales and temporal cycles. First, any claim to social position was based on complex genealogies which went back several hundred years before Kamehameha and for which different accounts can be checked against each other and prove to be generally consistent (Cachola-Abad 1993). Archaeology is the only means of access to periods prior to genealogical memory and a vital complement to this and written histories. The longer histories of Hawaii necessitate a combination of archaeology and history (Kirch 1994, Kirch and Sahlins 1992). There are the shorter-term cycles to do with the transformation of the individual within their life, such as that undergone by Kamehameha from warlike follower of a destructive Ku to a stable and beneficent ruler of a unified Hawaii. This transformation was underpinned by the use of the political and sacred landscape in which old temples were torn down and new ones constructed, emphasising the current powers. Kamehameha's transformation was also an echo of the yearly cycle from the wild form of Ku brought from the forests of the interior of the islands and domesticated through sacrifices in the temples, who then gave way to the fertilising powers of Lono. As with all changes in cosmic powers this was effected through human action in building and sacrificing at temples, which was a constant feature of Hawaiian life whether on a daily or a yearly scale. Cosmology and philosophy made no sense except in terms of action and it is within the landscape and the material culture it contained that action was worked out. We are looking at a mutual influence of thought and action, where old habits were created but within which startling innovation was possible, as the life of Kamehameha shows.

History is partly a matter of cultural style, deriving from the cosmological basis of a society and the aesthetics involved in putting such precepts into daily practice. Throughout this chapter I have left hints as to how material culture, landscape and aesthetics might be combined as people create worlds for themselves in the present, deriving partly from the means by which they construct their past. I shall end the chapter with a final example which will bring together some of these threads and also contrast with the Hawaiian histories we have just considered.

Styles of life

Northeast Arnhem Land is criss-crossed with Dreaming tracks, which are the routes taken by ancestral beings in the creation of the country. Inland from Trial Bay (Figure 7.4) is a place by the river called Wurlwurlwuy. The river had been created by a shark rushing inland after it had been speared by an ancestral harpoon. The shark became caught in a fish trap at Wurlwurlwuy, but escaped by breaking the trap apart and in the process the shark became transformed into various features of the landscape, so that his teeth became the trees that line the banks. The mouth of the same river was created by the fall of a massive stringy bark tree cut down inland by a female ancestral being. Any one place was created through the combined actions of the ancestors, who are still present in the landscape today (Morphy 1991, 1992: 125). The people who live in this landscape, known to outsiders as the Yolngu, are in some sense part of the landscape. For instance, on one occasion recounted by Morphy (1991: 200), a woman of the Marrakulu clan died at Yirrkala and her spiritual home was in Trial Bay (see Figure 7.4). Her funeral service and the songs, dances and paintings that accompanied it was constructed to both represent and to aid the journey of her spirit back to its home. Thus the painting on the coffin lid was of the shark to be found at Wurlwurlwuy and the entrance to the shade in which the coffin was painted was seen to represent the fish trap. Sticks were placed across its entrance and when the time came to move the body, the dancers acting as sharks burst suddenly out of the shade, carrying the coffin, smashing down the wall of sticks, thus recreating the Dreamtime events. The coffin was carried to the vehicle which was to drive it to the cemetery in a dance that evoked the rush of water after the fish trap was broken, but it also symbolised the soul's attempt to leave the body (Morphy

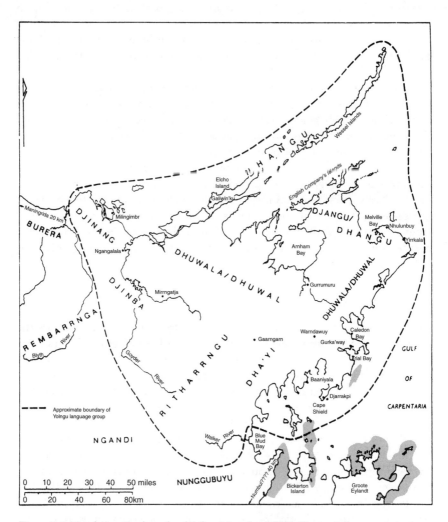

Figure 7.4 Northeast Arnhem land (after Morphy (1991): Figure 3.1)

1991: 200). The re-creation of the ancestral events was an aid to the struggles of the woman's spirit to free itself from bodily existence and to make its journey back to the sources of ancestral power at Trial Bay. The anger of the shark in the trap also allowed the mourners to purge themselves of their own feelings of loss and bereavement.

The funeral service was made up of painting, song and dance, all of which were part of the sacred law (*mardayin*) of the group, but which also could be constructed in a unique manner around this particular death. The mythical episode was appropriate to the circumstances of the death, using a series of mythical and aesthetic principles. Yolngu art and ritual, central to the life of the group, are constructed in any instance to achieve a set of effects appropriate to the context. As Morphy (1995) stresses, the most general background to people's life is the land. For the Yolngu, land is history at a number of different levels. As we have seen, the deepest of these in both an historical and a semantic sense is the ancestral landscape, providing continuity such that the Dreamtime still exists to structure contemporary action. Land is also genealogy, a set of links to known ancestors. A hunting or gathering expedition is never a purely pragmatic business, but a means by which young people get to know their past and older people maintain their links with the dead. The landscape has a group aspect, creating the history of the group as a whole, but it is also individual, as each person has their own unique set of links to the land, due to genealogy and the pattern of their life. The end of funeral rites often involves the burning of the country associated with a person, to make it safe for the living to enter.

People maintain links to the land by the use in ceremony of sacred objects and through creating dance, song and painting. The great strength of Morphy's analysis is to combine a picture of the general aspects of Yolngu life with a detailed analysis of painting. In looking at the paintings of the Manggalili clan, of which the famous artist Narritjin Maymuru was a member, Morphy is concerned with the links between the form of the paintings and their meanings. Meaning is not fixed or simple, but derives from the context in which the painting is made and used and, especially, from the knowledge of those looking at the painting. The knowledge of the viewers will range in a spectrum from senior, initiated men, to young men, women and children and finally to outsiders: one painting can evoke many different responses. Morphy (1991: chap. 10) looks at the paintings concerned with Djarrakpi, an important Manggalili clan centre (Figure 7.5). The salt lake at Djarrakpi has a sand bank to the west and a series of gullies to the north. These are seen to be formed of possum string (*burrkun*) by ancestral beings, one of whom was an ancestral woman Nyapililngu, who also formed the seaward dunes out of *burrkun*. The cashew trees (*marrawili*) surrounding the lake are connected with a cockatoo (the *guwak*), an ancestral figure with both bird and human aspects connected with funerary rites, and other trees have different associations. Morphy (1991: 236) renders these different aspects of the landscape as a template which underlies all paintings of Djarrakpi (Figure 7.6). One painting, by Narritjin, must stand for many and only a small portion of the meanings attached to this can be mentioned (Figure 7.7). Morphy's initial description of the painting is as follows:

> the three elongated figures are said to represent digging sticks, used by Nyapililngu to walk up and down the dunes. At a second level they mark the lake at Djarrakpi and the key features to either side. The left-hand digging stick represents the coastal dunes, the central stick the lake itself, and the right-hand stick the burrkun – the low sandbank on the inland side. Orienting the painting in a north–south direction, the bottom line (1)

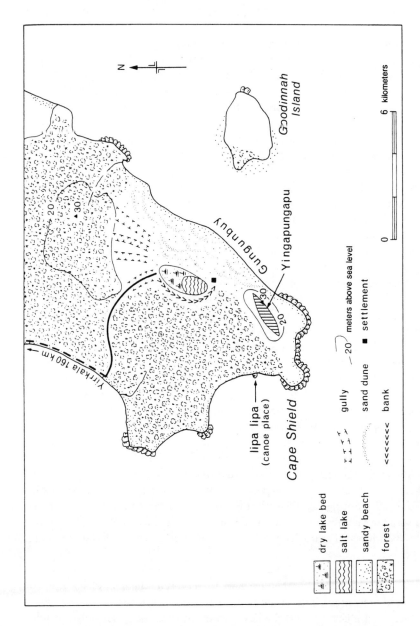

Figure 7.5 Map of Djarrakapi (after Morphy (1991): Figure 10.2)

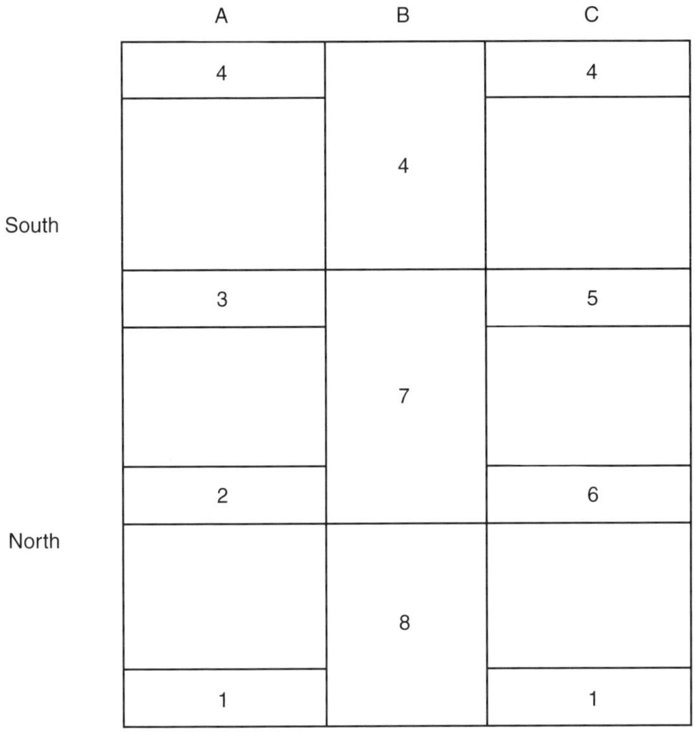

Figure 7.6 Template of meanings in Djarrakapi paintings (from Morphy (1991): Figure 10.10)

marks the head of the lake where the gullies run behind the dunes. The squares on the right-hand digging stick (6, 5, and 4) represent, respectively, the first cashew tree grove, the wild plum tress and the marrawili tree at the head of the lake. The equivalent positions on the other side represent the places where Nyapililngu spun possum-fur string and the marrawili tree.

(Morphy 1991: 238)

Each of the motifs on the painting has sets of meanings, so that, for example, the squares can represent camp sites or water holes, or the dashed infill on the digging sticks is a design used only by the Manggalili clan, the meanings of which are to do with possum fur and the claw marks of possums on trees (Morphy 1991: 238). The painting could be seen as a map and this would be its outside meaning, that a Yolngu person would be taught first. New and more hidden interpretations would involve the journey represented by the painting and the ancestral actions from which they result. For instance, gender differences are strongly encoded into all pictures about Djarrakpi: the eastern side of the lake has female connotations connected with Nyapililngu, the west

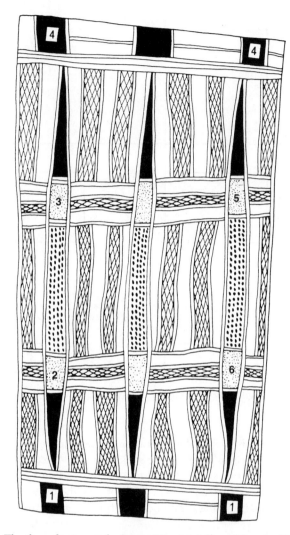

Figure 7.7 The three digging sticks (artist: Narritjin) (from Morphy (1991) : Figure 10.11)

with the male cockatoo. Any painting is only ever a part of the knowledge about Djarrakpi, with songs, dance and stories also conveying more detail. Each element tends to be learned separately and only later do people come to see the connections between them, this broader context deepening the understanding of each aspect of knowledge.

This is an example of a broader point, which is that all life is constructed through a particular aesthetic and an understanding of another way of life can only come through some appreciation of its style. Aboriginal life might be seen as too easy an example, in that life (and death) are so obviously constructed through aesthetic schemes. However, the Marakwet of the Cherangani Hills, the *kula* and Hawaiian history, which we have also looked at in this chapter, all represent aesthetics in action, both in the past and the present. Each group has their own sets of aesthetics and local means of constructing and dealing with history. In order to take the argument further it is necessary to clarify what is meant by the term aesthetic.

Gell (1992b, 1998) has criticised the use of the notion of aesthetics in the anthropology of art, as it comes with too much intellectual baggage connecting it to western notions of high culture and fine art. Whilst I would accept that we need to be cautious about exactly how we use the term, the idea of aesthetics is too useful to throw out. Aesthetics is partly about things that appeal to the senses, but as we have just seen it is much more than that. A particular aesthetic will guide the ways in which people use their bodies in action, according to a culturally based body language. It will also create sets of locales for actions, either through cloaking the landscape in a system of values or through the creation of a set of built environments, with their own sets of cues for action as analysed by Bell (1992). Finally, locales and the landscape as a whole can be linked together by the knowledgeable use of mobile material culture in which the functional and aesthetic will always combine. Sahlins saw colonial encounters in Hawaii as the meeting of two cultural logics, with the term 'logic' emphasising thought. I would prefer to see all encounters, colonial or not, as the meeting of cultural aesthetics, as this takes us away from how people think and interpret events, focusing on how they act within a landscape and through sets of material culture which involve both conscious meanings and habitual action.

Habitus gives us a set of learnt responses to the world, within which we learn what both pleasure and pain are, together with a myriad of other valuations. However, habitus comes not just from the early lessons of life, but is also transformed throughout our lives, as the relationships between the individual and the group change over time. Aesthetics is not just static style, but forms of transformations constantly reworking aspects of the human personality, such as sex and gender, together with the values attached to the material world.

Yolngu paintings now exist in a series of different dimensions outside Arnhem Land, one of which is the international art market. Bark paintings, a recent innovation, are sold all over the world and often command considerable prices (Morphy 1991: chap. 2). Many groups have moved off government and mission stations back on to their ancestral land in the last twenty-five years and now exist through a combination of hunting and gathering, social security payments and the sale of art to tourists and dealers. Morphy has shown that it is not the motifs of the paintings themselves, but knowledge of their interpretation that provides meanings. One painting can mean many different things, so that there is contradiction in selling works to outsiders that encode sacred meanings for the Yolngu themselves. The different appreciation of Yolngu art locally and globally is a microcosm of a relatively new set of problems facing anthropology and archaeology, raising questions about the point and purpose of both disciplines in a post-colonial world with far-reaching international connections. It is to problems of post-colonialism and globalism that I now turn.

8   Globalism, ethnicity and post-colonialism

As far as culture goes in Victoria things have done a complete turn around in the last 20 years. The land was taken off us, they stripped the land, raped the land, killed our people, but in the last 15 years the culture has revived out of all proportion. I've been Cultural Officer here for 12–13 years. I was one of the lucky ones as I was taught the culture by the older people and later when I spent years shearing or on drilling rigs I put it into practice. It's no shame to be black now, you are proud to be black. Once I busted this little white kid up at school and when I came home, my father asked me what I'd been fighting about. I told him this Gubba [non-Aboriginal] kid had called me a black and he swung me round and said 'Well ain't ya, ya silly black bastard!' And there and then I realised I was black and it was something to be proud of and I've tried to put it into practice the rest of my life.

(Darcy Pettit, Aboriginal Cultural Officer, Robinvale, Victoria, Australia, in Taylor 1988: 235)

European explorers moved into the area of northwest Victoria in southeastern Australia in the early nineteenth century, following the setting up of the colony at Botany Bay in 1788. The town of Robinvale, where Darcy Pettit is Aboriginal Cultural Officer today, stands near the confluence of the Murray and the Murrumbidgee, two of the major rivers of southeastern Australia. The river systems made the interior accessible to white settlers, who moved stock and equipment in on paddle steamers and barges. They initially encountered some of the densest Aboriginal populations in the whole continent. Many Aboriginal people died through fighting to defend their land, but far more were killed by introduced diseases such as measles and smallpox, such that it is estimated that 80 per cent of the population died within one generation. By the end of the last century most surviving Aboriginal people were on reserves and mission stations and were thought by whites to be destined to die out altogether (Griffiths 1996). Aboriginal people were employed as seasonal labourers on stock ranching properties and farms growing fruit and vegetables. In the early years of this century government policy changed, as it was realised that Aboriginal populations were not going to die out and Aboriginal children were raised in institutions or white families, often in ignorance of their Aboriginal background. This policy survived into the post-war period. However, increasing amounts of seasonal work in the 1930s and 1940s enabled some groups to move back to their homelands and they set up shanties along the rivers. Some kin group links were reforged during this period. In the post-war period some groups moved into towns, so that today 10 per cent of the 4,000 inhabitants of Robinvale are of Aboriginal descent. In these towns Aboriginal land councils or co-operatives have been set up and these have often formed part of the nucleus for reviving Aboriginal culture over the last two decades (Taylor 1988: 227–8). Throughout Australia the Bicentenary of white settlement in 1988 had the paradoxical effect of raising issues of Aboriginal culture and whether Australia as a nation could only look to the last 200 years of its history and ignore the previous 40,000 years, the now conservative estimate of the human occupation of the continent. The same is true of the 500-year anniversary of Columbus's 'discovery' of the Americas in 1492, which had the unlikely and beneficial effect of raising people's consciousness that many nations today were founded through colonial processes.

The history of this corner of Victoria is a microcosm of broader colonial (and now post-colonial) histories in many parts of the world. People in many parts of the world are rediscovering their own culture and a pride in their own culture. This is a reaction to the internalisation of feelings of inferiority and cultural doubt that were so often engendered by the colonial process. Indigenous people are now sometimes willing, and always able, to discuss their culture with people in other parts of the world. Increasingly frequently contact is made with the rest of the world directly – Twa pygmies in Rwanda have their own website, for instance, through which to present their culture and their plight to anyone who will take notice.

The global connections of colonial administration and empire are being replaced by new sets of connections made by transnational companies, easy air travel and new global media. Indigenous groups have a new sense of themselves and the lives they lead, feeling no need to have outsiders interpret their ways of life for the rest of the world. These changes together have created a totally new context for anthropology and archaeology. Both disciplines are attempting to catch up with the ways in which the world has changed and to re-orient their modes of operation, as well as to question the types of knowledge they produce. Anthropology has felt these changes soonest and most keenly, but similar dilemmas confront the post-colonial archaeologist. The changes have taken two main forms, which create the structure for this chapter. First, the methods and theories created in the early, colonial, days of anthropology were all to do with Us studying Them, where the Us in question were white, middle-class people in developed nations and They were small groups of far-away people, intriguing mainly due to their difference to ourselves. The major (implicit) model employed was that of an Island Culture where groups were seen to be small, self-contained or even isolated, internally organised in a coherent manner and, although they were allowed a few links to the outside world, they were seen to have little history. However, no group is an island even though they may live on one (see Terrell *et al.* 1997 for a critique of the dominant view that isolated island cultures were key to the human history of the Pacific) and each has its own history, linked to that of groups around it and to a wider world. There has been a shift in perception from cultures as ready-made, to cultures as always in a state of becoming, so that we have now jettisoned a belief in a relatively static 'primitive' which was different and prior to ourselves.

Secondly, there has been a decline, or even a collapse, in the belief of the superior nature of western knowledge. Old certainties, linked to the supposed objectivity of western knowledge, have been replaced by the belief that all knowledge is provisional, intimately linked to power relations, so that knowledge in the developed world is not inherently superior to anyone else's. Post-modernist thinkers such as Foucault, Derrida and Bourdieu have exposed and undermined the smug self-confidence of western thought and their ideas have entered both anthropology and archaeology since the 1960s. However, the original post-modernist thinkers did little to explore the colonial context in which western thought developed and they are now subject to critique along these lines. As we shall see below, Stoler (1995) has pointed out that it is impossible to understand the development of western sexuality over the last few hundred years without looking at its connection to race and colonialism and that Foucault (1981) in his history of sexuality ignores the colonial context almost totally. Thus although Clifford (1997: 39) has warned us against too easy an equation between post-modernist thought and the general post-colonial context in which we live, there are complex connections between them, particularly in the decline of the west as the sole economic power of importance and the concomitant decline in the certainties of western thought. I shall treat both of these issues in turn, taking the post-colonial global world in which we live first and turning to matters of thought and certainty later.

Globalism and economics

The rise of globalism has coincided with the movements of decolonisation which have brought us into the post-colonial world. Between the independence of India in 1947, through the independence of many African nations a decade or more later and the coming into being of smaller nations like Vanuatu in the last twenty years the old world order, dominated by empire, has been swept away. This trend has been accelerated by the break-up of the former Soviet Union and it is not impossible that China might one day fragment into its component parts. Imperial power, focused on a ruling nation state, has been replaced by the dominance of transnational companies, the largest of which have a main base in one nation (often either Japan or the US), but have operations in many parts of the world. So great is the scope of some of these companies that Mitsubishi is now calculated to be the fifth largest economy in the world, larger than all but the biggest of industrial nations. The international stock market also spans the globe and uncertainty in Japan can mean fear in New York. Modern capitalism is based around the rapid movement of money, information and the work force in a manner which makes nation boundaries irrelevant (see Harvey 1989: part 2 for an accessible account of recent trends). These changes have led to many academic debates: are we leaving the condition of modernity set up by the Industrial Revolution and entering a new phase of post-modernity? Harvey (1989) argues that this is not the case and that the present takes an earlier capitalist logic to a more exaggerated state. Of more relevance here is a linked debate over the role and future of the nation state on the one hand and local cultural differences on the other. Some feel that the state is about to wither away, others that rumours of its death have been exaggerated and that nations form a relatively cheap set of infrastructures as far as the transnational corporations are concerned and without which they could not survive (see the debates in *Theory, Culture & Society* over the last few years).

These debates, essentially over the economic role and context of the nation state are paralleled by arguments over human rights and citizenship. The nation state was the traditional means of protecting human rights (as well as the major threat to them – a paradox liberal thought has not done much to address), but now many indigenous groups and minorities are looking to international agencies, ranging from the UN to Amnesty International, to help them. Much internal state legislation is open to challenge in international courts. For instance, Australian land rights legislation for Aboriginal groups can be challenged internationally if it is held to breach conventions on human rights to which Australia has signed up. UNESCO provides some forum for discussion of issues of culture, heritage and rights, and many indigenous groups are setting up international organisations to oppose the nation states or transnational forces they feel are threatening them. For instance, the Rural Advancement Foundation International concerned with intellectual property rights to do with food plants and genetics (http://www.rafi.ca/misc/listserv.html) or Indigenous Knowledge run by the World Council of Indigenous Peoples. In the area of political activism, politics and culture become inextricably mixed, and it is to the fraught question of culture that I now turn.

Globalism and culture

The quote from Darcy Pettit, with which I started this chapter, emphasises culture as a central element in his life and work. This is true of many individuals around the world. Academia mirrors life and so culture has become a central term throughout the social sciences (see for instance, the rash of recent journals with culture in the title – *Public Culture, Cultural Studies, Theory, Culture & Society, Science as Culture, History and Culture, Cultural Anthropology* – or the rise of cultural studies as a sub- or meta-discipline depending on your point of view). The original home of the concept of culture as referring to habits of thought and action, rather than the state of being cultivated in mind and manners, is anthropology. As we saw in chapters 4 and 5 for much of this century American anthropology has developed a theory of culture in different ways. Paradoxically, anthropology seems rather embarrassed about this fact and increasingly uncertain itself about the limits of a term like 'culture' (Hannerz 1996: chap. 3). The root of this unease is in the distinction between the global and local and the possible relationship between the two. As anthropology grew up with an image of culture as always local, it is the global element which is now disturbing.

Global cultures have a number of different elements to them. Globality (this literature has created series of new nouns and adjectives, all created through a suffix attached to the word global – hence globalism, globalisation, globality, globalness) is often seen as manifested through a series of odd juxtapositions of items or habits derived from individual cultures and mixed. Hannerz (1996: 1–2) writes of his stay in Kafanchan, central Nigeria, where he was a resident of the Rosy Guest Inn and of his research assistant Ben who was a devotee of Kung Fu. One of Ben's older brothers had named his first son Gargarin, after the Soviet cosmonaut and Ben, wanting to out-do his brother named his first son Lenin. Later, Ben was interested in opening a corner shop, which as a proud father he wanted to call 'Lenin's Supermarket', a combination which had a perfect local logic, but to a more distanced view seems an odd juxtaposition of bourgeois values and stern revolutionary socialism. Such a mixture of values, combining different elements of public global culture in a local setting, are often presented as quaint and comic, but simultaneously sustain the critique of the old notion of an isolated culture. A second aspect of globalism is what we might call the global event. A prime example of this, in the cultural sphere, is Salman Rushdie's novel, *The Satanic Verses*. To quote Hannerz (1996: 11) again, '*The Satanic Verses* was originally published in Britain, first banned in India, and provoked riots in Pakistan; the *fatwa* was proclaimed in Iran. In Nigeria there were death threats against the Nobel laureate Wole Soyinka, who expressed his solidarity with Rushdie . . . .' Such events bring to mind McLuhan's (1964) phrase 'the global village' and although this sums up some of the connectedness we associated with a village, the image is far too pastoral for the world in which we live.

A third aspect of global life is that many communities do not just live in their places of origin. Mass movements of people this century through voluntary or forced migration have reinforced the millennia-old fact that people move. It is now as easy to study a Haitian community in Brooklyn as it is in Haiti, raising the question of Haitian identity and whether the original community is more rooted and real than the migrant one. Similarly, the recent Bosnian Muslim diaspora is partly held together through regular Internet communication (Lejla Somun pers. comm.), and while this does not have the same dynamic as an immediate face-to-face community, it is a real community although communing via the computer screen. Diasporas are a major feature of the modern world and cannot be studied by conventional ethnographic methods, based around living in one small community, learning the language and then writing the authoritative monograph which presents the community, whilst at the same time throwing light on central problems of anthropology (Clifford 1997: chap. 10).

A last, but not least, aspect of globalism takes us back to the economic, in that the products of transnationals are sold and bought everywhere, raising the question of whether these foreign items produced for profit are over-whelming local cultural products and forms. The present conventional answer is that televisions, ghetto blasters, outboard motors and fridges are appropri-ated according to local logics and add a new dimension to local life rather than submerging it (Miller 1995). There is much truth to this tribute to local resis tance and agency, which is a vital antidote to the nineteenth-century feeling that all local cultures were doomed to die out (Dilworth 1996). But it perhaps also needs stating that there is a massive loss of languages in the world today. It is calculated that of the roughly 6,000 languages in the world, 3,000 are in the process of dying out and 2,400 are endangered (P. Trudgill, *Times Higher Educational Supplement* 8 May 1998: 26). Given that language is central to cul-tural values, with the loss of language must go many aspects of cultural integrity and the causes of this loss have not been adequately probed, nor have the consequences. Nineteenth-century predictions of cultures dying out were predicated on the idea that small-scale societies could not possibly resist the forces of superior civilisations. This is clearly nonsense, but we may now be going too far in the other direction in saying that global forces will always be shaped and accommodated creatively within local cultures.

All these facets of global culture, and more, have raised a new problem cen-tral for anthropology: the relationship between the global and the local. On the one hand, there is the local situation (the Trobriand Islanders, the Nuer, the Zuñi) which was the traditional locus of study for anthropologists. On the other, is the new global culture (or perhaps a new realisation that there is a global culture). The conventional anthropological tools for approaching all problems are the key concepts of 'society' and 'culture'. Strathern (1995) feels that society, which is to do with relations between individuals and groups, is always a locally based concept. Society was a key means through which anthropologists linked parts of their data, for instance by looking at the con-nections between kinship and economic organisation, or wealth and the inher-itance of property (Strathern 1995: 158). Society served a range of purposes as an idea, but all of these were on a spatially restricted scale where anthro-pologists felt most confident. Culture is much trickier, being both about the diversity of forms of human life and at the root of people's sense of local identity. Culture partakes of both the local and the global and there is no easy means to distinguish between the two within the concept itself. Part of the problem is with the terms 'global' and 'local' and we need to decide if either is adequate to the different scales at which anthropologists must now work.

One way out of these dilemmas is to develop new forms of ethnographic study. Marcus (1986) has advocated a multi-site ethnography, where a local phenomenon can only be studied in terms of its connections to elsewhere, so that a team of field workers operate at different points within the system to understand its workings as a whole, some examples of which are given below. All these new forms of fieldwork are oriented to illuminating the problems of the contemporary world, rather than documenting the vanishing customs of primitive peoples as were the earliest forms of fieldwork. New areas of study also present themselves, such as the forms and mores of the scientific culture lying behind global forms (Martin 1996) and mass media so vital in making connections and promulgating cultural values (Das 1995, Abu-Lughod 1995). Nevertheless, they do not really get to grips with the differences between the global and the local. The relationship between the two is not just a question of scale: global culture (if it exists) is not just a bigger version of local cultures.

One dimension of the difference is to do with the nature of social life and interaction in either the local or the global sphere. A local culture can be seen to operate, at least partly, through face-to-face interaction, whereby people regularly meet, talk, fight or carry out ritual activity. People are known to each other and have the same sets of habits and taken-for-granteds. One aspect of the global culture, as we have seen above, is what is called space-time compression, whereby people can interact on a regular basis even though they are far from each other: phones, fax and the Internet facilitate such links. Air travel brings people together physically. In 1993 1.2 billion air travellers left their countries on international flights (compared with 400 million in 1989) and the rate of increase has at least been maintained since then (Cheater 1995: 124). However, although these people are mixed into some sort of community, it is not one of shared habits, values and well-known conflicts in the same way as a local culture is.

So much of anthropological thought was developed around the notion of the local that not just new methods of study, but also fresh attitudes to thought and knowledge are needed once the relative security of the small-scale and the local have been given up. My feeling is that problems of fitting together global and local scales of analysis cannot be tackled in the abstract but only through looking at specific cases where local action at any point on the globe is enmeshed in broader circumstances. Nevertheless, there is a new spirit and imagination in the air within anthropology to do with questioning the relationship of the metropolitan centres to the rest of the world and it is to this that I now turn.

Globalism, knowledge and representation

In the early days of anthropology the centre studied the periphery: the expedition to the Torres Strait, for instance, sent out a group of trained professionals who brought back information, objects, images and sound recordings to the British metropolitan centres from which they came. Haddon, Rivers and their team, although they were sympathetic to the locals whom they met, saw their task as taking folk knowledge and converting it into real scientific knowledge. This was the essence of Rivers' study of kinship: one could record the random and scattered knowledge of the natives and transform this into systematic knowledge of the structure of the society, to be represented in the form of a kinship diagram, which could then form the basis for understanding all sorts of social interactions and links, from the economy, to ritual and even sensory perceptions. But if we accept that all sorts of people and cultures can coexist and operate together in the new global culture, there is no reason to privilege one form of local knowledge over another, so that western forms of thought are not automatically regarded as inherently superior.

Once again this transforms the project of anthropology, or at least it would if it was taken seriously Moore (1996b: 3) has pointed out although many anthropologists have taken for granted that the people they study have internally consistent and logical forms of thought, these knowledges are seen as essentially local and cannot be taken to be forms of social science. This is partly because local forms of thought are seen to lack consistent self-criticism, they are thus folk knowledge and of local applicability only. Although these are not ideas that many would now subscribe to positively, they are demonstrated in negative fashion by the lack of citation of non-western scholars of schools of thought by anthropologists. Moore refers to a series of African thinkers, many of whom are theologians or historians, and none of whom are regularly cited by anthropologists, to make her point.

It not just in the area of thought that anthropological practice is changing. Anthropologists are becoming much more aware of the power of representation, which is not just a mode of presenting facts to the world, but one which channels the anthropologist's own perceptions of the world and has a determinate influence on those receiving the work. I want to return to the question of museum collections and how these now operate in a world of competing claims on cultural property and knowledge.

In chapter 2 we left museum collections with Pitt Rivers at the end of the nineteenth century. In this period museums were seen as means of displaying the primitive and exotic to an interested European, American and Australasian public. Museums were also vital in documenting ways of life about to die out under the pressures of colonialism (Griffiths 1996). The sole emphasis was on the needs of the western audience and the thought that the people being represented should have had some say in how they were portrayed would have seemed ridiculous to the majority of museum curators.

The indigenous voice can now attract the attention of the western ear, partly through a series of well-publicised cases. One of the best-known concerns the Glenbow Museum in Calgary, which put on an exhibition called 'The Spirit Sings: Artistic Traditions of Canada's First Peoples' to coincide with the Winter Olympics in January 1988. The Lubicon Lake Cree boycotted the Olympics and organised a series of demonstrations to draw world attention to a forty-year-old land claim. 'The Spirit Sings' exhibition became the centre of the boycott as its major sponsor was Shell Oil Canada Ltd, who were drilling for oil in the exact area of the land claim. As Bernard Ominayak, the Chief of the Lubicon Lake Cree said: 'The irony of using a display of North American Indian artifacts to attract people to the Winter Olympics being organised by interests who are still actively seeking to destroy Indian people, seems obvious' (quoted in Harrison 1988: 6). The curator's response was that 'Museums, like Universities, are expected by their constitutions, to remain non-partisan' (quoted in Harrison 1988: 8), to which the Lubicon Lake Cree replied that the acceptance of corporate sponsorship was already a political act. Such dramas, in which museums are seen (or unwittingly present themselves) as agents of western hegemony have been played out many times over the last twenty years, with some of the best-publicised cases based around the repatriation of cultural material. I shall look at just one such case.

The Maori ancestral house, Mataatua, was built in 1874 and was named after the canoe which first brought the descendants of all the Awa people who came to inhabit the Bay of Plenty area of the North Island of New Zealand. The house was built to cement an alliance of the Mataatua Confederation of tribes after kinship links had been fractured in the Land Wars (1860–72), when Maori fought Maori after government confiscation of land, at a time when the introduction of rifles had exacerbated tribal tensions, making their consequences more fatal. Mataatua was a meeting house for the new Confederation and a symbol of unity as tribes negotiated with the government over land in March 1875. Mataatua was in some sense a colonial product, but it also embodied much pre-colonial philosophy (see Neich 1996 for a general history of Maori meeting houses). Ancestors, viewed from a western perspective as being behind a person, are seen by Maori as being in front of them, together with the whole of the past (Allen 1998: 144). The future is created always with respect for the past, so that past and future mingle in a manner they do not in western thought. The meeting house symbolises these ancestral links.

> The front of the house is the face with an eye, the window, and mouth, the doorway, always open to welcome you inside. The gable mask is connected to the ridge pole, the backbone of the ancestor's body. From there the ribs connect to the side posts, *poupou* and the named ancestors carry their bloodlines to these *poupou* who are named, and define the powerful allegiances.
>
> (Allen 1998: 145)

The house is both a body and body politic, so that in the case of Mataatua the side-posts represented each of the ancestors of the major tribal groups. Meetings were held in the midst of the ancestors and only their power could allow correct and validated decisions to be made.

Maori houses, appreciated by westerners mainly for the beauty of the carving and construction, became common museum exhibits in the late nineteenth century. For Maoris the loss of a house always represented a diminution of identity, spiritual and political power, and social cohesiveness.

Mataatua was dismantled in 1879 and sent by the New Zealand government to the Sydney Exhibition, against the protest of many Ngati Awa, including the carvers of the house Apanui Te Hamaiwaho and his son Wepiha Apanui. Mataatua then went to the South Kensington Museum in 1882 (the South Kensington Museum was set up with money and exhibits from the Great Exhibition of 1851 and became the Victoria and Albert Museum in 1899, part of a complex of monuments to imperialism in South Kensington; see Barringer 1998). The house was originally exhibited in the quadrangle of the South Kensington Museum with the interior carvings turned outwards, to provide greatest appeal to the western audience, but further compromising the *mana* of a house already badly abused (Allen 1998: 149). A year later Mataatua was moved to the grounds of the Museum and four years later was dismantled and stored. The house was again displayed at the British Empire Exhibition in Wembley in 1924, but then, due to the efforts of Harry Skinner, who was instrumental in setting up both anthropology and archaeology in New Zealand, the house was returned to New Zealand for the New Zealand and South Seas Exhibition in Dunedin in 1925. After this Mataatua was given to the Otago Museum at which Skinner was Curator. In order to fit it within the museum Mataatua was shortened, losing sections connecting it to the Ranginui and Papatuanuku groups, thus obscuring its unique origins in a confederacy of tribes.

Of recent years there has been negotiation between Ngati Awa people and the Crown through the Treaty of Waitangi (a treaty set up in 1840 to reach agreements between Maori people and the Crown and which recently has come to have enormous importance as a means of creating new sets of relationships between government and Maori groups through the Waitangi Tribunal). In 1990, Ngati Awa published *Nga Karoretanga o Mataatua Whare* (*The Wanderings of the Carved House Mataatua*) and in 1994 presented their case to the tribunal (Allen 1998: 151). In 1996 the Waitangi Tribunal recommended to the Crown that Mataatua be returned to Ngati Awa, where it will be rebuilt on a new *marae*. Other houses have similarly been removed from tribal lands, such as the only complete house now in Britain, Hinemihi at Clandon Park in Surrey (Hooper-Greenhill 1998), except that in this case an agreement has been reached that this house should stay in Britain as a symbol of Maori culture and a point of reference for visiting Maori.

The transactions involving Mataatua form a sort of multi-site ethnography of the type advocated by Marcus (1986) involving agencies in many parts of the world, as well as the changing role of the social actors over time. Up until the Second World War the main role Maori people played in the public side of exhibitions was as living exhibits – for instance, there was a whole village of Maori at the Festival of the Empire in 1911, a form of exoticism of great appeal to a western audience. In the last few decades the major change has been for Maori people themselves to become active protagonists in the official side of museums and exhibits. The exhibition 'Te Maori: Treasures from New Zealand' which toured North America in 1984 and 1985 caused much debate about the degree of control Maori people should have over the way their cultural treasures are displayed. 'Te Maori' has also come to be seen as a model for indigenous involvement in creating exhibitions the world over.

All these issues together have caused a massive change in the ways in which indigenous peoples, museum professionals and the general public view the role of museums today. Gone is the notion that a museum displays other cultures, as exotic and radically different, which are of interest, but ultimately doomed to die out under the pressures of western expansion. The way forward for museums is not entirely clear, revolving as it does around negotiations between all interested parties, but it is changing rapidly and positively. Here Clifford's (1997: chap. 7) idea of the museum as a contact zone and an area of intercultural debate and exchange is a compelling one. The ethnographic museum collection is made up of objects crucial to the lives of many and embodying sets of skills and beliefs central to cultural values. Some groups want these objects returned, either for their intrinsic cultural value or for the aid they can bring in pursuing political struggles for land and cultural restitution. Other groups are happy for the artefacts to remain in museums as links between their culture and a different social world. Many groups want to set up continuing dialogue and relationships with museums so that there should be the movement of artefacts, people and information back and forth, not only between the museum and the local group concerned, but also between that group and the community within which the museum is located. Museums can thus become points for cultural interchange, rather than centres for the accumulation of cultural capital. The new information technology of Internet and CD-ROM is obviously going to be important here, moving information back and forth rapidly and bringing collections of artefacts and their related information together in virtual form in cases where this cannot be done physically.

Another important effect of the change in views of anthropological knowledge has been to make museums and anthropologists in general more self-conscious about means of representation. With this self-consciousness has come the realisation that the history of representation offers vital insights into the history of anthropology in general, a realisation most obvious in areas like photography and film. Photography for anthropological purposes started almost as soon as it was possible to take photographs, in the 1860s, and for several decades, until just after the First World War, photography was a dominant mode of documentation within anthropology (Edwards 1992). This is not to say that more photographs were taken then than later, but that in its early years photography was seen as a realistic documentary medium above all others, vital for recording the physical forms of people and everyday settings of action and material culture. Now early photographs are a dual record, both of the cultures they recorded, but equally of the people doing the recording. Not all photographers have been westerners and an early, famous example of a local photographer is George Hunt, a Kwakiutl Indian, supplied with camera and film by Boas (Jacknis 1992). Much can be learnt from looking at what was photographed, how scenes were arranged for the photographer and how photographs and lantern slides were used in publications and lectures to help bring the exotic home and as proof that what the anthropologist claimed to have recorded was actually there.

In confronting issues of representation museums may well form a micro-cosm of anthropology as a whole. Anthropology can no longer be one small section of the world talking about the rest, with complete confidence that its own views are superior or better grounded in reality. Rather, anthropological knowledge is one form of knowledge amongst many and is a set of negotiated understandings between professional and local people, with the professional picked out as having a set of skills in intercultural understanding and exchange. The future is about setting up forms of dialogue and negotiation between different bodies and types of knowledge, rather than anthropologists holding that their conclusions are superior, as more rational, systematically arrived at and open to criticism.

One important aspect of local values that we have not yet looked at is that of ethnic identity, which once seemed an unproblematical aspect of people's lives, but now with the old certainties gone, is open to question.

Ethnic identity

The problem of ethnicity is an easy one to recognise, but is difficult to define. Ethnicity has to do with differences between peoples and/or groups which have some sort of self-identity and boundedness from others. The notion of ethnicity overlaps with those of race and of nation, putting it at the heart of a whole series of questions to do with the parcelling up of human differences and their political or social significance. Both a strength and weakness of the idea of ethnicity is its wide range. Questions arise as to how and why Croats are different from Serbs, or Tutsis from Hutus; but also what are the nature or significance of black, white and hispanic differences in a multicultural nation like America. Within archaeology parallel queries concern whether the Celts of late prehistoric Europe were a people; do the Lapita assemblages of the western Pacific represent incoming Austronesian speakers; or how far is it pos-sible to trace back Native American groups known from the last few centuries into the prehistoric past? All these questions go under the rubric of ethnicity, but it is not at all clear whether they are problems of the same type and there is the suspicion that some of them may arise from the process of academic categorisation, rather than existing as real-world problems.

In a recent excellent review of anthropological approaches to ethnicity, Banks (1996) distinguishes three main attitudes to ethnicity: primordialism, instrumentalism and a category of the analyst's own making. Primordialism 'holds that ethnicity is an innate aspect of human identity' (Banks 1996: 39). Following the view that ethnic differences have always existed and will con-tinue to do so, the problem becomes one of description rather than explana-tion of the origin and form of ethnic differences. For many, ethnic identity arises from the attachments of kinship, through blood and marriage and the normative effects of shared custom and language, which can only result in people being bound together.

> These congruities of blood, speech and custom, and so on, are seen to have an ineffable, and at times overpowering, coerciveness in and of themselves. One is bound to one's kinsman, one's neighbour, one's fellow believer, *ipso facto*; as the result not merely of personal affection, practical necessity, common interest, or incurred obligation, but at least in great part by virtue of some unaccountable absolute import attributed to the very tie itself.
>
> (Geertz 1993a: 259)

A well-developed version of primordialism is found in the work of the Soviet theorist, Yulian Bromley, which was partly a response to the persistence of local differences within the Soviet Union despite Stalin's attempts to impose some sort of overriding Soviet culture. For Bromley (1980) an 'ethnos' (ethnic identity in an abstract sense) or 'ethnikos' (a specific manifestation of ethnic difference) have persisted through all the social formations identified by Marxist theory from primitive communism to present socialism. The Ukrainian or Georgian ethnikos can be traced back to the feudal period and beyond, but is also potent as a force in people's contemporary lives, partly as an element of resistance to the forces of homogenisation within the (then) contemporary Soviet Union. The importance of local differences has become even more important with the break-up of the Soviet Union and to be Chechen, Kirgiz or Tungus involves resistance to the dominant Russian power, but also necessitates the (re)invention of new cultural forms within an uncharted political present. Although mainly primordialist, Bromley's approach to ethnicity also held within it elements of instrumentalism or situationalism, both labels for the view that ethnic differences are created or emphasised when it is politically or economically advantageous for people to do so.

The work of Fredrick Barth, the most influential of all recent writers on ethnicity, also combines elements of both primordialism and situationalism, although with a stress firmly on the situational aspects of ethnicity. Barth (1969: 10–11) outlines what he sees as the most common elements of a definition of ethnic groups in the literature to that date: that they are biologically self-perpetuating, bounded, sharing fundamental social values in common, forming a field of communication more intense than with those outside the group and conscious of an identity also recognised by others. Barth argued that we should look less at the markers of ethnic difference in terms of dress, food, language or custom, and more at how the boundaries of groups are created and maintained despite the flow of people, information and materials across these boundaries. One of his best-known examples of the importance of boundaries comes from his own work in the 1950s on the Pathan

population of western Pakistan and Afghanistan. The Pathans live in a territory of roughly 180,000 square km, which is ecologically varied and divided
between two nation states. Pathans have lots of different ways of making a living, as pastoralists, settled agriculturalists, urban migrants or mobile traders,
and keep up a mass of contacts with other groups. Given this diversity of
ecology, economy, contacts and nationhood, how far can Pathans claim to be
a single group?

In attempting an answer Barth concentrated on the boundaries of the
Pathan group. The southern boundary of the Pathan territory was most
important, where the Pathan met the Baluchis. The latter were an expanding
group, moving northward, a movement which was complemented by a steady
number of Pathans who became Baluchi (although the reverse never seemed to
have happened). Baluchis, according to Barth, had a means of incorporating
people from other groups, as they were organised into client groups under
chiefs and sub-chiefs. Anyone submitting to a leader could become a Baluchi
and this contrasted with Pathan views of their group, which was seen to be
descended from a common ancestor so that only this blood link entitles individuals to be Pathans. Barth felt that numbers of Pathans were being displaced
from their social positions through war, crime and accident and thus faced a
choice either to become a marginalised member of their own group or to
become Baluchi. In a society where male honour was paramount, the latter
was often the preferable alternative in Barth's view. Banks (1996: 16) has criticised Barth's stress on the voluntary nature of Pathan movements, saying that
an alternative explanation is to see the Baluchis as an expansionary group
moving into Pathan territory, who are able to categorise the incomers as members of their own group.

The structure of Barth's explanation fits in well with his overall view of ethnicity and the persistence of ethnic boundaries as a form of adaptation to an
ecological or socio-economic niche. In a different example, Barth (1969:
19–26) took up Haaland's (1969) analysis of the Fur and the Baggara in the
Darfur region of Sudan. The Fur engage in sedentary hoe agriculture of millet, whilst the Baggara are nomadic cattle herders and there is little competition between them. However, some Fur have adopted the lifestyle and identity
of the Arabic Baggara as a response to the lack of opportunities in their agricultural economy and live by the potentially greater rewards of cattle herding.
In both the Pathan and the Fur cases Barth saw ethnicity as a strategy, either as
a means of getting out of a difficult situation, or as a way into a better one.
This is the heart of the instrumentalist view whereby ethnicity is seen as a collectively organised strategy for the enhancement or protection of political or
economic interests. Barth, however, has something of a bet both ways in
stressing instrumentalism, but at the same time not questioning the ethnic
categories of Pathan, Baluchi, Baggara and Fur which gives his work some
element of primordialism.

A more thoroughgoing instrumentalism is found in the work of people like
Cohen (1969), who sees not just that people will swap ethnic identities for

reasons of advantage, but will reconfigure ethnic identity if this is necessary to further the social strategies they are pursuing, thus making ethnicity a much more plastic element of human identity. Cohen worked among the Hausa of newly independent Nigeria in the early 1960s, focusing his work on the Hausa traders of Ibadan, a southern Nigerian town. The Hausa of Ibadan are migrants from the north, but are unlike other migrant communities to southern Nigeria in that they display a tightly organised set of communities differentiated from the Yoruba majority. Cohen sees the reasons for this distinctiveness in the Hausa need to maintain a monopoly over the trade in cattle and kola nuts. The trade in kola nuts (chewed as a stimulant throughout west Africa) is between Hausa traders in the south and Hausa in the north. This trade reflects patterns of production in that the nuts are only grown in the south, but much used in the north. Cattle move in the reverse direction, as the tseste fly in the south mean that cattle cannot be raised there. Both forms of trade require high degrees of trust, credit and co-operation and these are much easier to achieve amongst people who all consider themselves Hausa than between people from differing groups.

Trade is a small part of a complex story in which identity has played a large part. In the lead-up to Nigerian independence Hausa integrity in the south was being eroded, partly through the Yoruba majority adopting Islam, which had previously been the preserve of the Hausa. The southern Hausa response was to retribalise (Cohen 1969: 1–3) and almost all of them became members of the Tijaniyya order, a particular Muslim Brotherhood. In order to accommodate to changes in Yorubaland the Hausa of Ibadan differentiated themselves from the Hausa of the north, so that new migrants from the north had to learn how to be Hausa in Ibadan. Also, those originally from other groups can become Hausa as long as they can speak Hausa, claim origin from a place within Hausaland, are Muslim and have no facial scars or other bodily features that would assign them to another group. Cohen's study is a rich and rounded one, showing that identity responds not just to the economic imperatives of trade, but also the complex inter-group rivalries and differences brought about by both colonialism and subsequent political independence. If we were to write the conclusions of his study large, we would have to conclude that African tribal identity is not a primordial fact, surviving into the present as a relic from pre-colonial days, but rather a vital element in the struggle between colonialist and colonised and various groups vying for position in a fast-changing world.

The third possible position on ethnicity, to return to Banks, is that it is simply a category in the analyst's head and has little or no existence out there in the world. Many tools of analysis (kinship being a prime example; see Needham 1971) have been shown to be simply that, and anthropologists have been in danger of mistaking their model of reality for reality itself. However, to take this view too much to heart would mean expunging the term ethnicity totally from our intellectual vocabularies and this would leave too much unsaid, even if this is partly due to the fact that we are used to viewing the world in ethnic terms. Banks' (1996: 189–90) recommendation, with which I agree, is that it is too late to stop using the term, but that we should only continue its use if we are aware that the instrument of study is shaping both the world and our perception of that world.

Archaeology and ethnicity

In archaeology the notion of ethnicity has only recently come to the fore and this is because both race and culture, concepts used to categorise human difference since the nineteenth century, have been rejected in a variety of ways and for many different reasons as the century has gone on. The idea of race had a complex field of thought surrounding it in the last century, but it has never come back into favour again since the abuses of the Nazi period. The New Archaeology rejected a view of culture as representing different peoples, stressing instead local adaptations to the environment and culture as a set of functional purposes. Post-processualism reinstated a human world made up of differences in identity and the work of Barth was very influential in inspiring work on boundaries between groups, conceived in ethnic terms (although the word 'ethnic' itself was not used often).

There is no space here to go into the tangled history of thought on race in the last century, but certain points need to made either to explore the absence of the concept now or the manner in which the space left by its absence has been filled by other ideas. Stocking (1987: 19) has pointed out that until the early nineteenth century there was no real idea that human beings were divided into a series of different cultures each with their own different world. Once people were seen to be incommensurably different, the way was opened up for the discussion of the difference in physical terms as well as in language, artefacts or customs. The developing study of human anatomy allowed people such as Cuvier to create racial categories on the basis of physiological differences (Stocking 1968). The most extreme view on the importance of racial differences was held by the polygenesists, who felt that different races had distinct origins and varying human groups derived from variations in people's mental and physical abilities. The monogenesists, on the other hand, saw all humans as having a single origin, with subsequent divergences due to environmental differences. Language was the key to how and when people diverged, as the data from linguistics was thought to span much of human history.

Both monogenesist and polygenesist thought were thrown into new perspective by the recognition of high human antiquity and the acceptance of Darwin's theories in the middle of the century. The culture-evolutionary stages of Morgan, Tylor and Spencer emphasised cultural and technological differences, rather than variation in physical type. Race did not go away, however, but formed the unexamined background to all other forms of difference and many made an equation between race, language and culture. Of course, the general background of colonialism contributed to the unconscious reinforcement of the link between cultural, linguistic and physical differences –

the White Man's Burden was a male, paternalistic view, but also one that used skin colour to stand for physical differences as a whole. As Clifford (1988: 234) says the dominance of a notion of culture has come about partly as a liberal alternative to the term 'race'.

It was the Nazis' use of race that has made it such a dangerous term for all those who came after. Kossina's work and its use by the National Socialists was aimed to demonstrate the historical importance of the German 'master race'. Himmler founded the SS organisation, *Deutsches Ahnenerbe* (German Ancestral Inheritance) which carried out excavations designed to demonstrate the expansion of Germans into Poland, southern Russia and the Caucasus in prehistory and later, which acted as historical justification for the invasion of those countries in the last war (Arnold 1990, McCann 1990). Childe, who had written on the Aryans himself, wrote a critique of the nascent Nazi ideas to distance himself from them (Childe 1933). Although there has been little other criticism until recently (see Jones 1997: chap. 1 for an overview of literature past and present), any equation between race and culture (or other biological difference) has been absent through the middle of this century and more recent attempts to link the two, such as sociobiology, have struggled continuously to insist on a non-racist use of biology. Here the main attempt has been to show that non-genetic aspects of human groups (material culture, language and customs) are influenced to a great degree by bounded genetic groups, with kin relations seen as the link between culture and biology (van den Berghe 1978). Sociobiological ideas have had little impact on archaeology or anthropology as a whole, but this may change with the increasing influence of DNA work which will have the net effect of making biology more prominent within the social sciences.

Ethnicity started to come back on to the intellectual agenda within archaeology with post-processualist critiques of the functionalist approach to culture on the part of New Archaeology. Binford and others, as representatives of New Archaeology, stressed the functional and adaptive aspects of culture and style was mainly an adornment which received some study in terms of how patterns of artefact types were transmitted from one generation to the next (Flannery 1976, Plog 1978, 1983). Sackett was the only internal critic of approaches to group difference within New Archaeology, an argument he pursued mainly in terms of the understanding of style (Sackett 1977, 1985). The most influential critique has been that of Hodder (1979, 1982) where he looked at the nature of boundaries between groups through ethnoarchaeological work. The overall thrust of the work was to show that identity is created by symbolic means and is negotiated and manipulated, rather than existing as an unproblematical category. In this Hodder is in tune with the instrumentalist approaches to ethnicity within anthropology, and his stress on boundaries derives some inspiration from Barth. Even so, there is very little explicit discussion of ethnicity in Hodder's work and it is only in more recent work that the term is central to archaeological analysis.

Prime amongst these is Jones' (1997) review of the concept of ethnicity in archaeology and the possible influence of anthropology on archaeological ideas. Jones starts from the view that material culture is active in creating people's identities and she cites MacKenzie's work on *bilums*, amongst other studies, to show how complex is the relationship between things and people. Jones (1997: 120) also criticises many instrumentalist views of ethnicity as not looking at the relationship between culture and ethnicity, without which there is no basis for understanding the generation of ethnicity and the specific forms it takes. Jones takes the theory of practice and particularly the notion of habitus as a means to understand how ethnicity is generated and deployed, deriving as it does from both the conscious and unconscious dispositions that people have inculcated within them. Viewed in terms of archaeological evidence, prime amongst which is the distribution of material culture, there may be occasions (such as in Hodder's [1982b] Baringo study) where boundaries between assemblages of items indicate ethnic boundaries and there may be other occasions where there is little correlation between ethnic groups and the material culture they make and use. Ethnicity is also linked to other forms of identity, such as social hierarchy and gender (Jones 1997: 125). The links between these different facets of identity can be judged through looking at the specific history of a region, as ethnicity arises from intersections in the similarities and differences in people's *habitus* and allows one to look at how unconscious patterns of life are transformed in self-consciously used symbols. Groups are never static entities but always in the process of becoming.

These concerns tie in to the issue of nationalism and its multiple effects on archaeology. Nationally based traditions have affected archaeological studies in different countries, and also the results from archaeology have been used as justification for the existence and continuation of the nation state (Díaz-Andreu and Champion 1996, Graves-Brown *et al.* 1996, Kohl and Fawcett 1995).

The example Jones uses is that of the Romanization of southern Britain in the Iron Age. Jones's first step is to do away with the ethnic groups generally assumed for the late Iron Age and Roman periods – native and Roman or the various tribal groups thought be in existence (the Iceni, the Durotriges, etc.). Instead she looks at the different contexts and locales (rural settlements, nucleated settlements, forts and so on) in which different classes of material culture were used. She concentrates on certain well-excavated and published sites (Kelvedon, Skeleton Green, Gorhambury and King Harry Lane) which date to the late Iron Age and Roman periods. In looking at these sites much heterogeneity is apparent, which contradicts the idea of Romanization as a uniform process. Broad changes in architecture are found, for instance, such as the move to masonry construction and greater symmetry in the lay-out of the buildings, but there are lags in rural areas and differences in speed of change between one region and another. Skeleton Green shows early changes and, whereas similar changes occur in Gorhambury, these are not until later. Pottery assemblages change in terms of both form and fabric over both Essex and Hertfordshire, but changes show up differently in various contexts, suggesting that change is modified by the role and status of the people using the pottery. These statuses cannot be glossed straightforwardly as Roman versus native, but rather can be viewed as being part of an integrated cultural field in which all involved, incomers and locals, found themselves involved in new relationships and becoming new people as a result. The Romans were as much a product of the Empire as the natives, so that the Roman Empire as a whole can be seen as constantly creating and recreating new identities as it expanded across Eurasia and Africa, rather than simply bringing into contact existing groups who met, but preserved the differences they brought to the meeting. Roman colonialism is one instance of imperialism at work, which has provided something of a model for later colonial structures. It is to the most recent forms of colonialism, or rather post-colonialism that I now turn.

Post-colonial theory: Said, Spivak and Bhabha

In getting to grips with the new sets of relationships in the present world, both archaeologists and anthropologists are coming to terms with its decolonised state and are drawing on bodies of literature, partly deriving from literary studies, social theory and history to develop tools of thought for tackling the post-colonial world.

Many have argued that the present state of the world, where colonies are few but the colonial legacy is omnipresent, requires new forms of thought and discussion. These new forms go jointly under the name of post-colonial theory, although, as we shall see, a single title is misleading for such a complex phenomenon. Complexity is partly due to the variety of theoretical influences, but also to the shape-shifting nature of colonialisms and their subsequent histories. Some threads can be followed and, at the theoretical level, these are provided by the pervasive influence of French social theorists, the most influential of whom are Derrida and Foucault. Foucault's ideas on power and Derrida's analysis of discourse have been used by people such as Edward Said, Gayatri Spivak and Homi Bhabha to uncover the Eurocentric biases of much First World discussion of colonialism, the nature of global culture and marginality within that culture in the present, the roots of contemporary global connections in the colonialisms of last five centuries and how far marginal groups are coming to have a voice within the global cacophony of competing interests. I shall start with the theory, as this is the prior basis for analysis, but also because it is subject to considerable reconstruction through application to post-colonial problems, as we shall see later.

Although Derrida, Foucault and others, such as Lacan, have helped structure much of post-colonial theory in the last two decades, there has also been some resistance to their ideas as putting straightforward propositions in an incomprehensible form – the charge that has been raised against their ideas almost everywhere. As Derek Walcott said of French theory, 'It convinces one that Onan was a Frenchman' (Walcott 1989: 141). More serious is the tension between Marxism, in its various forms, and French theory. Many see that it is impossible to understand colonial histories purely through analysis of discourse and regimes of knowledge, without acknowledging the violence of original dispossession, the ensuing economic exploitation and continued recourse to armed force by all colonial regimes. Marxism, with its emphasis on the economic and social relations involved in exploitation, is seen as the means for understanding the hardest realities of colonialism. However, such are the complexities of the field that others reject Marxism as shot through with western schemes of history of millennial hopes for the future and attempting to impose universal values on the world as a whole (Moore-Gilbert 1997: 3).

Foucault was concerned with the links between power and knowledge. People are created as subjects within particular regimes of knowledge and discourse, so that their views of themselves, their place in the world and the nature of that world itself are structured by particular symbolic schemes which give shape and meaning to the world. Power and knowledge are intimately linked, because 'discourse produces reality; it produces domains of objects and rituals of truth' (Foucault 1979: 194). In his view the last few centuries have seen a change from a complex set of medieval powers to the rise of state-dominated societies which work through series of rationalist habits of thought codified in scientific discourse, the rule of law and the records of centralised bureaucracies. These powers do not form a coherent and consistent whole, but are animated by some of the same principles of rationalism and control. They also do not represent a repressive structure imposed from above, but rather the general atmosphere of thought and appreciation within which all live. In this sense power can be creative: creating particular views of the world, aesthetic appreciations of social and physical relations and systematised means of investigation of both social and physical phenomena. As people are created as subjects within particular regimes of knowledge and power, they take these for granted and assume that they are natural. The all-pervasive nature of knowledge/power leaves little scope for resistance and overall Foucault's thought is pessimistic, seeing history as the movement from one regime of domination to another. Whether such pessimism is warranted and whether the notion of all-pervasive regimes of power/knowledge is a good model for colonial relations are both questions open to debate, as we shall see. Foucault had a major influence on post-colonial theory and this was first expressed in the work of Edward Said.

Said can be seen as the most influential of the post-colonial theorists. His book, *Orientalism* (Said 1978), has attracted enormous attention, negative as well as positive. His basic premise is a simple one: the west has created and maintained a simplified, clichéd and essentialised view of the east through much of its history. Continuing structures of representation produce the east as inferior, being variously voiceless, sensual, female, despotic, irrational and backward, as against the west's view of itself as masculine, democratic, rational, moral, dynamic and progressive. These characterisations come through even in the writing of people who are sympathetic to the east. Said uses Foucault to show how the academic and cultural apparatus of the west produced this 'truth' about the East, so that cultural works joined seamlessly to political action and the writings of Kipling might subtly reinforce claims to intervene in, or further westernise, conquered territories. Like Foucault, Said is pessimistic about the possibility of resistance, either by subject peoples or those within the west who reject the dominant stereotype and he sees Orientalism as dating back to the Greeks, at least, so that this cliché has become a natural part of the west's perception of the non-western world.

Said's work has had a major influence on people in the west, writing on eastern history and culture. *Orientalism* has also come in for much criticism: it is said to be bad history, creating a stereotype out of much more varied views of the east by the west; it leaves out the dimension of gender and it only analyses western discourse and argues with western academics ignoring the voice of the colonised and their discourse (Clifford 1988, Young 1990). Said (1993) has gone on to look at the general effect that imperialism has had on western culture and the lack of acknowledgement of this influence. He also now sees the existence of a common culture throughout the world rooted in the experience of colonialism, linking colonised and coloniser alike. Working through this common history can lead to a common dialogue of liberation.

Derrida had a major influence in shaping the thought of the second of the post-colonial theorists I shall consider, Gayatri Spivak. Derrida concentrates almost exclusively on the manner in which meaning is constructed and the means by which dominant meanings might be disrupted. The notion of text is crucial to his view and by this he means not just written texts, but all structures of signification through which meanings are created. Derrida starts from the margins of texts, eschewing more conventional forms of criticism which concentrate on the overall structure of the plot and the intentions of the author. Derrida focuses on what authors did not intend, those revealing slips of the tongue or loose ends in construction, which at first sight seem irrelevant but on further consideration provide a vital clue to the whole. Derrida seizes on a loose end to deconstruct the text, to unravel its basic assumptions and logic, but also to highlight the things which the text passes over in silence. His deconstructive method is perfectly suited to analysis of the influence of colonialism in European thought and the post-colonial theorists have seized on deconstruction as a means of showing the vital presence of colonialism at the margins of the core texts of western culture. Colonial forms of life provide background shadow and shade to highlight the development of the notion of the rational, controlled, individualised white male which lies at the heart of western liberal humanism. Such a figure could only be developed through implicit contrasts with a black mass of people, swayed by their emotions and imperfectly individuated to be found, it was thought, in all areas outside Europe. The deconstructive method, highlighting the contrasts necessary to create western humanism, poses considerable challenges for both archaeology and anthropology as both are outgrowths of liberal philosophy, and are engaged in the conscious study of the Other which has played such a major role in the unconscious creation of western thought.

In contrast to Said, Spivak takes her main inspiration from Derrida and not Foucault, wanting to address the notion that Foucault deals with real history, but Derrida only with texts. For Spivak deconstruction is not the exposure of error, but is rather about how truths are produced . This investigation into the creation of truth is to ensure that other, more liberating truths are produced. Deconstructing classic colonial texts and revealing their logics will prevent radical politics unwittingly reproducing the habits of thought they seek to undermine. Following Derridean deconstruction Spivak employs a number of strategies, such as the seeking out of minor characters like St John Rivers, the missionary to India, found in *Jane Eyre*. Or the monster in *Frankenstein*, who is not so much a minor character, as a misunderstood one: it is commonly believed that the monster took the name of its creator, rather than being a nameless other, the antithesis of civilisation. A further technique is catachresis, which involves ripping ideas and images out of their normal contexts and deploying them randomly and unexpectedly. This is the antithesis of the creation of essentialised figures, such as the Indian or the Asian, who appear constantly in colonial literature. Essentialism of this type is impossible, because of the unstable nature of all subjects. Following Lacan, who sees all individuals as emerging through a symbolic order inscribed in language, Spivak feels that all human subjects are multiple, made up of the conflictual meanings of the codes which help construct them. In a colonial situation, where coloniser and colonised alike are continually constructing different codes in opposition to each other, character is by no means straightforward, but continually re-ordered through changing sets of relationships.

Spivak, by contrast, has created no all-embracing scheme for colonial discourse, such as is found in *Orientalism*, nor is she confident of the millennial outcome to which Said now looks forward. Rather she concentrates on the variety of colonial experiences and histories and a major element seen to structure this variety is gender, so that women's experiences loom large. She also gives more place to local voices, with much less of a concentration on colonial conversations. There is considerable acknowledgement of change over time in colonial regimes, so that the diasporas created through slavery are seen as very different to the diasporas resulting from economic migrations in the post-war period. Furthermore, Spivak makes a point of exploring her position as a western-based critic of colonialism in a 'workplace engaged in the ideological production of neo-colonialism' (Spivak 1987: 210). Such a varied range of emphases in her work derives in part from the disparate nature of the theoretical positions Spivak draws on, mixing feminism, deconstructionism and a political economic strand of Marxism. Her links with the Subaltern Studies Group (Guha 1988) have also led to influence from Gramsci (who coined the term 'subaltern'), but also to a critique of their revisionist histories (Spivak 1987).

Spivak's emphasis on the symbolic construction of individuals and reality as a whole comes into conflict with her more Marxist analysis of the political and economic realities underlying colonial relations. It is very difficult to hold simultaneously that there are certain objective conditions of exploitation and repression, but that also the whole is constructed through symbolic schemes creating particular reality effects. To her credit, Spivak acknowledges, and even revels in, such contradictions which might help illuminate some of the contradictory aspects of the colonial process (Moore-Gilbert 1997: 99). A further complication is how far Spivak is guilty of 'nativism', that is claiming privileged insight into the Indian point of view through being Indian herself, albeit based in the US and far removed from the oppressed women of that sub-continent. At different times within her writings she appears as a representative of Third World women and as distanced academic, although this is a problem all cultural analysts share, as the position of analyst almost always distances the writer from those being analysed.

Further ambiguities are to be found in the work of Homi Bhabha, the third of our triad of post-colonial theorists. Bhabha, like Spivak, is concerned to expose the creation of simplified and cliched views of the colonial world. Complexity existed at the level of identity and also in the domain of knowledge, where contradiction was common. The native could be:

> both savage (cannibal) and yet the most obedient and dignified of servants (the bearer of food); he is the embodiment of rampant sexuality and yet innocent as a child; he is mystical, primitive, simple-minded and yet the most worldly and accomplished liar and manipulator of social forces.
>
> (Bhabha 1994: 82)

For Bhabha, too great a concentration on the division between coloniser and colonised is pernicious. Both patrol officer and native were involved in complex sets of negotiations and mutualities and each operated through 'forms of multiple and contradictory beliefs' about the other (Bhabha 1994: 95). However, as a measure of control the colonisers attempted to both fix the identity of the colonised in their own minds, and to alter it, with the Anglicised Indian being a case in point. However, although some Indians were encouraged to develop features of English culture this does not mean that English culture was a static entity and it too was a colonial product. Colonial contacts helped create Englishness and it was not just the Indians that were Anglicised, but also the English themselves. This is the point that Jones (1997) made about the Roman Empire: the Romans came into being as Romans through their empire. Perhaps this is a truth about all forms of imperialism; rather than being simply the imposition of the colonial culture on the natives, native and coloniser are created through the relations of colonialism. The colonial experience was much more contradictory and complex than contained in simple histories emphasising either domination or resistance.

Not only were everyday aspects of cultural life created through colonialism, but also trends of thought. It has only recently started to be realised how much subtle influence colonial relations have had on political, economic and social philosophies. It is also ironical that post-modernism, which has set itself up as a general critique of current ways of life, often sees western values as the norm. Only the west has taken part in the creation of modernity and equally only the western world has created the conditions of post-modernity, leaving out any non-western agency in the creation of global culture and relations. If in fact, as Bhabha holds, all cultures have hybrid origins and are creole forms, then all cultures in the world today are created through modernity and have played a part in creating the modern world. Lacan, Derrida and Foucault can all be criticised for assuming western culture as a norm in their work. For instance, Lacan could be criticised for not recognising that different modes of forming individual identities exist throughout the globe and for not recognising the specificity of varying forms of gender, race and class and the multitude of historical and social contexts in which these are created. It is odd that Said, Spivak and Bhabha do not subject their French influences to the same criticism as they do other works.

Whilst all three theorists excavate evidence of colonial influences in nineteenth-century novels and other writings, point out its hidden but pervasive influence or the Eurocentrism of the authors, they are much less likely to do so in the cases of Derrida, Foucault and Lacan. This is a problem with different levels. The first of these concerns how far specific analytical frameworks can be borrowed from any of the French thinkers and applied to the colonial world. To concentrate on Foucault, is it useful to apply his notion of knowledge as power to any colonial context? Foucault holds that for Europe people were formed as subjects through particular regimes of truth, coming to see the world in particular ways. Only a tiny fraction of Indian, African or Australasian colonial populations were formed as subjects through the operation of western regimes of truth. For most people the colonisers' culture remained foreign, with its own strange logic, and was an external power in their lives, rather than an internalised set of values. Power and knowledge in the colonial world were not linked in the same way as in Europe and this gave the operation of power a more straightforwardly repressive appearance in the colonies than at home. French revolutionaries, new to the ideas of liberty, equality and fraternity were still able to put down a revolt in the colony of Haiti in a bloody manner, when an export of these ideas could only have resulted in an end to colonialism in this instance (Moore-Gilbert 1997: 123). Also, Foucault's genealogy of the modern world was based on history in Europe and runs counter to changes in Europe's rule abroad. Foucault dates the emergence of the modern regime of power to around 1760 and sees the power of the spectacle (public hanging and punishment) being replaced by more bureaucratic forms of power, which incarcerated the criminal and hid the operation of power. However, 1760 is almost exactly the period of the British take-over in India, which inaugurated a whole series of spectacles of imperial pomp and punishment alike.

There are also more basic problems, which pose a challenge for all forms of western thought about colonialism. If the west's whole cultural and theoretical apparatus was constructed in a global context of colonialism how many sins of omission and commission are we committing in any social analysis? For instance, in her re-evaluation of Foucault's *History of Sexuality* Stoler (1995) points out that Foucault omits the colonial dimension totally, and in doing so allows for no systematic discussion of the links between sex and race in European history. As Bhabha says, coloniser and colonised have been mutually creating, yet European cultural and intellectual history is always written as if Europe is a self-contained entity with a history deriving from the Greeks and without any fundamental influence from the rest of the world. To do this is to bracket out 500 years of intense, unequal and complex relations with the rest of the world, and to tell a very partial story of Europe's history and its present.

Having started with colonialism in chapter 2 we have now come full circle, ending with the complexities of the present post-colonial world. Archaeology and anthropology are the products of colonialism in their genesis and early years. What we are inclined to forget is that these colonial influences are still with us. Even though many reading this book will have been born into a post-colonial world we have all been created as colonial subjects. The independence of colonies did not immediately end the influences of colonialism and make us truly post-colonial in thought and by instinct. In this sense archaeology and anthropology are engaged in two sets of tasks at once: one is to learn about the state of the modern world and its antecedents; the second is to unlearn the habits of thought which we bring to bear on the world through a thorough examination of their histories and antecedents. This process of unlearning will be helped by the realisation that the set of unequal relations which compose the modern world is just the latest in a series of global relations, historical and prehistorical.

Creating the world by way of an ending

The framework I have been starting to sketch out over the last few chapters is one which allows us to understand how people create worlds for themselves. This is not a matter of each generation creating the world anew. But people do take the world they are born into and refashion it. This is not done by individuals alone, or under circumstances of people's own choosing, but, nevertheless, people deploy their bodily skills in the physical settings available to them in order to come up with forms of life which make sense to them and within which they can act. The raw materials for the creation of a world might be purely local, but more often derive in part from the movement of materials and ideas over longer distances. I have used the notion of aesthetics as a means of encapsulating a feeling of rightness about the world, enjoining correct styles of action and response. Sahlins (1985) has put forward the idea of a cultural logic, a structure of thought and understanding underlying cultural forms. I would like to substitute the notion of a cultural aesthetics, as this takes us away from what happens in people's heads, focusing rather on a more holistic generation of culture which includes both body and mind, while attempting to erode the distinction between the two.

I have also tried to argue for the benefits of a relational view of culture, with individuals and groups crystallising as entities in some situations, but being radically transformed in others. This adds many extra dimensions immediately to what I was saying above: people are not unitary entities when they create worlds for themselves; our qualities of gender, ethnicity and rank are not born with us to remain immutable throughout our lives, but are continuously transformed by the cultural relations we enter. The worlds people create are not one thing, but many: a series of linked locales of action which have their own special properties but which take on extra significances from their position within the cultural whole. Culture is about the values that attach to people, places and things and the processes that create and change such values (Munn 1986).

Anthropology is very good at providing us with detailed knowledge of how people create worlds for themselves in the present. Although the variability of contemporary human life is vast, it is still only a tithe of that seen throughout human history. To understand how people create their lives in the present requires an understanding of the past. For instance, part of the problem of the global versus the local within anthropology today is due to an imperfect learning of the lessons of history. An archaeologist would say that for many parts of the world there has never been a purely local culture, in that people always and everywhere have been enmeshed in broader systems of exchange and contact. The new forces of globalism do not threaten local cultures, as these do not exist. From the Palaeolithic onwards there have been long-distance movements of objects and, perhaps, people (Gamble 1986). From the Bronze Age on, in Eurasia there grew up what have been called world systems within which materials moved very long distances, as did ideas and people (Chase-Dunn and Hall 1991, Frank 1993). Roman pottery has been found in Lombok in eastern Indonesia, having come via India. Similar systems of exchange operated elsewhere in the world, such as Mesoamerica and the Pacific.

However, the lessons of history go in both directions and archaeologists are coming to realise that it is impossible to take ways of life found today and use them as direct analogues through which to understand the past, as the hunter-gatherer revisionist debate shows (chap. 5). Perhaps we all need to learn the lessons of history more seriously. One way of doing this is to highlight problems of colonialism and power. Modern colonialism is just the latest and largest of a set of colonial forms found throughout history and prehistory. Just as modern-day hunter-gatherers are not 'pristine' due to their involvement in the modern world system, the same can be said of Central Asian hunter-gatherers who had relations with the Bronze Age cities of the south or north Australian groups who had regular trade relations with Indonesian states. A serious consideration of the nature of previous world systems will throw light on the nature of global and local relations in the past and their possible continuing effects into the present. The tangled natures of these histories also throws into doubt any simple notion of the origin of cultural forms, with hybridity being recently emphasised by Rowlands (1994a, 1994b) when writing on European cultural origins and in the controversial writings of Bernal (1991) on the origins of classical civilisation.

Archaeology and anthropology are making something of a return to nineteenth-century concerns with history, in which past and present can be compared, although the spirit of the enterprise is now quite different. A broad comparative project of human history can be used today to understand earlier phases of human existence and throw light on present predicaments. Together the two disciplines have considerable areas of overlap, but also a division of labour between past and present. Both are crucial in setting up forms of intercultural communication through which different versions of history can be exchanged and contrasted. Organisations such as the World Archaeological Congress are vital in creating channels of communication (Ucko 1987, 1995).

In this book I hope to have explored some of the reasons why archaeology and anthropology can usefully collaborate, despite differences in basic data and timescales. The two disciplines are drawing on and developing similar bodies of theory, in a way which they have not done for a century, around the body, aesthetics and practice. People using such theory are probably still a minority in each discipline, but a large enough minority for dialogue to take place. Whether co-operation will be long lasting, only time will tell, although it seems likely that both disciplines will change out of all recognition over the coming years. What is important for now is that past and present are so intermingled in the understanding of the contemporary scene, that both perspectives are vital; to understand the past we need to know more about how we are situated in the present.

References

Abu-Lughod, L. 1995. 'The objects of soap opera: Egyptian television and the cultural politics of modernity', in D. Miller (ed.) *Worlds Apart: Modernity Through the Prism of the Local*: 190–210. London: Routledge.

Allen, N. 1998. 'Maori vision and the imperialist gaze', in T. Barringer and T. Flynn (eds) *Colonialism and the Object: Empire, Material Culture and the Museum*: 144–152. London: Routledge.

Althusser, L. and E. Balibar. 1970. *Reading Capital*, trans. B. Brewster. London: New Left Books.

Appadurai, A. 1981. 'Gastro-politics in Hindu south Asia', *American Ethnologist* 8: 494–511.

Appadurai, A. 1988. 'How to make a national cuisine: cookbooks in contemporary India', *Comparative Studies in Society and History* 30: 3–24.

Arnold, B. 1990. 'The past as propaganda: totalitarian archaeology in Nazi Germany', *Antiquity* 64: 464–78.

Asad, T. 1973. *Anthropology and the Colonial Encounter*. London: Ithaca Press.

Banks, M. 1996. *Ethnicity: Anthropological Constructions*. London: Routledge.

Barnes, B. 1986. *About Science*. Oxford: Blackwell.

Barringer, T. 1998. 'The South Kensington Museum and the colonial project', in T. Barringer and T. Flynn (eds) *Colonialism and the Object: Empire, Material Culture and the Museum*: 11–27. London: Routledge.

Barth, F. 1969. 'Introduction', in F. Barth (ed.) *Ethnic Groups and Boundaries: The Social Organisation of Cultural Difference*: 9–38. Bergen/London: Universitets Forlaget/ George Allen and Unwin.

Barth, F. 1987. *Cosmologies in the Making: A Generative Approach to Cultural Variation in Inner New Guinea*. Cambridge: Cambridge University Press.

Bateson, G. 1936. *Naven: A Survey of the Problems Suggested by a Composite Picture of the Culture of a New Guinea Tribe Drawn from Three Different Points of View*. Cambridge: Cambridge University Press.

Bell, A. R. 1990. 'Separate people: speaking of Creek men and women', *American Anthropologist* 92: 332–45.

Bell, C. 1992. *Ritual Theory, Ritual Practice*. Oxford: Oxford University Press.

Benedict, R. 1943. 'Obituary of Franz Boas', *Science* 97: 60–2.

Bernal, M. 1987. *Black Athena I: The Fabrication of Ancient Greece 1785–1985*. New Brunswick: Rutgers University Press.

Bernal, M. 1991. *Black Athena II: The Archaeological and Documentary Evidence*. New Brunswick: Rutgers University Press.

Bhabha, H. 1994. *The Location of Culture*. London: Routledge.

Biersack, A. (ed.) 1991. *Clio in Oceania: Toward a Historical Anthropology*. Washington: Smithsonian Institution Press.

Binford, L. R. 1962. 'Archaeology as anthropology', *American Antiquity* 28: 217–25.

Binford, L. R. 1967. 'Smudge pits and hide smoking: the use of analogy in archaeological reasoning,' *American Antiquity* 32: 1–12.

Binford, L. R. 1972. *An Archaeological Perspective*. New York: Seminar Press.

Binford, L. R. 1978. *Nunamiut Archaeology*. New York: Academic Press.

Binford, L. R. 1980. 'Willow smoke and dogs' tails: hunter-gatherer settlement systems and archaeological site formation', *American Antiquity* 45: 4–20.

Bloch, M. 1984. *Marxism and Anthropology: The History of a Relationship*. Oxford: Oxford University Press.

Boas, F. 1897. *The Social Organization and Secret Societies of the Kwakiutl Indians*. Washington: Report of the US National Museum.

Boas, F. 1982 (1889). 'On alternating sounds', in G. W. Stocking (ed.) *A Franz Boas Reader*: 72–7. Chicago: University of Chicago Press.

Bohannon, P. and L. Bohannon. 1968. *Tiv Economy*. Harlow: Longmans.

Boon, J. A. 1990. *Affinities and Extremes: Crossing the Bittersweet Ethnology of East Indies History, Hindu-Balinese Culture and Indo-European Allure*. Chicago: University of Chicago Press.

Borofsky, R. 1987. *Making History: Pukapukan and Anthropological Constructions of Knowledge*. Cambridge: Cambridge University Press.

Bourdieu, P. 1984. *Distinction: A Social Critique of the Judgement of Taste*. London: Routledge and Kegan Paul.

Bourdieu, P. 1988. *Homo Academicus*. Cambridge: Polity Press.

Bourdieu, P. 1990. *The Logic of Practice*. Cambridge: Polity Press.

Bromley, Y. 1980. 'The object and subject matter of ethnography', in E. Gellner (ed.) *Soviet and Western Anthropology*: 151–60. London: Duckworth.

Butler, J. 1990. *Gender Trouble: Feminism and the Subversion of Identity*. London: Routledge.

Butler, J. 1993. *Bodies that Matter: On the Discursive Limits of 'Sex'*. London: Routledge.

Byrne, R. and A. Whiten (eds). 1988. *Machiavellian Intelligence: Social Expertise and the Evolution of Intellect in Monkeys, Apes and Humans*. Oxford: Clarendon Press.

Cachola-Abad, C. K. 1993. 'Evaluating the orthodox dual settlement model for the Hawaiian Islands: an analysis of artefact distribution and Hawaiian oral traditions', in M. W. Graves and R. C. Green (eds) *The Evolution and Organisation of Prehistoric Society in Polynesia*: 13–32. Auckland: New Zealand Archaeological Association Monograph 19.

Chagnon, N. 1997. *Yanomami*. Fort Worth: Harcourt Brace Publishers.

Chapman, W. R. 1985. 'Arranging ethnology: A. H. L. F. Pitt Rivers and the typological tradition', in G. W. Stocking (ed.) *Objects and Others*: 15–48. Madison: University of Wisconsin Press.

Chase-Dunn, C. and T. D. Hall. (eds) 1991. *Core/Periphery Relations in Precapitalist Worlds*. Boulder, CO: Westview Press.

Cheater, A. P. 1995. 'Globalisation and the new technologies of knowing: anthropological calculus or chaos?', in M. Strathern (ed.) *Shifting Contexts: Transformations in Anthropological Knowledge*: 117–30. London: Routledge.

Childe, V. G. 1925. *The Dawn of European Civilization*. London: Kegan Paul.

Childe, V. G. 1929. *The Danube in Prehistory*. Oxford: Oxford University Press.

Childe, V. G. 1930. *The Bronze Age*. Cambridge: Cambridge University Press.

Childe, V. G. 1933. 'Races, peoples and cultures in prehistoric Europe', *History* 18: 193–203.

Chorley, R. and P. Haggett (eds). 1967. *Models in Geography*. London: Methuen.

Claassen, C. and R. A. Joyce (eds). 1997. *Women in Prehistory: North America and Mesoamerica*. Philadelphia: University of Pennsylvania Press.

Clark, J. G. D. 1954. *Excavations at Star Carr*. Cambridge: Cambridge University Press.

Clarke, D. L. 1968. *Analytical Archaeology*. London: Methuen.

Clarke, D. L. (ed.). 1977. *Spatial Archaeology*. London: Methuen.

Clifford, J. 1988. *The Predicament of Culture: Twentieth-Century Ethnography, Literature and Art*. Cambridge, MA: Harvard University Press.

Clifford, J. 1997. *Routes: Travel and Translation in the Late Twentieth Century*. Cambridge, MA: Harvard University Press.

Clifford, J. and G. E. Marcus (eds). 1986. *Writing Culture: The Poetics and Politics of Ethnography*. Berkeley: University of California Press.

Cohen, A. 1969. *Custom and Politics in Urban Africa: A Study of Hausa Migrants in Yoruba Towns*. London: Routledge and Kegan Paul.

Comaroff, J. 1985. *Body of Power, Spirit of Resistance: The Culture and History of a South African people*. Chicago: University of Chicago Press.

Conkey, M. W. and J. D. Spector. 1984. 'Archaeology and the study of gender', in M. B. Schiffer (ed.) *Advances in Archaeological Method and Theory*, vol. 7: 1–38. New York: Academic Press.

Connell, R. W. 1995. *Masculinities*. Cambridge: Polity Press.

Coote, J. 1992. '"Marvels of everyday vision": the anthropology of aesthetics and the cattle-keeping Nilotes', in J. Coote and A. Shelton (eds) *Anthropology, Art and Aesthetics*: 245–73. Oxford: Clarendon Press.

Crapanzano, V. 1980. *Tumahi: Portrait of a Moroccan*. Chicago: University of Chicago Press.

Crapanzano, V. 1986. 'Hermes' dilemma: the masking of subversion in ethnographic description', in J. Clifford and G. E. Marcus (eds) *Writing Culture: The Poetics and Politics of Ethnography*: 51–76. Berkeley: University of California Press.

Das, V. 1995. 'On soap opera: what kind of anthropological object is it?', in D. Miller (ed.) *Worlds Apart: Modernity Through the Prism of the Local*: 169–89. London: Routledge.

Descola, P. 1996. *In the Society of Nature: A Native Ecology in Amazonia*. Cambridge: Cambridge University Press.

Díaz-Andreu, M. and T. Champion (eds). 1996. *Nationalism and Archaeology in Europe*. London: UCL Press.

Dilworth, L. 1996. *Imagining Indians in the Southwest: Persistent Visions of a Primitive Past*. Washington: Smithsonian Institution Press.

Douglas, M. 1970. 'The healing rite', *Man* 5: 302–8.

Douglas, M. and B. Isherwood. 1979. *The World of Goods*. London: Allen Lane.

duCros, H. and L. Smith (eds). 1993. *Women in Archaeology: A Feminist Critique*. Occasional Papers in Prehistory, no. 23. Canberra: Research School of Pacific and Asian Studies, Australian National University.

Duff, W. 1975. *Images in Stone BC: Thirty Centuries of Northwest Coast Indian Sculpture*. Seattle: University of Washington Press.

Durkheim, E. 1965. *The Elementary Forms of the Religious Life*, trans. J. W. Swain. New York: The Free Press.

Durkheim, E. and M. Mauss. 1963. *Primitive Classification*. Chicago: University of Chicago Press.

Edwards, E. (ed.). 1992. *Anthropology and Photography 1860–1920*. New Haven, CT and London: Yale University Press in association with the Royal Anthropological Institute.

Ekholm, K. 1972. *Power and Prestige: The Rise and Fall of the Kongo Kingdom*. Uppsala: Skriv Service.

Engels, F. 1940. *The Origins of the Family, Private Property and the State*. London: Lawrence and Wishart.

Engelstadt, E. 1991. 'Images of power and contradiction: feminist theory and post-processual archaeology', *Antiquity* 65: 502–14.

Evans-Pritchard, E. E. 1950. 'Social anthropology: past and present', *Man* 50: 118–24.

Fabian, J. 1983. *Time and the Other: How Anthropology Makes its Objects*. New York: Columbia University.

Favret-Saada, J. 1980. *Deadly Words: Witchcraft in the Bocage*. Cambridge: Cambridge University Press.

Flannery, K. (ed.) 1976. *The Early Mesoamerican Village*. London: Academic Press.

Foley, R. 1982. 'A reconsideration of the role of predation on large mammals in tropical hunter-gatherer adaptation', *Man* 17: 393–402.

Forge, A. 1973. 'Style and meaning in Sepik art', in A. Forge (ed.) *Primitive Art and Society*: 169–92. London: Oxford University Press.

Foster, R. 1995. *Social Reproduction and History in Melanesia: Mortuary Ritual, Gift Exchange and Custom in the Tanga Islands*. Cambridge: Cambridge University Press.

Foucault, M. 1979. *Discipline and Punish: The Birth of the Prison*, trans. A. Sheridan. Harmondsworth: Peregrine.

Foucault, M. 1981. *The History of Sexuality, Volume I: An Introduction*. Harmondsworth: Penguin Books.

Frank, A. G. 1993. 'Bronze Age world systems cycles', *Current Anthropology* 34: 383–429.

Frankenstein, S. and M. Rowlands. 1978. 'The internal structure and regional context of early Iron Age society in south-western Germany', *Bulletin of the Institute of Archaeology* 15: 73–112.

Freeman, D. 1984. *Margaret Mead and Samoa: The Making and Unmaking of an Anthropological Myth*. Harmondsworth: Penguin Books.

Friedman, J. and M. J. Rowlands. 1978. 'Notes towards an epigenetic model of the evolution of "civilisation" ', in J. Friedman and M. J. Rowlands (eds) *The Evolution of Social Systems*: 201–76. London: Duckworth.

Gamble, C. 1986. *The Palaeolithic Settlement of Europe*. Cambridge: Cambridge University Press.

Geertz, C. 1983. ' "From the native's point of view": on the nature of anthropological understanding', in *Local Knowledge*: 55–70. New York: Basic Books.

Geertz, C. 1993a (1973). 'The integrative revolution: primordial sentiments and civil politics in the new states', in *The Interpretation of Cultures*: 255–310. London: Fontana.

Geertz, C. 1993b (1973). 'Deep play; notes on the Balinese cockfight', in *The Interpretation of Cultures*: 412–53. London: Fontana.

Geertz, C. 1993c. 'After the revolution: the fate of nationalism in the new states', in *The Interpretation of Cultures*: 234–54. London: Fontana.

Gell, A. 1992a. 'Inter-tribal commodity barter and reproductive gift-exchange in old Melanesia', in C. Humphrey and S. Hugh-Jones (eds) *Barter, Exchange and Value: An Ethnographic Approach*: 142–68. Cambridge: Cambridge University Press.

Gell, A. 1992b. 'The technology of enchantment and the enchantment of technology', in J. Coote and A. Shelton (eds) *Anthropology, Art and Aesthetics*: 40–63. Oxford: Clarendon Press.

Gell, A. 1992c. *The Anthropology of Time: Cultural Construction of Temporal Maps and Images*. Oxford: Berg.

Gell, A. 1998. *Art and Agency: Towards a New Anthropological Theory*. Oxford: Clarendon Press.

Gero, J. and M. W. Conkey (eds). 1991. *Engendering Archaeology: Women and Prehistory*. Oxford: Basil Blackwell.

Gibson, K. R. and T. Ingold (eds). 1993. *Tools, Language and Cognition in Human Evolution*. Cambridge: Cambridge University Press.

Giddens, A. 1984. *The Constitution of Society: Outline of the Theory of Structuration*. Cambridge: Polity Press.

Giddens, A. 1992. *The Transformation of Intimacy: Sexuality, Love and Eroticism in Modern Societies*. Cambridge: Polity Press.

Gilchrist, R. 1994. *Gender and Material Culture: The Archaeology of Religious Women*. London: Routledge.

Gilchrist, R. 1996. 'Virgin territory: gender archaeology and medieval religious women' (in a review feature on Gilchrist 1994), *Cambridge Archaeological Journal* 6: 120–2.

Godelier, M. 1977. *Perspectives in Marxist Anthropology*. Cambridge: Cambridge University Press.

Golson, J. 1982. 'The Ipomoean revolution revisited: society and the sweet potato in the Upper Wahgi Valley', in A. Strathern (ed.) *Inequality in New Guinea Highland Societies*: 109–36. Cambridge: Cambridge University Press.

Goodman, J. 1993. *Tobacco in History*. London: Routledge.

Goodman, J., P. E. Lovejoy and A. Sherratt (eds). 1995. *Drugs in history and anthropology*. London: Routledge.

Goody, J. 1982. *Cooking, Cuisine and Class*. Cambridge: Cambridge University Press.

Gordon, R. 1992. *The Bushman Myth: The Making of a Namibian Underclass*. Boulder, CO: Westview Press.

Gosden, C. 1994. *Social Being and Time*. Oxford: Blackwell.

Graves-Brown, P., S. Jones and C. Gamble (eds). 1996. *Cultural Identity and Archaeology: The Construction of European communities*. London: Routledge.

Gregory, C. A. 1982. *Gifts and Commodities*. London: Academic Press.

Griffiths, T. 1996. *Hunters and Collectors: The Antiquarian Imagination in Australia*. Cambridge: Cambridge University Press.

Guha, R. (ed.). 1988. *Selected Subaltern Studies*. Oxford: Oxford University Press.

Haaland, G. 1969. 'Economic determinants in ethnic processes', in F. Barth (ed.) *Ethnic Groups and Boundaries*: 58–73. Oslo: Universitetsforlaget.

Hager, L. D. (ed.). 1997a. *Women in Human Evolution*. London: Routledge.

Hager, L. D. 1997b. 'Sex and gender in paleoanthropology', in L. Hager (ed.) *Women in Human Evolution*: 1–28. London: Routledge.

Hall, M. 1988. 'At the frontier: some arguments against hunter gathering and farming modes of production in Southern Africa', in T. Ingold, D. Riches and J. Woodburn (eds) *Hunters and Gatherers 1: History, Evolution and Social Change*: 137–47. Oxford: Berg.

Hannerz, U. 1996. *Transnational Connections: Culture, People, Places*. London: Routledge.

Harris, D. R. (ed.). 1994. *The Archaeology of Gordon Childe*. London: UCL Press.

Harris, M. 1968. *The Rise of Anthropological Theory*. New York: Thomas Y. Crowell Company.

Harrison, J. D. 1988. 'The Spirit Sings and the future of anthropology', *Anthropology Today* 4: 6–9.

Harvey, D. 1989. *The Condition of Post-modernity: An Enquiry into the Origins of Cultural Change*. Oxford: Basil Blackwell.

Held, D. 1980. *Introduction to Critical Theory: Horkheimer to Habermas*. London: Hutchinson.

Herdt, G. H. (ed.). 1982. *Rituals of Manhood: Male Initiation in Papua New Guinea*. Berkeley: University of California Press.

Herdt, G. H. (ed.). 1984. *Ritualized Homosexuality in Melanesia*. Berkeley: University of California Press.

Higgs, E. S. (ed.). 1972. *Papers in Economic Prehistory*. Cambridge: Cambridge University Press.

Higgs, E. S. and M. R. Jarman. 1969. 'The origins of agriculture: a reconsideration', *Antiquity* 43: 31–41.

Hill, J. N. 1968. 'Broken K pueblo: patterns of form and function', in S. R. Binford and L. R. Binford (eds) *New Perspectives in Archaeology*: 103–43. Chicago: Aldine.

Hindness, B. and P. Q. Hirst. 1975. *Pre-Capitalist Modes of Production*. London: Routledge and Keegan Paul.

Hinsley, C. M. 1981. *Savages and Scientists: The Smithsonian Institution and the Development of American Anthropology 1846–1910*. Washington, DC: Smithsonian Institution Press.

Hinsley, C. M. 1983. 'Ethnographic charisma and scientific routine: Cushing and Fewkes in the American southwest 1879–1893', in G. W. Stocking (ed.) *Observers Observed*: 53–69. Madison: University of Wisconsin Press.

Hinsley, C. M. 1985. 'From shell-heaps to stelae: early anthropology at the Peabody Museum', in G. W. Stocking (ed.) *Objects and Others: Essays on Museums and Material Culture*: 49–74. Madison: University of Wisconsin Press.

Hodder, I. 1979. 'Economic and social stress and material culture patterning', *American Antiquity* 44: 446–54.

Hodder, I. 1982a. *The Present Past: An Introduction to Anthropology for Archaeologists*. London: Batsford.

Hodder, I. 1982b. *Symbols in Action*. Cambridge: Cambridge University Press.

Hodder, I. 1997. '"Always momentary, fluid and flexible": towards a reflexive excavation methodology', *Antiquity* 71: 691–700.

Hodder, I. and C. Orton. 1976. *Spatial Analysis in Archaeology*. Cambridge: Cambridge University Press.

Hoffman, C. 1984. 'Punan foragers in the trading networks of southeast Asia', in C. Shrire (ed.) *Past and Present in Hunter-Gatherer Studies*: 123–49. Orlando, FL: Academic Press.

Hooper-Greenhill, E. 1998. 'Perspectives on Hinemihi: a Maori meeting house', in T. Barringer and T. Flynn (eds) *Colonialism and the Object: Empire, Material Culture and the Museum*: 129–43. London: Routledge.

Humphrey, C. and J. Laidlaw. 1994. *The Archetypal Actions of Ritual*. Oxford: Clarendon Press.

Humphrey, N. 1976. 'The social functions of intellect', in P. P. G. Bateson and R. A. Hinde (eds) *Growing Points in Ethology*: 303–17. Cambridge: Cambridge University Press.

Ingold, T. 1992. 'Editorial', *Man* 27: 693–6.

Ingold, T. 1993a. 'The temporality of the landscape', *World Archaeology* 25: 152–74.

Ingold, T. 1993b. 'Tool-use, sociality and intelligence', in K. R. Gibson and T. Ingold (eds) *Tools, Language and Cognition in Human Evolution*: 429–45. Cambridge: Cambridge University Press.

Jacknis, I. 1985. 'Franz Boas and Exhibits: On the Limitations of the Museum Method of Anthropology', in G. W. Stocking (ed.) *Objects and Others: Essays on Museums and Material Culture*: 75–111. Madison: University of Wisconsin Press.

Jacknis, I. 1992. 'George Hunt, Kwakiutl photographer', in E. Edwards (ed.) *Anthropology and Photography 1860–1920*: 143–51. New Haven, CT and London: Yale University Press in association with the Royal Anthropological Institute.

Jones, S. 1997. *The Archaeology of Ethnicity: Constructing Identities in the Past and Present.* London: Routledge.

Josephides, L. 1985. *The Production of Inequality: Gender and Ritual Exchange among the Kewa.* London: Tavistock.

Kame'eleihiwa, L. 1992. *Native Land and Foreign Desires.* Bishop Museum Press: Honolulu.

Kelly, R. L. 1995. *The Foraging Spectrum: Diversity in Hunter-Gatherer Lifeways.* Washington, DC: Smithsonian Institution Press.

Kirch, P. V. 1994. *The Wet and the Dry.* Chicago: University of Chicago Press.

Kirch, P. V. and M. Sahlins. 1992. *Anahulu: The Anthropology of History in the Kingdom of Hawaii. The Archaeology of History.* Chicago: University of Chicago Press.

Knorr-Cetina, K. D. and M. Mulkay (eds). 1983. *Science Observed: Perspectives on the Social Study of Science.* London: Sage Publications.

Kohl, P. L. and C. Fawcett (eds). (1995). *Nationalism, Politics and the Practice of Archaeology.* Cambridge: Cambridge University Press.

Kossina, G. 1911. *Die Herkunft der Germanen.* Leipzig: Kabitsch.

Krader, L. 1972. *The Ethnological Notebooks of Karl Marx.* Assen: Van Gorcum.

Kroeber, A. L. 1916. 'Zuñi potsherds', *Anthropological Papers of the American Museum of Natural History* 18: 7–37.

Kroeber, A. L. 1944. *Configurations of Culture Growth.* Berkeley: University of California Press.

Kroeber, A. L. 1959. 'Franz Boas: the man', in W. Goldschmidt (ed.) *The Anthropology of Franz Boas*: 14. American Anthropological Association, Memoir 89.

Kroeber, A. L. and C. Kluckhohn. 1952. *Culture: A Critical Review of Concepts and Definitions.* Cambridge: Papers of the Peabody Museum of American Archaeology and Ethnology, vol. XLVII.

Kulick, D. and M. Wilson (eds). 1995. *Taboo: Sex, Identity and Erotic Subjectivity in Anthropological Fieldwork.* London: Routledge.

Kuper, A. 1996. *Anthropology and Anthropologists*, 3rd edn. London: Routledge.

Laqueur, T. 1992. *Making Sex: Body and Gender from the Greeks to Freud.* Cambridge, MA: Harvard University Press.

Latour, B. 1987. *Science in Action.* Cambridge, MA: Harvard University Press.

Latour, B. and S. Woolgar. 1986. *Laboratory Life: The Social Construction of Scientific Facts.* Princeton: Princeton University Press.

Leach, E. 1973. 'Concluding address', in C. Renfrew, *The Explanation of Culture Change: Models in Prehistory*: 761–71: London: Duckworth.

Leach, J. W. and E. Leach. 1983. *The Kula: new perspectives on Massim Exchange.* Cambridge: Cambridge University Press.

Lee, R. B. 1968a. 'What hunters do for a living, or how to make out on scarce resources', in R. B. Lee and I. DeVore (eds) *Man the Hunter*: 30–48. Chicago: Aldine.

Lee, R. B. 1968b. 'Commentary', in S. R. Binford and L. R. Binford (eds) *New Perspectives in Archaeology*: 343–6. Chicago: Aldine.

Lee, R. B. and I. DeVore (eds) 1968. *Man the Hunter*. Chicago: Aldine.

Leone, M. P. 1968. 'Neolithic economic autonomy and social distance', *Science* 162: 1150–1.

Lévi-Strauss, C. 1966. *The Savage Mind*. Chicago: University of Chicago Press.

Lévi-Strauss, C. 1969a. *The Elementary Structures of Kinship*. London: Eyre and Spottiswoode.

Lévi-Strauss, C. 1969b. *The Raw and the Cooked*. London: Jonathan Cape.

Lévi-Strauss, C. 1987. *Introduction to the Work of Marcel Mauss*. London: Routledge and Kegan Paul.

Lévi-Strauss, C. and D. Eribon. 1991. *Conversations with Lévi-Strauss*. Chicago: University of Chicago Press.

Linnekin, J. 1990. *Sacred Queens and Women of Consequence*. Ann Arbor: The University of Michigan Press.

Longacre, W. A. 1968. 'Some aspects of prehistoric society in East-Central Arizona, in S. R. Binford and L. R. Binford (eds) *New Perspectives in Archaeology*: 89–102. Chicago: Aldine.

Lubbock, J. 1912. *Pre-historic Times*, 6th edn. London: Williams and Norgate.

McCann, W. J. 1990. '"Volk and Germanentum": the presentation of the past in Nazi Germany', in P. Gathercole and D. Lowenthal (eds) *The Politics of the Past*: 74–88. London: Unwin Hyman.

MacGregor, A. 1983a. 'The Tradescants: gardeners and botanists', in A. MacGregor (ed.) *Tradescant's Rarities*: 3–16, Oxford: Clarendon Press.

MacGregor, A. 1983b. 'Collectors and collections of rarities in the sixteenth and seventeenth centuries', in A. MacGregor (ed.) *Tradescant's Rarities*: 70–97, Oxford: Clarendon Press.

MacKenzie, M. 1991. *Androgynous Objects: String Bags and Gender in Central New Guinea*. Chur, Switzerland: Harwood Academic Publishers.

McLuhan, M. 1964. *Understanding Media*. New York: McGraw-Hill.

McMahon, M. 1984. *The Making of a Profession*. New York: IEEE.

Malinowski, B. 1922. *The Argonauts of the Western Pacific: An Account of Native Enterprise and Adventure in the Archipelagos of Melanesian New Guinea*. London: Routledge and Kegan Paul.

Malinowski, B. 1926. *Crime and Custom in Savage Society*. London: Allen and Unwin.

Malinowski, B. 1929. *The Sexual Life of Savages in Northwestern Melanesia*. London: Routledge and Kegan Paul.

Malinowski, B. 1935. *Coral Gardens and their Magic*, 2 vols. London: Allen and Unwin.

Malinowski, B. 1967. *A Diary in the Strict Sense of the Term*. London: Routledge and Kegan Paul.

Marcus, G. E. 1983. 'The fiduciary role in American family dynasties and their institutional legacy: from the law of trust to trust in the Establishment', in G. E. Marcus (ed.) *Elites: Ethnographic Issues*: 221–56. Albuquerque: University of New Mexico Press.

Marcus, G. E. 1986. 'Contemporary problems of ethnography in the modern world system', in J. Clifford and G. Marcus (eds) *Writing Culture: The Poetics and Politics of Ethnography*: 165–93. Berkeley: University of California Press.

Marcus, G. E. and M. M. J. Fischer. 1986. *Anthropology as Cultural Critique: An Experimental Moment in the Human Sciences*. Chicago: University of Chicago Press.

Mark, J. 1980. *Four Anthropologists: An American Science in its Early Years.* New York: Science History Publications.

Marriott, M. 1976. 'Hindu transactions: diversity without dualism', in B. Kapferer (ed.) *Transaction and Meaning*: 108–42. Philadelphia: ISHI Publications (ASA Essays in Anthropology 1).

Marshall, Y. (ed.). 1998a. 'Intimate Relations', Special Issue, *World Archaeology* 29.

Marshall, Y. 1998b. 'By way of introduction from the Pacific Northwest coast', *World Archaeology* 29: 311–16.

Martin, E. 1996. 'Interpreting electron micrographs', in H. L. Moore (ed.) *The Future of Anthropological Knowledge*: 16–36. London: Routledge.

Mauss, M. 1969. *The Gift*. London: Routledge and Kegan Paul.

Mauss, M. 1979. *Sociology and Psychology*. London: Routledge and Kegan Paul.

Mead, M. 1939. *From the South Seas: Studies of Adolescence and Sex in Primitive Societies.* New York: William Morrow and Company.

Meggers, B. 1960. 'The law of cultural evolution as a practical research tool', in G. Dole and R. Carneiro (eds) *Essays in the Science of Culture*: 302–16. New York: Thomas Y. Crowell.

Meillassoux, C. 1981. *Maidens, Meal and Money: Capitalism and the Domestic Economy.* Cambridge: Cambridge University Press.

Meltzer, D. J., J. M. Advasio and T. D. Dillehay. 1994. On a Pleistocene occupation at Pedra Furada, Brazil. *Antiquity* 68: 695–714.

Meskell, L. 1998a. 'Running the gamut: gender, girls and goddesses', *American Journal of Anthropology* 102: 181–5.

Meskell, L. 1998b. 'Intimate archaeologies: the case of Kha and Merit', *World Archaeology* 29: 363–79.

Miller, D. 1987. *Material Culture and Mass Consumption*. Oxford: Blackwell.

Miller, D. 1988. 'Appropriating the state on the council estate', *Man* 23: 353–72.

Miller, D. 1995. 'Consumption as the vanguard of history: a polemic by way of an introduction', in D. Miller (ed.) *Acknowledging Consumption: A Review of New Studies*: 1–57. London: Routledge.

Mintz, S. W. 1974. *Caribbean Transformations*. Chicago: Aldine.

Mintz, S. W. 1985. *Sweetness and Power: The Place of Sugar in Modern History.* Harmondsworth: Penguin.

Moore, H. 1988. *Feminism and Anthropology*. Cambridge: Polity Press.

Moore, H. 1994. *A Passion for Difference*. Cambridge: Polity Press.

Moore, H. 1996a. *Space, Text and Gender: An Anthropological Study of the Marakwet of Kenya.* New York: The Guilford Press.

Moore, H. 1996b. 'The changing nature of anthropological knowledge: an introduction', in H. L. Moore (ed.) *The Future of Anthropological Knowledge*: 1–15. London: Routledge.

Moore, J. and E. Scott. (eds). 1997. *Invisible People and Processes: Writing Gender and Childhood into European Archaeology.* London: Leicester University Press.

Moore, R. I. 1987. *The Formation of a Persecuting Society: Power and Deviance in Western Europe, 950–1250.* Oxford: Oxford University Press.

Moore-Gilbert, B. 1997. *Postcolonial theory: contexts, practices, politics*. London: Verso.

Morgan, L. H. 1985 (1877). *Ancient Society*. Tucson: University of Arizona Press.

Morphy, H. 1991. *Ancestral Connections: Art and an Aboriginal System of Knowledge.* Chicago: University of Chicago Press.

Morphy, H. 1992. 'From dull to brilliant: the aesthetics of spiritual power among the

Yolngu', in J. Coote and A. Shelton (eds) *Anthropology, Art and Aesthetics*: 181–208. Oxford: Clarendon Press.

Morphy, H. 1995. 'Landscape and the reproduction of the ancestral past', in E. Hirsch and M. O'Hanlon (eds) *The Anthropology of Landscape: Perspectives on Place and Space*: 184–209. Oxford: Clarendon Press.

Morris, I. 1994. 'Archaeologies of Greece', in I. Morris (ed.) *Classical Greece: Ancient Histories and Modern Archaeologies*: 9–47. Cambridge: Cambridge University Press.

Morris, R. C. 1995. 'All made up: performance theory and the new anthropology of sex and gender', *Annual Review of Anthropology* 24: 567–92.

Moser, S. 1995. 'Archaeology and its disciplinary culture: the professionalistion of Australian prehistoric archaeology', unpublished PhD thesis, University of Sydney.

Munn, N. 1977. 'The spatiotemporal transformation of Gawa canoes', *Journal de la Société des Océanistes* 54–5: 39–53.

Munn, N. 1983. 'Gawan kula: spatiotemporal control and the symbolism of influence', in J. Leach and E. Leach (eds) *The Kula: New Perspectives on Massim Exchange*: 277–308. Cambridge: Cambridge University Press.

Munn, N. 1986. *The Fame of Gawa*. Cambridge: Cambridge University Press.

Munn, N. 1990. 'Constructing regional worlds in experience: kula exchange, witchcraft and Gawan local events', *Man* 25: 1–17.

Munn, N. 1992. 'The cultural anthropology of time: a critical essay', *Annual Reviews of Anthropology* 21: 93–123.

Needham, R. 1971. 'Introduction', in R. Needham (ed.) *Rethinking Kinship and Marriage*: xiii–cxvii. London: Tavistock.

Neich, R. 1996. *Painted Histories*. Auckland: Auckland University Press.

Ngati Awa. 1990. *Nga Karoretanga o Mataatua Whare (The Wanderings of the Carved House Mataatua)*, Research report no. 2. Auckland: Te Runanga o Ngati Awa.

Nickles, T. 1989. 'Integrating the science studies disciplines', in S. Fuller, M. de Mey and T. Shinn (eds) *The Cognitive Turn: Sociological and Psychological Perspectives on Science*: 225–56. Dordrecht: Kluwer Academic.

Obeyesekere, G. 1992. *The Apotheosis of Captain Cook*. Princeton: Princeton University Press.

Orme, B. 1981. *Anthropology for Archaeologists: An Introduction*. London: Duckworth.

Øvrevik, S. 1991. 'Engendering archaeology', *Antiquity* 65: 738–41.

Pagden, A. 1982. *The Fall of Natural Man*. Cambridge: Cambridge University Press.

Perry, W. J. 1923. *The Children of the Sun*. London: Methuen.

Pfaffenberger, B. 1988. 'Fetishised objects and humanised nature: towards an anthropology of technology', *Man* 23: 236–52.

Phillips, S. 1994. 'The outer world of the European Middle Ages', in S. B. Schwarz (ed.) *Implicit Understandings*: 23–63. Cambridge: Cambridge University Press.

Pinch, T. 1986. *Confronting Nature: The Sociology of Solar Neutrino Detection*. Dordrecht: D. Reidel.

Pinney, C. 1995. 'Moral topophilia: the significations of landscape in Indian oleographs', in E. Hirsch and M. O'Hanlon (eds) *The Anthropology of Landscape: Perspectives on Place and Space*: 78–113. Oxford: Clarendon Press.

Plog, S. 1978. 'Social interaction and stylistic similarity: a re-analysis', in M. B. Schiffer (ed.) *Advances in Archaeological Method and Theory* 1: 143–82. New York: Academic Books.

Plog, S. 1983. 'Analysis of style in artefacts', *Annual Review of Anthropology* 12: 125–42.

Polanyi, K. 1957. 'The economy as an instituted process', in K. Polanyi, C. Arensburgh and H. Pearson (eds) *Trade and Market in the Early Empires*: 243–70. Glencoe: Free Press and Falcon's Wing Press.

Povinelli, E. 1992. '"Where we gana go now": foraging practices and their meanings among the Belyuen Australian Aborigines', *Human Ecology* 20: 169–201.

Povinelli, E. 1993. *Labor's Lot: The Power, History and Culture of Aboriginal Action*. Chicago: University of Chicago Press.

Pratt, M. L. 1992. *Imperial Eyes: Travel Writing and Transculturation*. London: Routledge.

Radcliffe-Brown, A. R. 1922. *The Andaman Islanders: A Study in Social Anthropology*. Cambridge: Cambridge University Press.

Radcliffe-Brown, A. R. 1930–1. 'The social organization of Australian tribes', *Oceania* 1. 34 63, 207 46, 322 41, 426 56.

Radcliffe-Brown, A. R. 1952. *Structure and Function in Primitive Society*. London: Cohen and West.

Radcliffe-Brown, A. R. 1958. 'The comparative method in social anthropology', in M. N. Srinivas (ed.) *Method in Social Anthropology: Selected Essays*: 108–29. Bombay: Asia Publishing House.

Rathje, W. L. 1974. 'The Garbage Project: a new way of looking at the problems of archaeology', *Archaeology* 27: 236–41.

Renfrew, A. C. 1973a. *Before Civilization: The Radiocarbon Revolution and Prehistoric Europe*. London: Cape.

Renfrew, A. C. (ed.). 1973b. *The Explanation of Culture Change: Models in Prehistory*. London: Duckworth.

Renfrew, A. C. 1975. 'Trade as action at a distance: questions of integration and communication', in J. A. Sabloff and C. C. Lamberg-Karlovsky (eds) *Ancient Civilization and Trade*: 3–59. Albuquerque: University of New Mexico Press.

Renfrew, C. 1980. 'The Great Tradition versus the Great Divide: archaeology as anthropology?', *American Journal of Archaeology* 84: 287–98.

Renfrew, C. 1984. *Approaches to Social Archaeology*. Edinburgh: Edinburgh University Press.

Renfrew, A. C. and J. Cherry (eds). 1986. *Peer Polity Interaction and Sociopolitical Change*. Cambridge: Cambridge University Press.

Rivers, W. H. R. 1906. *The Todas*. London: Macmillan.

Rivers, W. H. R. 1914. *The History of Melanesian Society*, 2 vols. Cambridge: Cambridge University Press.

Rivers, W. H. R. 1926 (1911). 'The ethnological analysis of culture', in G. E. Smith (ed.) *Psychology and Ethnology*: 120–40. London: Kegan Paul, Trench and Trubner.

Rivière, P. 1995. *Absent-Minded Colonialism: Britain and the Expansion of Empire in Nineteenth-Century Brazil*. London: Tauris Academic Studies.

Rosaldo, R. 1980. *Ilongot Headhunting 1883–1974: A Study in Society and History*. Stanford: Stanford University Press.

Rowlands, M. 1987. 'The concept of Europe in prehistory', *Man* 22: 558–9.

Rowlands, M. 1994a. 'Childe and the archaeology of freedom', in D. R. Harris (ed.) *The Archaeology of V. Gordon Childe*: 35–54. London: UCL Press.

Rowlands, M. 1994b. 'The politics of identity in archaeology', in G. C. Bond and A. Gilliam (eds) *Social Construction of the Past: Representation as Power*: 129–143. London: Routledge.

Rowlands, M., M. Larsen and K. Kristiansen. 1987. *Centre and Periphery in the Ancient World*. Cambridge: Cambridge University Press.

Sackett, J. R. 1977. 'The meaning of style in archeology: a general model', *American Antiquity* 42: 369–80.

Sackett, J. R. 1985. 'Style and ethnicity in the Kalahari: a reply to Weissner', *American Antiquity* 50: 154–60.

Sahlins, M. D. 1958. *Social Stratification in Polynesia*. Seattle: University of Washington Press.

Sahlins, M. D. 1963. 'Poor man, rich man, big man, chief: political types in Melanesia and Polynesia', *Comparative Studies in Society and History* 5: 285–300.

Sahlins, M. D. 1972. *Stone Age Economics*. New York: Aldine.

Sahlins, M. 1981. *Historical Metaphors and Mythical Realities*. Ann Arbor: University of Michigan Press.

Sahlins, M. 1985. *Islands of History*. Chicago: University of Chicago Press.

Sahlins, M. 1991. 'The return of the event, again', in A. Biersack (ed.) *Clio in Oceania*: 37–99. Washington: Smithsonian Institution Press.

Sahlins, M. 1995. *How 'Natives' Think*. Chicago: University of Chicago Press.

Sahlins, M. D. and E. R. Service (eds). 1960. *Evolution and Culture*. Ann Arbor: University of Michigan Press.

Said, E. W. 1978. *Orientalism*. New York: Vintage.

Said, E. W. 1993. *Culture and Imperialism*. New York: Knopf.

Sauer, C. 1963. 'The morphology of landscape', in J. Leighly (ed.) *Land and Life: A Selection of the Writings of Carl Sauer*: 315–50. Berkeley: University of California Press.

Schiffer, M. B. 1976. *Behavioral Archeology*. New York: Academic Press.

Schwarz, S. B. (ed.). 1994. *Implicit Understandings*. Cambridge: Cambridge University Press.

Service, E. R. 1962. *Primitive Social Organisation: An Evolutionary Perspective*. New York: Random House.

Service, E. R. 1971. *Cultural Evolutionism: Theory in Practice*. New York: Holt, Rinehart and Winston, Inc.

Shennan, S. 1989. 'Archaeology as archaeology or as anthropology? Clarke's *Analytical Archaeology* and Binford's *New Perspectives in Archaeology* 21 years on', *Antiquity* 63: 831–5.

Shostak, M. 1981. *Nisa: The Life and Words of a !Kung Woman*. Cambridge, MA: Harvard University Press.

Sigaut, F. 1994. 'Technology,' in T. Ingold (ed.) *Companion Encyclopedia of Anthropology*: 420–59. London: Routledge.

Smith, B. 1985. *European Vision and the South Pacific*. New Haven, CT: Yale University Press.

Smith, C. A. (ed.). 1976. *Regional Analysis*. New York: Academic Press.

Smith, P. J. 1997. 'Grahame Clark's new archaeology: the Fenland Research Committee and Cambridge prehistory in the 1930s', *Antiquity* 71: 11–30.

Soja, E. 1989. *Postmodern Geographies*. London: Verso.

Soja, E. 1996. *Thirdspace: Journeys to Los Angeles and Other Real-and-Imagined Places*. Oxford: Blackwell.

Spencer, W. B. and F. Gillen. 1899. *The Native Tribes of Central Australia*. London: Macmillan.

Spier, L. 1917. *An Outline for a Chronology of Zuñi Ruins*. New York: Anthropological Papers of the Museum of Natural History.

Spivak, G. 1987. *In Other Worlds: Essays in Cultural Politics*. London: Routledge.

Spriggs, M. (ed.). 1984. *Marxist Perspectives in Archaeology*. Cambridge: Cambridge University Press.

Spriggs, M. 1997. 'Who taught Marx, Engels and Morgan about Australian Aborigines?', *History and Anthropology* 10: 185–218.

Steward, J. H. 1936. 'The economic and social basis of primitive bands', in R. H. Lowie (ed.) *Essays in Anthropology Presented to Alfred Louis Kroeber*: 331–50. Berkeley: University of California Press.

Stocking, G. W. 1968. *Race, Culture and Evolution: Essays in the History of Anthropology*. London: Collier-Macmillan.

Stocking, G. W. 1987. *Victorian Anthropology*. New York: The Free Press.

Stocking, G. W. 1992. 'The ethnographer's magic: fieldwork in British anthropology from Tylor to Malinowski', in G. W. Stocking (ed.) *Observers Observed: Essays on Ethnographic Fieldwork*: 70–120. Madison: University of Wisconsin Press.

Stocking, G. W. 1996. *After Tylor: British Social Anthropology 1888–1951*. London: Athlone Press.

Stoler, A. L. 1995. *Race and the Education of Desire: Foucault's History of Sexuality and the Colonial Order of Things*. Durham, NC: Duke University Press.

Strang, V. 1997. *Uncommon Ground: Cultural Landscapes and Environmental Values*. Oxford: Berg.

Strathern, A. 1979. *Ongka: A Self-Account by a New Guinea Big-Man*. London: Duckworth.

Strathern, M. 1988. *The Gender of the Gift: Problems with Women and Problems with Society in Melanesia*. Berkeley: University of California Press.

Strathern, M. 1995. 'The nice thing about culture is that everyone has it', in M. Strathern (ed.) *Shifting Contexts: Transformations in Anthropological Knowledge*: 153–76. London: Routledge.

Swallow, D. 1982. 'Production and control in the Indian garment export industry', in E. Goody (ed.) *From Craft to Industry*: 138–65. Cambridge: Cambridge University Press.

Tambiah, S. J. 1976. *World Conqueror and World Renouncer: A Study of Buddhism and Polity in Thailand against an Historical Background*. Cambridge: Cambridge University Press.

Taylor, P. (ed.). 1988. *After 200 Years*. Canberra: Aboriginal Studies Press.

Taylor, T. 1996. *The Prehistory of Sex*. London: Fourth Estate.

Taylor, W. W. 1948. *A Study of Archaeology*. Menshasa, WI: Memoir Series of the American Anthropological Association, no. 69.

Terray, E. 1973. 'Classes and class consciousness in the Abron Kingdom of Gyaman', in M. Bloch (ed.) *Marxist Analyses and Social Anthropology*: 85–135. London: Malaby Press.

Terrell, J. E., T. L. Hunt and C. Gosden. 1997. 'The dimensions of social life within the Pacific', *Current Anthropology* 38: 155–95.

Thomas, J. 1993. 'The politics of vision and the archaeologies of landscape', in B. Bender (ed.) *Landscape: Politics and Perspectives*: 19–48. Oxford: Berg.

Thomas, K. 1984. *Man and the Natural World: Changing Attitudes in England 1500–1800*. Harmondsworth: Penguin.

Thomas, N. 1989. *Out of Time: History and Evolution in Anthropological Discourse*. Cambridge: Cambridge University Press.

Thomas, N. 1991. *Entangled Objects: Exchange, Material Culture and Colonialism in the Pacific*. Cambridge, MA: Harvard University Press.

Tilley, C. 1994. *A Phenomenology of Landscape: Places, Paths and Monuments*. Oxford: Berg.

Tilley, C. 1996. *An Ethnography of the Neolithic: Early Prehistoric Societies in Scandinavia*. Cambridge: Cambridge University Press.

Toby, R. P. 1994. 'The "Indianness" of Iberia and changing Japanese iconographies of other', in S. B. Schwarz (ed.) *Implicit Understandings*: 323–51, Cambridge: Cambridge University Press.

Trigger, B. G. 1989. *A History of Archaeological Thought*. Cambridge: Cambridge University Press.

Turner, V. 1977. *The Ritual Process: Structure and Anti-Structure*. Ithaca, NY: Cornell University Press.

Tylor, E. B. 1871. *Primitive Culture: Researches into the Development of Mythology, Philosophy, Religion, Language, Art and Custom*. London: J. Murray.

Tylor, E. B. 1888. 'On a method of investigating the development of institutions, applied to laws of marriage and descent', *Journal of the Anthropological Institute* 18: 245–72.

Ucko, P. 1987. *Academic Freedom and Apartheid: The Story of the World Archaeological Congress*. London: Duckworth.

Ucko, P. (ed.) 1995. *Theory in Archaeology: A World Perspective*. London: Routledge.

Valeri, V. 1991. 'The transformation of transformation', in A. Biersack (ed.) *Clio in Oceania*: 101–64. Washington, DC: Smithsonian Institution Press.

van den Berghe, P. L. 1978. 'Race and ethnicity: a sociobiological perspective', *Ethnic and Racial Studies* 1: 401–11.

Vasey, P. L. 1998. 'Intimate sexual relations in prehistory: lessons from the Japanese macaques', *World Archaeology* 29: 407–25.

Veblen, T. 1924. *The Theory of the Leisure Class: An Economic Study of Institutions*. London: Allen and Unwin.

Wagner, R. 1994. 'The fractal person', in M. Strathern and M. Godelier (eds) *Big Men and Great Men: The Personifications of Power in Melanesia*: 159–73. Cambridge: Cambridge University Press.

Walcott, D. 1989. 'Caligula's horse', in S. Slemon and H. Tiffin (eds) *After Europe: Critical Theory and Post-colonial Writing*: 135–42. Mundelstrup: Dangaroo.

Wallerstein, I. 1974. *The Modern World System, I*. New York: Academic Press.

Wallerstein, I. 1980. *The Modern World System, II*. New York: Academic Press.

Weiner, A. B. 1977. *Women of Value, Men of Renown: New Perspectives in Trobriand Exchange*. St Lucia: University of Queensland Press.

Weiner, A. B. 1980. 'Stability in banana leaves: colonisation and women in Kiriwina, Trobriand Islands', in M. Etienne and E. Leacock (eds) *Women and Colonisation: Anthropological Perspectives*: 270–93. New York: Praeger.

Whallon, R. 1982. 'Editorial introduction', *Journal of Anthropological Archaeology* 1: 1–4.

White, H. 1973. *Metahistory*. Baltimore, MD: Johns Hopkins University Press.

White, H. 1978. *Tropics of Discourse*. Baltimore, MD: Johns Hopkins University Press.

White, J. P. with F. F. O'Connell. 1982. *A Prehistory of Australia, New Guinea and Sahul*. Sydney: Academic Press.

White, L. 1959. *The Evolution of Culture*. New York: McGraw-Hill.

White, L. 1963. *The Ethnology and Ethnography of Franz Boas*, Bulletin of the Texas Memorial Museum, no. 6. Austin: Texas Memorial Museum.

Willey, G. R. and P. Phillips. 1958. *Method and Theory in American Archaeology*. Chicago: University of Chicago Press.

Willey, G. R. and J. A. Sabloff. 1980. *A History of American Archaeology*, 2nd edn. San Francisco: W. H. Freeman and Co.

Wilmsen, E. N. 1992. 'A myth and its measure', *Current Anthropology* 33: 611–14.

Wilmsen, E. N. and J. Denbow. 1990. 'Paradigmatic history of San-speaking peoples and current attempts at revision', *Current Anthropology* 31: 489–524.

Wolf, E. 1971. *Peasant Wars of the Twentieth Century*. London: Faber and Faber.

Wolf, E. 1982. *Europe and the People without History*. Berkeley: University of California Press.

Worsley, P. 1957. *The Trumpet Shall Sound*. London: MacGibbon and Kee.

Wright, R. P. (ed.). 1996. *Gender and Archaeology*. Philadelphia: University of Pennsylvania Press.

Wylie, A. 1991. 'Gender theory and the archaeological record: why is there no archaeology of gender?' in J. Gero and M. Conkey (eds) *Engendering Archaeology*: 31–54. Oxford: Blackwell.

Yates, T. 1990. 'Archaeology through the looking-glass', in I. Bapty and T. Yates (eds) *Archaeology after Structuralism: Post-structuralism and the Practice of Archaeology*: 154–202. London: Routledge.

Young, R. 1990. *White Mythologies: Writing History and the West*. London: Routledge.

Index

colonialism 102–3; functionalism 78–83; institutionalisation of anthropology 40–2, 50–2
Malthus, T.R. 105
Manggalili clan 173–6
manipulation 127–8
Manutasopi case 159
Maori people 187–9
Marakwet 154–8
Marcus, G.E. 78, 184–5
marriage 67–8, 111–12
Marshall, Y. 146
Marx, K. 105–8, 114
Marxism 86, 105–11, 114, 197–8
Mary the Virgin, St 141, 142
mass consumption 165–6
Mataatua 187–8
material anthropology 152–78
material culture 30, 55–7, 120, 160–7; consumption 163–7; ethnicity 196–7; production 160–3; *see also* artefacts, exchange
Mauss, M. 76, 77–8, 111, 124–5, 135
Mead, M. 84, 149
meaning 111–16; art and 173–6, 177–8; negotiation of 59–60
mechanical solidarity 76
Medici collections 19
medieval period 16–18
megaliths 74
Meggers, B. 88–9
Melanesia 132–6
Merit 143–6
Meskell, L. 143–6
migration 96, 98, 183–4
Miller, D. 165–6
Mintz, S.W. 108, 165
Mitsubishi 181
mobility 96, 98, 183–4
modes of production 107–8
monogenesists 194
Montagu, 51
Moore, H. 154–8, 186
Morgan, L.H. 45, 55, 67, 68, 70, 105–6; evolutionism 63–4
Morphy, H. 171–5, 177
Morris, I. 22
mound studies 54–5
Mountain Ok 136–9
multi-site ethnography 184–5
Munn, N. 158–9
museum collections *see* collections
mystics, female 141
myth 113–14

Nagda 154
Napoleon I 25
Narritjin Maymuru 173–5, 176
nation state 92, 182
nationalism 196
nativism 201
Nazism 195
negotiation of meanings 59–60
neo-evolutionism 88–100
Neolithic 8
nervous system 67
New Archaeology 57, 94–100, 194, 195
Ngati Awa people 188
Nickles, T. 34
North America *see* United States
Notes and Queries on Anthropology 40–1
numaym 71
Nunamiut 5
nunneries 141–3
nunnery churches 142–3, 144, 145

Obeyesekere, G. 168
objectivity 58–9
Omarakana 42, 79
Ominayak, B. 186–7
order: and change 167–70
orders of difference 15–18
organic solidarity 76
Orientalism 198–9
Otago Museum 188
other, self and 16, 23, 25
Owen, W. 50

Palowahtiwa 43
Papa 169
Papua New Guinea 103–5
participant observation 41–2
Pathans 191–2
Peabody Museum 55
Pengelly, W. 28
perception 150–1
performance-based rituals 131
Perry, W.J. 74, 75
Pettit, D. 179, 182
Pfaffenberger, B. 160, 161
Phillips, P. 4
photography 189–90
Pinney, C. 154
Pitt Rivers, A.H. 22, 25–32, 52
pleasure, sex and 149–50
Plot, R. 22, 24
plurality 133
Polanyi, K. 91
Polo, Marco 17